EMPLOYMENT LAW HANDBOOK

A Complete Reference for Business

Stephen L. Berry
Dawn S. Hyde
Ann L. Lamdin
Michael F. Marino
Martin C. Mead
Thomas P. Murphy
Francis W. Palmieri

Eric Paltell
Andrew C. Peterson
Cynthia Marcotte Stamer
Jacqueline Stanley
Michael Starr
John L. Thurman

Government Institutes, Inc.
Rockville, MD
1993

Government Institutes, Inc., Rockville, Maryland 20850

Copyright © 1993 by Government Institutes. All rights reserved.
Published December 1993.

98 97 96 95 94 93   5 4 3 2 1

No part of this work may be reproduced or transmitted in any form or by any means, electronic or mechanical, including photocopying, recording, or any information storage and retrieval system, without permission in writing from the publisher. All requests for permission to reproduce material from this work should be directed to Government Institutes, Inc., 4 Research Place, Suite 200, Rockville, Maryland 20850.

The authors and publisher make no representation or warranty, express or implied, as to the completeness, correctness or utility of the information in this publication. In addition, the authors and publisher assume no liability of any kind whatsoever resulting from the use of or reliance upon the contents of this book.

Printed in the United States of America.

Library of Congress Cataloging-in-Publication Data

Employment law handbook: a complete reference for business/Stephen L. Berry... [et al.].
    p. cm.
Includes index.
ISBN 0-86587-361-5
    1. Labor laws and legislation--United States. 2. Affirmative action programs--Law and legislation--United States. I. Berry, Stephen L.
KF3455.E473   1993
344.73'01--dc20
[347.3041]   93-42334
                                                                        CIP

SUMMARY TABLE OF CONTENTS

Chapter 1: **AFFIRMATIVE ACTION** 1
Dawn S. Hyde

Chapter 2: **FAMILY & MEDICAL LEAVE ACT OF 1993** 21
Francis W. Palmieri
John L. Thurman

Chapter 3: **AMERICANS WITH DISABILITIES ACT OF 1990: EMPLOYER RESPONSIBILITIES** 44
Michael Starr

Chapter 4: **WAGES AND SALARIES** 77
Eric Paltell

Chapter 5: **EMPLOYEE BENEFIT COMPLIANCE MATTERS** 99
Frank Palmieri

Chapter 6: **OSHA CONCERNS** 139
Andrew C. Peterson
Martin C. Mead

| Chapter 7: | WORKPLACE DRUG TESTING PROGRAMS 160
Stephen L. Berry |

| Chapter 8: | IMMIGRATION AND VISAS FOR WORKERS 183
Ann L. Lamdin |

| Chapter 9: | DEALING WITH PROBLEM EMPLOYEES 206
Michael F. Marino |

| Chapter 10: | PERSONNEL POLICY MANUAL AND EMPLOYEE HANDBOOKS 229
Jacqueline D. Stanley |

| Chapter 11: | PERSONNEL AUDITS 248
Thomas P. Murphy |

| Chapter 12: | WORKERS' COMPENSATION...... 257
Cynthia Marcotte Stamer |

INDEX 308

TABLE OF CONTENTS

Chapter 1
AFFIRMATIVE ACTION

1.0 AN HISTORICAL PERSPECTIVE	1
1.1 Title VII of the Civil Rights Act of 1964	2
1.2 The Promulgation of Executive Orders 11246 and 11375	2
1.3 Rehabilitation Act of 1973	3
1.4 Americans with Disabilities Act of 1990	4
1.5 The Vietnam Era Veterans Readjustment Assistance Act of 1974	4
2.0 THE OFFICE OF FEDERAL CONTRACT COMPLIANCE PROGRAMS	4
2.1 Jurisdictional Requirements—Executive Orders 11246 and 11375	5
2.2 Written Affirmative Action Plans	6
3.0 THE SUPREME COURT AND AFFIRMATIVE ACTION	6
4.0 WHAT IS INCLUDED IN A WRITTEN AFFIRMATIVE ACTION PLAN?	6
5.0 STEPS TO BUILD AN AFFIRMATIVE ACTION PLAN	7
6.0 GUIDELINES FOR AFFIRMATIVE ACTION STATISTICAL COMPONENTS	8
6.1 Employees to be Included	8
6.2 Personnel Actions	10
6.3 Positive Actions	10

6.4 Negative Actions 10
   6.5 Applicant Flow 11
   6.6 Who is Considered an Applicant? 11
7.0 BASIC PLAN PREPARATION 12
8.0 AFFIRMATIVE ACTION NARRATIVE
    REPORTS 13
9.0 NARRATIVE COMPONENTS OF MINORITY
    AND FEMALES PLAN 13
   9.1 Preface 13
   9.2 Introduction 13
   9.3 Policy Statement 14
   9.4 Dissemination of Policy 14
   9.5 Responsibility for Implementation of the Plan .. 14
   9.6 Identification of Problem Areas 14
   9.7 Development and Execution of
       Action-Oriented Programs 14
   9.8 Internal Auditing and Reporting System 15
   9.9 Support of Community Action Programs 15
   9.10 Compliance with Sex Discrimination
        Guidelines 15
   9.11 Compliance with Religion, National
        Origin Guidelines 15
   9.12 Consideration of Minorities and Females
        Not in the Workforce 15
   9.13 Conclusion 15
10.0 DOCUMENTING AFFIRMATIVE ACTION
     COMMUNICATION, TRAINING AND GOOD
     FAITH EFFORTS 16
11.0 OFCCP AUDITS 17
   11.1 The Review or Audit Process 18
   11.2 Possible Review Outcomes 19
12.0 A REVIEW OF CURRENT AFFIRMATIVE
     ACTION PRACTICES 19
13.0 CONCLUSION 20

Chapter 2
FAMILY & MEDICAL LEAVE ACT OF 1993

1.0 INTRODUCTION	21
2.0 EMPLOYERS SUBJECT TO THE FMLA	22
2.1 The 50-Employee Threshold	22
2.2 Common Law Employees	23
2.3 Related Companies and Successor Employers	24
3.0 EMPLOYEES ELIGIBLE FOR FAMILY LEAVE	25
4.0 EMPLOYEE ENTITLEMENTS UNDER THE FMLA	26
4.1 Circumstances in Which Family Leave May Be Taken	27
4.2 Types of Leave Available to Employees	29
4.3 Notice and Certification Requirements Under the FMLA	30
4.4 Treatment of Employee Benefits Under FMLA	33
4.5 Coordination of Family Leave with Paid Leave	35
4.6 Job Security Under FMLA	36
5.0 REASONS FOR WHICH FAMILY LEAVE MAY BE DENIED	38
6.0 PENALTIES FOR VIOLATIONS OF THE FMLA	39
7.0 MISCELLANEOUS	40
7.1 Notice to Employees	40
7.2 Spouses Employed by Same Employer	41
7.3 Clarification of Employment Status	41
7.4 Coordination with State Family Leave Laws	42
7.5 Effective Date of the FMLA	42
8.0 FMLA APPROVAL MATRIX	42

Chapter 3
AMERICANS WITH DISABILITIES ACT OF 1990: EMPLOYER RESPONSIBILITIES

1.0 OVERVIEW	44

2.0 QUALIFIED PERSONS WITH DISABILITIES ... 45
   2.1 The Definition of Disability 45
      2.1.1 Physical or Mental Impairment 46
      2.1.2 Substantially Limits a Major Life Activity . 47
      2.1.3 Past and Suspected Impairments 48
   2.2 Otherwise Qualified for Employment 49
   2.3 Essential Job Functions 49
      2.3.1 Criteria of Essential Functions 49
      2.3.2 Evidence of Essential Functions 50
      2.3.3 Job Descriptions 51
   2.4 Drug and Alcohol Abusers 51
   2.5 Other Exceptions 52
3.0 HIRING AND SELECTION REQUIREMENTS ... 53
   3.1 Pre-Employment Inquiries 53
      3.1.1 Aptitudes and Abilities 53
      3.1.2 Nature and Severity of Disabilities 54
   3.2 Medical Examinations 55
      3.2.1 Scope of Medical Inquiries 55
      3.2.2 Confidentiality Requirements 56
   3.3 Employment Standards 56
      3.3.1 Selection Criteria 57
      3.3.2 Preferences Based on Qualifications 57
      3.3.3 Physical and Mental Qualifications 58
      3.3.4 Religious Preferences 58
   3.4 Workplace Safety 58
      3.4.1 The "Direct Threat" Standard 59
      3.4.2 Food-Handling Employees 59
   3.5 Testing Abilities, Not Disabilities 59
4.0 THE DUTY TO MAKE REASONABLE
    ACCOMMODATIONS 60
   4.1 The Concept of Reasonable Accommodation ... 60
   4.2 The Range of Reasonable Accommodation 61
   4.3 Accommodation and Job Performance 62
      4.3.1 Job Restructuring 63
      4.3.2 Modified Work Schedules 63
      4.3.3 Reassignment to a Vacant Position 64
      4.3.4 Adaptive Equipment or Devices 65
      4.3.5 Personal Assistants 65

4.4 The Process for Selecting a Reasonable
    Accommodation 66
    4.4.1 Identifying the Limitation 66
    4.4.2 Employee Consultation 67
    4.4.3 Selecting an Accommodation 68
4.5 The "Undue Hardship" Defense 68
    4.5.1 Disrupting Business Operations 69
    4.5.2 Excessive Cost 70
    4.5.3 The Employing Unit 71
5.0 EQUAL ACCESS TO EMPLOYMENT
    OPPORTUNITIES 71
    5.1 Non-Segregated Facilities 72
    5.2 Health Insurance 72
        5.2.1 Permissible Benefit Limitations 72
        5.2.2 Disability-Based Distinctions 73
    5.3 Leave Policies 74
    5.4 Contractual Arrangements 74
    5.5 Relationship and Association 75
    5.6 Retaliation and Interference 76

Chapter 4
WAGES AND SALARIES

1.0 INTRODUCTION 77
2.0 FAIR LABOR STANDARDS ACT 78
    2.1 Covered Employees and Employers 78
        2.1.1 Employees 78
        2.1.2 Employers 79
        2.1.3 Public Sector Employers 79
    2.2 Exemptions from Coverage 79
        2.2.1 Employee Exemptions 79
        2.2.2 Industry Exemptions 80
    2.3 Hours Worked and Compensation 81
        2.3.1 Minimum Wage 81
        2.3.2 Overtime 81
        2.3.3 Compensable Hours Worked 84
        2.3.4 Compensatory Time 87
    2.4 Record-Keeping Requirements 87

2.5 Penalties 88
      2.5.1 Civil Penalties 88
      2.5.2 Criminal Penalties 88
   2.6 Enforcement 88
   2.7 Child Labor Prohibitions 89
      2.7.1 Child Labor Standards for 16- and
            17-Year-Old Youths 90
      2.7.2 Child Labor Standards for 14- and
            15-Year-Old Youths 90
      2.7.3 Penalties 91
3.0 EQUAL PAY ACT OF 1963 91
   3.1 Requirements 91
   3.2 Enforcement 92
4.0 PREVAILING WAGE LAWS 92
5.0 STATE WAGE AND HOUR LAWS 93
   5.1 Overtime, Minimum Wage, and
       Child Labor Laws 93
   5.2 "Payment of Wages" Laws 93
6.0 WHITE COLLAR EXEMPTION CHECKLIST
    (APPENDIX A) 94
   6.1 Executive Employees 94
   6.2 Administrative Employees 95
   6.3 Professional Employees 96
7.0 OVERTIME CALCULATION CHART
    (APPENDIX B) 97
8.0 FLSA RECORDKEEPING CHECKLIST
    (APPENDIX C) 97

Chapter 5
EMPLOYEE BENEFIT COMPLIANCE MATTERS

1.0 OVERVIEW 99
2.0 RETIREMENT PLANS 100
   2.1 Qualified Retirement Plans 100
   2.2 Defined Benefit Plans 100
   2.3 Defined Contribution Plans 101
   2.4 Nonqualified Retirement Programs 102

   2.5 ERISA Retirement Plans 103
3.0 WELFARE BENEFIT PLANS 104
4.0 REPORTING AND DISCLOSURE RULES 104
   4.1 Form 5500 Requirements 105
   4.2 Exemptions from Filing 105
   4.3 When and Where To File 107
   4.4 Audit Requirements 107
   4.5 Sanctions for Failure to Obtain Audit 108
   4.6 Penalties for Failure to File 108
5.0 DISCLOSURES TO PARTICIPANTS 108
   5.1 Summary Plan Description 108
   5.2 Summary of Annual Report 110
6.0 TAX QUALIFICATION REQUIREMENTS 110
   6.1 Eligibility Requirements 110
   6.2 Minimum Coverage Rules 111
   6.3 General Nondiscrimination Rules 113
   6.4 Minimum Participation Requirements 114
   6.5 Vesting Rules 114
   6.6 Funding Requirements 115
   6.7 Section 415 Limitations on Benefits and
       Contributions 115
   6.8 401(k) Plan Testing 116
   6.9 Separate Line of Business Rules 119
7.0 MISCELLANEOUS AND TAX-RELATED
     ISSUES 121
   7.1 Highly Compensated Employees 121
   7.2 Rules for Top-Heavy Plans 122
   7.3 Compensation Limitation 124
   7.4 Pension Benefit Guaranty Corporation
       Premiums 125
   7.5 Antialienation Provisions and Qualified
       Domestic Relations Orders 125
8.0 COBRA REQUIREMENTS 125
   8.1 Purpose 126
   8.2 Effective Date 126
   8.3 Employers Subject to COBRA 126
   8.4 Definitional Considerations 127
   8.5 COBRA Coverage 128
   8.6 Election 129

8.7 Period of Coverage 129
8.8 Termination of Coverage 130
8.9 Notifications 130
8.10 Premium 131
8.11 Sanctions 131

Chapter 6
OSHA CONCERNS

1.0 INTRODUCTION 139
2.0 GENERAL INDUSTRY SAFETY AND HEALTH STANDARDS 140
  2.1 Standards of Universal Application 140
  2.2 Specific Safety Standards 143
    2.2.1 Structural Conditions 143
    2.2.2 Machinery 144
    2.2.3 Hazardous Materials 145
    2.2.4 Fire Protection 145
  2.3 Specific Health Standards 145
    2.3.1 Environmental Controls 146
    2.3.2 Toxic and Hazardous Substances 146
    2.3.3 Blood-Borne Diseases 147
    2.3.4 Process Safety 147
    2.3.5 Confined Spaces 148
    2.3.6 Special Industries 148
3.0 GENERAL DUTY CLAUSE 148
4.0 RECORDKEEPING AND REPORTING REGULATIONS 150
  4.1 General Requirements 150
  4.2 Fatalities or Multiple Hospitalizations 152
  4.3 Injuries and Illnesses 153
  4.4 Enforcement of Recordkeeping and Reporting Requirements 154
5.0 UNLAWFUL DISCRIMINATION 155
6.0 VARIANCES 156
7.0 EMPLOYER DEFENSES TO CITATIONS FOR VIOLATION OF OSHA STANDARDS 156
  7.1 The Infeasibility of Compliance Defense 157

7.2 The Isolated Incident Defense 157
7.3 The Greater Hazard Defense 158
7.4 The Multi-Employer Work Site Defense 158

Chapter 7
WORKPLACE DRUG TESTING PROGRAMS

1.0 INTRODUCTION 160
2.0 DRUG TESTING UNDER THE ADA 161
   2.1 Pre-Employment Medical Inquiries and
       Examinations 161
   2.2 Medical Examinations of Current Employees ... 162
   2.3 Employer Conduct Allowed by the ADA 162
3.0 DRUG TESTING UNDER THE U.S.
      CONSTITUTION 165
   3.1 Balancing Test Applied 165
   3.2 Application of the Legal Test to Specific
       Workplace Drug Testing Programs 166
       3.2.1 Applicant Testing 166
       3.2.2 Current Employees 168
       3.2.3 Fitness-for-Duty Testing 168
       3.2.4 Reasonable Suspicion Testing 168
       3.2.5 Post-Accident Testing 170
       3.2.6 Random Testing 170
4.0 MINIMIZING THE RISK OF LIABILITY 173
   4.1 Determine the Company's Need for an
       Alcohol and Drug Abuse Program 173
   4.2 Design an Alcohol and Drug Policy which
       Fits Your Company's Needs 173
   4.3 Draft a Comprehensive Company Policy
       Concerning Drugs, Alcohol, Controlled
       Substances and Searches 174
   4.4 Establish and Follow Proper Guidelines for
       Conducting Substance or Other Medical Tests .. 174
   4.5 Inquiries which Employers Should Make of
       Prospective Laboratories 175

4.6 Clearly Articulate Company Policy
to Employees 177
4.7 Train Supervisors to Deal Effectively and
Appropriately with Employees Who Appear
to be Under the Influence of or Abusing Drugs,
Alcohol or other Controlled Substances 177
4.8 Establish and Follow Appropriate Procedures
for Conducting Searches 178
4.9 Keep Information Confidential 181
4.10 If the Company is Unionized,
Involve the Union 182

Chapter 8
IMMIGRATION AND VISAS FOR WORKERS

1.0 OVERVIEW OF THE UNITED STATES
IMMIGRATION SYSTEM 183
  1.1 Determining Immigration Status 183
    1.1.1 United States Citizen 183
    1.1.2 Permanent Resident of the United States .. 184
    1.1.3 Temporary Resident 185
    1.1.4 Asylee 185
    1.1.5 Holder of Temporary Protected Status 185
    1.1.6 Nonimmigrant 186
    1.1.7 Illegal Aliens 186
  1.2 Determining an Individual's Entitlement to
Lawful Status in the United States 186
2.0 OBTAINING PERMANENT RESIDENCE IN THE
UNITED STATES THROUGH EMPLOYMENT ... 187
  2.1 Priority Workers 188
    2.1.1 Aliens of Extraordinary Ability in
the Arts, Sciences, Education, Business
or Athletics 188
    2.1.2 Outstanding Professors and Researchers ... 189
    2.1.3 Multinational Executives or Managers 190
  2.2 Professionals Holding Advanced Degrees
or Aliens of Exceptional Ability 191

      2.2.1 Professionals Holding Advanced Degrees .. 191
      2.2.2 Aliens of Exceptional Ability in the
           Sciences, Arts, and Business 192
  2.3 Other Workers 192
      2.3.1 Professional Employees with Bachelor's
           Degrees 193
      2.3.2 Skilled Workers 193
      2.3.3 Unskilled Workers 193
  2.4 Special Immigrants 193
  2.5 Investors 194
3.0 SATISFYING THE LABOR CERTIFICATION
     REQUIREMENT 194
4.0 OBTAINING TEMPORARY VISAS FOR
     WORK IN THE UNITED STATES 196
  4.1 B-1 Business Visitor Visa 196
  4.2 L-1 Intracompany Transferee Visa 197
  4.3 E-1 and E-2 Treaty Visas 197
  4.4 H-1B Temporary Worker Visa for Aliens
      Employed in Specialty Occupations 199
  4.5 H-3 Temporary Trainee Visa 200
  4.6 J-1 Exchange Visitor Visa 201
  4.7 O Visa for Aliens of Extraordinary Ability 202
  4.8 Q Visas for Participants in International
      Cultural Exchange Programs 202
5.0 THE IMPACT OF THE IMMIGRATION
     REFORM AND CONTROL ACT OF 1986
     ON EMPLOYERS IN THE UNITED STATES 202
  5.1 Verification Requirements 203
  5.2 Employer Penalties 204
  5.3 Discrimination Issues 204

Chapter 9
DEALING WITH
PROBLEM EMPLOYEES

1.0 OVERVIEW 206
2.0 SIGNS TO LOOK FOR 207
3.0 REAFFIRMING YOUR "AT WILL" STATUS 208

4.0 MINIMIZE PROBLEM EMPLOYEES:
CAREFULLY SCREEN CANDIDATES
THROUGH APPLICATIONS AND
INTERVIEWS 209
    4.1 Arrest and Conviction Inquiries 210
    4.2 Reference Checks 212
    4.3 Credit Checks 212
        4.3.1 Consumer Reports 213
        4.3.2 Investigative Consumer Reports (ICR) 213
    4.4 Polygraph Testing 214
    4.5 Psychological Tests 215
    4.6 Honesty Tests 216
    4.7 Prior Military Service 216
    4.8 Driving Records 217
5.0 TOOLS FOR THE EMPLOYER TO UTILIZE
DURING EMPLOYMENT IN DEALING WITH
PROBLEM EMPLOYEES 218
6.0 INVESTIGATION OF THE FACTS 219
7.0 SPECIAL TOOLS FOR MONITORING
PROBLEM EMPLOYEES 220
    7.1 Surveillance 220
        7.1.1 Surveillance at Work 220
        7.1.2 Surveillance at Home 223
    7.2 Drug Screens 225
    7.3 Searches 226

Chapter 10
PERSONNEL POLICY MANUAL AND EMPLOYEE HANDBOOKS

1.0 OVERVIEW 229
2.0 BENEFITS 229
3.0 WHO SHOULD WRITE IT? 230
4.0 ADOPTING POLICIES 231
    4.1 Does the Policy Make Sense? 231
    4.2 Does the Policy Pertain to Organizational
        Operations? 232
    4.3 Can the Policy be Consistently Applied? 232

4.4 Can the Policy be Easily Enforced by
   Supervisors or Followed by Employees? 233
4.5 Can the Policy Adapt to a Broad Range of
   Circumstances? 234
5.0 POLICY SOURCES 234
6.0 DRAFTING CONSIDERATIONS 235
7.0 OPEN VS. CLOSED POLICY STATEMENTS 238
8.0 FORMS 239
9.0 REVIEW AND REVISION 239
10.0 LOCATION 240
11.0 EMPLOYEE HANDBOOK 241
   11.1 What Information Should be Included in an
   Employee Handbook? 242

Chapter 11
PERSONNEL AUDITS

1.0 THE VALUE OF SELF-AUDITS 248
2.0 WHO SHOULD DO THEM? 249
3.0 TECHNIQUES TO PINPOINT YOUR
   COMPANY'S STRENGTH'S AND
   WEAKNESSES 250
4.0 UNION VULNERABILITY ASSESSMENT 255
5.0 EMPLOYEE ATTITUDE SURVEY 256
6.0 THE IMPORTANCE OF FOLLOWING UP
   ON VULNERABILITIES IDENTIFIED BY
   THE AUDIT 256

Chapter 12
WORKERS' COMPENSATION

1.0 INTRODUCTION 257
2.0 HISTORICAL EVOLUTION
     OF WORKERS' COMPENSATION 258
3.0 FEDERAL WORKERS' COMPENSATION LAWS......... 262

4.0	STATE WORKERS' COMPENSATION LAWS	265
	4.1 Covered Employments	266
	4.2 Compensable Injuries	270
5.0	COMPENSATION AND BENEFITS	275
	5.1 Medical Expense Compensation	276
	5.2 Wage Loss Compensation	277
	5.3 Permanent Disablement Compensation	280
	5.4 Death Compensation For Survivors	282
	5.5 Miscellaneous Benefits	283
	5.6 Prohibitions Against Discrimination Against Employees Claiming Workers' Compensation Benefits	284
	5.7 Administration and Dispute Resolution	285
	5.8 Financial Security Requirements	285
	5.9 Compulsory Nature of Workers' Compensation	287
6.0	COORDINATION OF STATEWORKERS' COMPENSATION LAWS	291
	6.1 Duty to Maintain Workers' Compensation Coverage in a Foreign State	291
	6.2 Coordination of Workers' Compensation Coverage in Multiple States	292
7.0	RELATED FEDERAL LAWS	294
	7.1 The Americans With Disabilities Act and Other Disability Discrimination Laws	294
	7.2 Employee Retirement Income Security Act of 1974	296
8.0	OSHA	298
9.0	THE WORKERS' COMPENSATION CRISIS	299
10.0	CONCLUSION	306
INDEX		308

ABOUT THE AUTHORS

Stephen L. Berry

Stephen L. Berry is an attorney in the Los Angeles office of Paul, Hastings, Janofsky & Walker, where he specializes in labor and employment law, representing management.

Mr. Berry has advised numerous employers in the development of drug and alcohol policies, and has defended employers on federal and state court lawsuits challenging their drug testing programs and in adverse employment actions based on those programs.

Dawn S. Hyde

Dawn S. Hyde is president of Berkshire Associates, a Washington, D.C. area human resources management consulting firm specializing in affirmative action services.

Ms. Hyde has more than ten years experience working with legal, business, and governmental communities in the preparation of affirmative action programs, development of outreach programs, and on-site audit consultation during OFCCP audits.

An acknowledged expert in her field, Ms. Hyde holds a Master of Administrative Science degree from the Johns Hopkins University, and has extensive experience in affirmative action programs, and co-authored the *Affirmative Action Handbook* for Government Institutes.

Ann L. Lamdin

Ann L. Lamdin is an attorney in the Baltimore, Maryland, office of Piper & Marbury. Ms. Lamdin advises businesses and individuals in all aspects of immigration law, including family and employment based immigrant visas, nonimmigrant visas for business and pleasure visits to the United States, business immigration planning, and compliance with the employer sanctions and anti-discrimination provisions of U.S. immigration laws.

Ms. Lamdin received her J.D. with honors from the University of Maryland School of Law and her bachelor's degree in business management, *magna cum laude*, also from the University of Maryland at College Park.

Michael F. Marino

Michael F. Marino is deputy head of the Labor and Employment Law Section of the national law firm of Reed Smith Shaw & McClay in the McLean, Virginia, office. Mr. Marino is labor counsel to national corporations and area businesses. He also represents management in collective bargaining negotiations, union organizing campaigns, arbitrations, NLRB, FLSA, OSHA, and EEOC matters, and DOL investigations.

Mr. Marino received his Master of Laws degree in labor law from Georgetown University Law Center, his J.D. from Syracuse University, and his B.S. from Cornell University School of Industrial and Labor Relations. He also served in the United States Marine Corps as a judge advocate and later as assistant general counsel of the Navy for employment matters. He is also a frequent lecturer and author on employment-related matters.

Martin C. Mead

Martin C. Mead practices in the area of representation of private and public employers in all aspects of employment law, including wrongful discharge and fair employment practice litigation; Occupational Safety and Health matters; arbitrations; and EEOC, workers' compensation, and wage/hour matters.

Mr. Mead is a graduate of Birmingham-Southern College in Alabama and received his law degree from Harvard Law School.

Thomas P. Murphy

Thomas P. Murphy is a partner in the McLean, Virginia and Washington, D.C., offices of Reed Smith Shaw & McClay, where he specializes in representing management in labor and employment law matters.

Mr. Murphy handles all types of labor and employment law matters for private and public sector clients. He serves as labor counsel to a number of regional and national corporations, including those engaged in manufacturing, energy, retail, health care and the defense industry.

Mr. Murphy received his J.D. from Vermont Law School and a B.S. in industrial management from Clarkson College of Technology. He is also a frequent lecturer and author on labor and employment law matters.

Francis W. Palmieri

Francis W. Palmieri is a partner in the law firm of Palmieri & Eisenberg, specializing in the practice of tax and ERISA employee benefit matters. He also headed the employee benefits practice for a major accounting firm in the Philadelphia region.

Mr. Palmieri has extensive experience in both tax and ERISA employee benefit matters, including retirement plans, compensation plans for taxable and tax-exempt organizations, healthcare cost containment, compensation programs, and medical and COBRA benefit matters.

Mr. Palmieri is an instructor at the Philadelphia Institute for Employee Benefits Training. He also has written extensively and is a co-author of *Complying With The Family And Medical Leave Act Compliance Guide* by Government Institutes, Inc.

Mr. Palmieri is a graduate of St. John's University School of Law and has an advanced law degree in taxation (LL.M.) from New York University School of Law. He is also a graduate of St. John's University College of Business Administration and is a Certified Public Accountant.

Eric Paltell

Eric Paltell is an attorney specializing in the representation of management in the fields of employment and labor relations law. He is an associate in the law firm of Piper & Marbury.

Mr. Paltell is an experienced labor and employee relations lawyer, representing both public and private employers in personnel and employment law matters, wrongful discharge litigation, union avoidance, NLRB proceedings, collective bargaining negotiations, grievance arbitration, EEO suits, and wage and hour cases.

Mr. Paltell obtained his undergraduate and law degrees from the University of Virginia.

Andrew C. Peterson

Andrew C. Peterson is a partner in the Los Angeles office of Paul, Hastings, Janofsky & Walker. He represents private and public employers in all aspects of employment law, including wrongful discharge, fair employment practice, and labor management litigation; Occupational Safety and Health matters; organizing campaigns; labor negotiations; arbitrations; matters before the Equal Employment Opportunity Commission, Fair Employment and Housing Commission, Office of Federal Contract Compliance Programs, and National Labor Relations Board; and wage/hour matters.

He has written and lectured extensively on a variety of employment matters and authored the *California OSHA Compliance Handbook* for Government Institutes.

Mr. Peterson received his A.B. degree from Wesleyan University, and his J.D. degree from the University of Chicago Law School. Before attending law school, he served in the U.S. Navy.

Cynthia Marcotte Stamer

Cynthia Marcotte Stamer is an associate with the firm of Gardere & Wynne. In the firm's Employee Benefits, Insurance and Health Care Section, Ms. Stamer helps employers design and administer cost-effective employment, employee health, worker's compensation and other employee benefit programs. She specializes in employee welfare and pension benefit plans, executive compensation, employee and personal insurance, trusts, ERISA litigation, labor and employment, tax, exempt organization and health law matters.

Ms. Stamer advises companies about the design, implementation and administration of self-insured and insured employee welfare benefit and workers compensation programs to meet their budgetary goals and employee benefit objectives.

Ms. Stamer is a graduate of Arizona State University and a graduate of Loyola Law School. She joined Gardere & Wynne in 1988 after practicing employee benefits law in Los Angeles, California and Phoenix, Arizona.

Jacqueline Stanley

Jacqueline Stanley is a freelance legal writer in Greensboro, North Carolina. She writes extensively and specializes in developing personnel policy manuals and employee handbooks.

A graduate of Wake Forest University Law School, Ms. Stanley also teaches legal research and writing courses at a local college. In addition to being a member of the Greensboro and North Carolina Bar Associations, Ms. Stanley is the vice chair of publications for the Career and Family Committee of the American Bar Association.

Michael Starr

Michael Starr is labor counsel to Parker Chapin Flattau & Klimpl in New York City. He practices in all areas of labor and employment relations law emphasizing litigation of employment-discrimination and labor-management disputes, and labor aspects of corporate transactions. He has spoken and written extensively in matters relating to employment discrimination, preventive employee relations, and individual employee rights.

Mr. Starr graduated from Yale Law School, where he was an editor of the *Yale Law Journal* and holds a doctorate in philosophy from the University of Michigan. He has served on the Labor & Employment Law Committee of the Association of the Bar of the City of New York and is a member of the Human Resources Committee of the New York Chamber of Commerce and Industry.

John L. Thurman

John L. Thurman is a partner with Mason, Griffin & Pierson in Princeton, New Jersey, where he is co-chair of the Labor & Employment Practice Group. Mr. Thurman consults with human resources professionals and inhouse counsel on difficult wrongful discharge, EEO, ERISA, and affirmative action compliance matters and provides training to executives and managers on the prevention and effective management of employment litigation.

Mr. Thurman lectures at the Rutgers University Center for Management Development and is a frequent speaker to employer groups and professional organizations. He is a graduate of the Vanderbilt University School of Law, and holds degrees from Oberlin College and Harvard Divinity School. He also has co-authored the *Complying With The Family And Medical Leave Act Compliance Guide* for Government Institutes, Inc.

Chapter 1
AFFIRMATIVE ACTION

Dawn S. Hyde
Berkshire Associates Inc.

1.0 AN HISTORICAL PERSPECTIVE

Affirmative action programs have become a part of the fabric of day-to-day business life. Most employers understand that affirmative action is not only essential in keeping their government business, but is also an important part of operating a successful business. In 1986, the Department of Labor published a study entitled Workforce 2000, in which it analyzed the number of new entrants to the workforce for the years 1985 through 2000. The analysis showed that of those who would be newly entering the workforce, only 15 percent would be white males. Clearly, the ability to hire and retain the other 85 percent will be increasingly important to business success.

This trend toward widespread implementation of affirmative action is the end product of a process that began in 1964 with the passage of Title VII of the Civil Rights Act. This and related federal laws pertinent to affirmative action are summarized as follows:

1.1 Title VII of the Civil Rights Act of 1964

Title VII of the Civil Rights Act prohibits discrimination on the basis of race, color, religion, sex and national origin.[1] During the extensive debate concerning that then-controversial statute, some of the most virulent opposition concerned the possible granting of preferences to individuals on the basis of their protected status. Throughout the debate, supporters of Title VII, including Senator Hubert Humphrey, repeatedly stated that Title VII would not permit any requirement that an employer give preferential treatment to any minority group. Senator Humphrey stated:

> Contrary to the allegations of some opponents of the Title, there is nothing in it that will give any power to the Commission or to any Courts to require hiring, firing, or promotion of employees in order to meet racial "quota" or to achieve a certain racial balance.[2]
> It is claimed that the Bill would require racial quotas for all hiring, when in fact it provides that race shall not be a basis for making personnel decisions.[3]

It seemed, then, that Title VII could not serve as a vehicle for affirmative action. Some other method of addressing the nation's systemic employment inequities was needed.

1.2 The Promulgation of Executive Orders 11246 and 11375

One year after Title VII, President Johnson, recognizing that it would not be possible to get an affirmative action statute through Congress, decided to require government contractors to take affirmative action in employment for minorities. To that end, he promulgated Executive Order 11246 on September 24, 1965. Later, Executive Order 11375 imposed the same rules for women.

---

[1] 42 U.S.C. §2000e.
[2] 110 Cong. Rec. 6549 (1964).
[3] *Id.* at 6553.

The Executive Orders required the inclusion of an equal opportunity clause in all subcontracts and purchase orders by government contractors. They also provided for sanctions and penalties and for enforcement by "rules, regulations, or orders as the Secretary of Labor may issue and adopt."

1.3 Rehabilitation Act of 1973

The Rehabilitation Act of 1973 requires federal contractors or subcontractors having contracts in excess of $2,500 to take affirmative action in employment for individuals with handicaps. The Rehabilitation Act defines an individual with handicaps as a person who: (1) has a physical or mental impairment which substantially limits one or more of such person's major life activities; (2) has a record of such impairment; or, (3) is regarded as having such impairment. By "major life activity" the definition means activities like walking, talking, breathing, or working. An example of someone with a "record" of an impairment is a person who has recovered from cancer but who is discriminated against because of her past disability. An example of a person who is "regarded as having an impairment" is someone who has a significant burn on his face which does not actually limit him in any major life activity, but who is nonetheless discriminated against because of the disfigurement.

An employer must make reasonable accommodations for any covered disabilities. If an employer can effect some modification in a job's requirements, and this modification will allow the individual with handicaps to do the job, then the change should be made. Some examples of reasonable accommodations include job restructuring, acquisition or modification of equipment or devices, and reassignment to vacant positions.

An employer can demonstrate that the accommodation would impose undue hardship. An undue hardship is an action that requires significant difficulty or expense for the employer. Among the factors are the nature and costs of the accommodation, the number of persons employed, the type of operation of the employer, and the number, type or location of the employer's facilities. If the balance of these factors makes it unreasonably burdensome to accommodate an employee with handicaps, it is probably not necessary to make the accommodation.

1.4 Americans with Disabilities Act of 1990

Effective July, 1992, the Americans with Disabilities Act of 1990 (ADA) makes discrimination against persons with disabilities illegal. The definitions and rules are virtually identical to those under the Rehabilitation Act. The primary difference is that the Rehabilitation Act applies only to government contractors, whereas the ADA applies to all covered employers.

1.5 The Vietnam Era Veterans Readjustment Assistance Act of 1974

Employers with a federal contract or subcontract for $10,000 or more are covered by Section 402 of the Vietnam Era Veterans Readjustment Assistance Act of 1974. The requirements for affirmative action under the veterans act largely parallel those under the rehabilitation act.

The veterans act requires government contractors and subcontractors to take affirmative action to employ and advance in employment qualified disabled veterans and veterans of the Vietnam era. A disabled veteran is a person entitled to a disability compensation under laws administered by the Veterans Administration for disability rated at 30 percent or more, or a person whose discharge or release from active duty was for a disability incurred or aggravated in the line of duty. A qualified disabled veteran is a veteran who is capable of performing a particular job with a reasonable accommodation to his or her disability.

A veteran of the Vietnam Era is a person who has served on active duty for a period of more than 180 days, a part of which occurred between August 5, 1964 and May 7, 1975.

2.0 THE OFFICE OF FEDERAL CONTRACT COMPLIANCE PROGRAMS

In 1978 President Carter consolidated the responsibility for monitoring affirmative action within the Office of Federal

Contract Compliance Programs (OFCCP), a division of the Department of Labor. The OFCCP issued regulations that are contained at Chapter 60 of Part 41 of the Code of Federal Regulations. Those regulations, which are some 120 pages in length, generally cover all issues within the jurisdiction of the OFCCP.

2.1 Jurisdictional Requirements—Executive Orders 11246 and 11375

Under the regulations, the requirements of the Executive Orders are imposed only on government contractors and subcontractors who have a single contract for supplies, services, or the use of real or personal property in the amount of $10,000 or more. An indefinite quantity contract that provides for continual supply in excess of $10,000 is also covered.

Under the regulations, banks and other financial institutions, however, which serve as depositories of federal funds in any amount or as issuing and paying agents for U.S savings bonds, or who are covered by the Federal Deposit Insurance Corporation (FDIC), are also covered by the Equal Opportunity Clause of the Executive Orders regardless of any dollar amount.

There has been a major controversy as to whether having federal deposit insurance alone should be enough. When the OFCCP proposed its regulations, both the FDIC and the Federal Reserve Board opposed them. Recently, an administrative law judge held that such insurances alone are not enough to provide coverage, but the OFCCP continues to adhere to its position in the regulations. It may be, however, that if deposit insurance is the only contract, the OFCCP will refer any matters to the Equal Employment Opportunity Commission or the Department of Justice.

It is important to recognize that because the Executive Order extends to subcontractors, there is a tier effect. A major government contractor may receive a multi-million dollar contract and through subcontractors implicate literally hundreds of suppliers who have subcontracts that in some way relate to the overall contract if their subcontract exceeds $10,000.

Another important aspect of the Executive Orders is that once a contractor is covered, the entire entity of the contractor may come under the Executive Orders.

2.2 Written Affirmative Action Plans

Those contractors or subcontractors having contracts over $50,000 and who have 50 or more employees must prepare written affirmative action plans. Banks that serve as depositories of federal funds or which are issuing and paying agents for U.S. savings bonds, or are FDIC-insured must have written plans.

As with rules for coverage under the $10,000 contract provision, there is no aggregating of contracts. Moreover, state and local governments are exempted from preparing a written plan except for educational institutions, utilities, or medical facilities.

3.0 THE SUPREME COURT AND AFFIRMATIVE ACTION

The case history indicates that the Supreme Court will generally uphold affirmative action efforts as long as it satisfies their affirmative action test. The test as it stands today has three parts, a demonstrated underutilization or history of discrimination, a plan that is temporary and designed to remedy the problem, and the rights of the non-protected people are not unnecessarily trammeled.

4.0 WHAT IS INCLUDED IN A WRITTEN AFFIRMATIVE ACTION PLAN?

An affirmative action plan is prepared on a yearly basis and includes a statistical analysis of the current workforce compared to availability and narrative sections on the company's policy, who has responsibility and what affirmative action programs are in place. Major elements of the statistical portion of the Plan include:

- Analyses of the workforce by department and job group to determine the representation of women and minorities.

- An availability analysis which determines by job group the percentage of minorities and women who might be available for employment by or promotion within the organization.
- A utilization analysis to determine if minorities or women are currently being underutilized in any job group. "Underutilization" is defined as having fewer minorities or women in a particular job group than would reasonably be expected based on their availability. Where minorities and women are underutilized, goals are developed to correct these deficiencies. Special actions are planned to ensure the employment and/or promotion of qualified minorities and women to meet the goals.
- All personnel actions are reviewed to ensure that they are in accord with the Company's commitments to a policy of Equal Employment Opportunity.

5.0 STEPS TO BUILD AN AFFIRMATIVE ACTION PLAN

Steps to build an affirmative action plan include the following:

1. Determine the employees to include in the plan.
2. Review the list of data requirements. Audit the data to determine which data can be used in its present format and which needs to be corrected or developed. Recordkeeping systems should be updated as needed to ensure the collection and maintenance of data required for future reports.
3. Decide which census areas to use for availability analyses.
4. Prepare Workforce Analysis and Lines of Progression.
5. Prepare Job Group Analysis by determining the number and percent of employees in each job group, by job title, ethnic group and sex. A job

group is one or more jobs having similar skills, job content, wage rates, and promotional opportunities. Job groups should generally not include jobs from more than one EEO category. EEO categories or job groups of less than 30 generally should not be subdivided.
6. Complete the Eight Factor Availability Analysis by determining the percent of availability for each factor. Value weights for each factor to determine the final availability for each job group.
7. Determine areas of underutilization and calculate standard deviation of availability to utilization to determine significant problem areas.
8. Establish goals on availability percentages for hiring plus promotions into underutilized areas.
9. Analyze the personnel actions, such as promotions and transfers, and the applicant flow. Perform four/fifths analyses to determine whether there is adverse impact from your selection and termination processes.
10. Prepare a Goal Attainment Analysis and two written narratives, one for minorities and females and one for veterans and the disabled.

6.0 GUIDELINES FOR AFFIRMATIVE ACTION STATISTICAL COMPONENTS

Compliance with affirmative action regulations begins with the collection of certain information about the Company's employee base which will provide the foundation for statistical reports as well as a solid defense for personnel activity. Affirmative action data considerations include the employees to be included and specific data requirements about both the employee base and applicant flow.

6.1 Employees to be Included

For single facility groups, the affirmative action plan will include all full- and part-time employees and any temporary employees expected to remain on the company payroll for more than thirty days.

For multi-location groups, divide the organization into facility locations. Similar to the EEO-1 Report requirements, plan to prepare a statistical analysis for the headquarters facility. Include the following in this report:

(1) all employees in the same geographic area who work at the headquarters location. Depending upon location and similarity of business units, local facilities with fewer than fifty employees may be included in the headquarters plan; and,

(2) facility employees at outlying locations (such as a plant manager or regional sales manager) who were hired and/or are directly supervised by a member of headquarters staff. This is referred to as the Corporate Initiative.

A separate statistical analysis for every facility which employs fifty or more people must be completed. A written affirmative action plan is not required for outlying facilities with less than 50 employees.

Once determinations have been made about the type and number of affirmative action plans required, data gathering, organizing and evaluation will begin. Data requirements include:

- Roster of Employees
- Personnel Actions (new hires, applicants, promotions, transfers, terminations, etc.)
- Applicant Flow (list of applicants)
- Data Tables or Directories
  —Position Table (job title directory)
  —Department Table
  —Applicant Disposition Table
  —Termination Table
  —Gender/Race (gender/ethnicity) Table

6.2 Personnel Actions

For the purpose of affirmative action, personnel action data should be gathered for the 12-month period prior to the annual plan date.

Personnel action data to be analyzed as a part of the affirmative action plan includes the following:

6.3 Positive Actions

Hires—Workers added to the organization's payroll. Employees placed on the payroll for a short-term, temporary basis (less than 30 days) are not included as hires.

Promotions—Any personnel activity resulting in movement to a position affording higher pay or greater rank, and/or providing for greater skill or responsibility, or the opportunity to attain such.

Transfers—A personnel action which results either in movement from one department to another or a lateral position change within a department which is not otherwise classified as a promotion.

Recalls—The return of workers to the payroll following layoff but prior to a complete break in service.

Other—Significant positive personnel actions which are often recorded and evaluated for the purpose of affirmative action include training, additional compensation or bonuses, accommodations, good faith and volunteer efforts. When possible, specific information regarding these activities should be recorded and evaluated as any other positive personnel action to ensure and document affirmative action implementation.

6.4 Negative Actions

Terminations—Separation of an employee from the active and inactive payroll.

Lay Offs—The separation of an employee from the active payroll during a reduction in force.

Demotions—Any management-initiated personnel activity resulting in movement to a position affording lower pay, rank, or responsibility.

Other—Significant negative personnel actions which are often recorded and evaluated for the purpose of affirmative action include disapproval of training, denial of additional compensation or bonuses, refusal to accommodate and disciplinary actions.

6.5 Applicant Flow

Applicant flow is a record of applicants for employment during the plan year showing specific members of each racial, ethnic, and sex group who applied for positions.

6.6 Who is Considered an Applicant?

An applicant for the purpose of affirmative action reporting should be defined to ensure conformance to the regulations and to comply with organizational policy and procedures. Many firms define an applicant as an individual who completes and submits an approved company application. Other firms consider individuals who have submitted resumes to be applicants, provided they complete and return an applicant identification form. Many firms will not accept unsolicited resumes and will consider solicited resumes only if they are timely and contain sufficient information.

To limit applicant flow liability, more and more organizations accept applications only for open positions and targeted recruitment or difficult-to-fill positions. In addition, many organizations accept applications only at selected locations, on specific days, during assigned hours and allow individuals to apply and be considered for only one position at a time. The following rules should be considered when developing applicant definitions and procedures:

1. Applicant flow data should be collected from each applicant for each position sought.
2. While pre-employment submission of race, sex and ethnic identity is generally considered to be a voluntary action on the part of the applicant, applicants should be encouraged to complete the requested information.
3. Applicant self-identification information should be separated from each application for recording purposes, not circulated or made part of the information considered during the hiring process.
4. If applicant identification information appears to be incorrect, the applicant may be asked to review it for accuracy. In general, racial/ethnic identification should not be questioned and in no case should it be permissible for a company employee to change applicant information in any way.
5. Do not allow an individual to apply or be considered for "any" position; insist they apply for a specific position.

7.0 BASIC PLAN PREPARATION

The following table shows the reports which are required for the preparation of an affirmative action plan, plus the data needed to prepare the these reports.

REQUIRED REPORTS	Workforce Analysis Lines of Progression	Job Group Analysis Availability/Utilization Goals	Personnel Actions Other Reports
DATA NEEDED	—Roster of Employees —Department Table —Job Title/Code Table	—Roster of Employees —Job Table —Job Grouping —Census Data —Promotions (if possible)	—Job Title/Code Table —Job Groupings —Personnel Actions

8.0 AFFIRMATIVE ACTION NARRATIVE REPORTS

The completed plan will include two narrative reports which include a statement of the policy, how the policy has been disseminated internally and externally, basic findings, and action programs. One report will address the issues for minorities and females and a second report will address the issues of veterans and disabled employees.

9.0 NARRATIVE COMPONENTS OF MINORITY AND FEMALES PLAN

The OFCCP regulations provide a useful outline of the narrative components of an affirmative action plan.[4] While the regulations do provide guidance, the contractor should not recite or paraphrase the bland language of the regulations. The OFCCP is looking for activities specific to the contractor which have been carefully planned to achieve real affirmative action and increased employment opportunities for minorities and females.

9.1 Preface

The Preface includes several legal points about the language and preparation of the plan to position the contractor favorably against reverse discrimination charges, disclosure of confidential information, and use of the plan by litigants.

9.2 Introduction

The Introduction is an optional summary of contractor's business, positive compliance history, or affirmative action accomplishments. This is an opportunity to create a positive, upbeat view of the firm and its affirmative action record, progress, and status. During recessionary times, the Introduction can be used to explain lack of opportunity or poor business conditions which have limited affirmative action activities and successes.

---

[4] 41 C.F.R., Sec. 60-2.

9.3 Policy Statement

A Policy Statement signed by the CEO, reaffirms commitment to equal employment opportunity for all personnel actions, designates affirmative action officer, and identifies an internal reporting and monitoring procedure.

9.4 Dissemination of Policy

A Dissemination of Policy describes the steps taken internally and externally to widely communicate the policy.

9.5 Responsibility for Implementation of the Plan

Responsibility for Implementation of the Plan outlines the job duties of the affirmative action officer.

9.6 Identification of Problem Areas

One of the most sensitive and comprehensive sections of the AAP, this is supposed to be a critical self-analysis where the contractor reviews in detail job groups and organizational units to determine whether there is any adverse impact in personnel actions against minorities or women and also reviews virtually all other phases of its compliance. While the contractors should know the problem areas best, since the affirmative action program is not guaranteed confidentiality and non-disclosure under the Freedom of Information Act, in practice contractors must use extraordinary care in crafting this section.

9.7 Development and Execution of Action-Oriented Programs

Action-oriented programs must be designed to address the actual problem areas identified including specific programs to increase the employment or promotion opportunities for the affected class(es). For example, the OFCCP evaluates these programs as to whether they were sufficiently specific to accomplish the aim for which they were created and whether they were properly executed.

9.8 Internal Auditing and Reporting System

Cited in the policy statement, this section describes the process of monitoring AAP progress, management input and accountability, and internal auditing systems.

9.9 Support of Community Action Programs

Here the focus is on the contractor's and employees' support of external action programs that would foster training or employment opportunities for any protected class.

9.10 Compliance with Sex Discrimination Guidelines

Compliance with Sex Discrimination Guidelines discusses contractor's compliance with OFCCP's guidelines.[5]

9.11 Compliance with Religion, National Origin Guidelines

Compliance with Religion, National Origin Guidelines states efforts to insure non-discrimination along these guidelines.

9.12 Consideration of Minorities and Females Not in the Workforce

A paragraph primarily stating that the contractor identifies itself as an equal employment opportunity/affirmative action employer in the media and advertisements.

9.13 Conclusion

Like the Introduction, the Conclusion is not required but is an opportunity to cite progress and show the contractor in a favorable light.

---

[5] 41 C.F.R., Part 60-20.

10.0 DOCUMENTING AFFIRMATIVE ACTION COMMUNICATION, TRAINING AND GOOD FAITH EFFORTS

In preparation for monitoring check points, an OFCCP audit, or the annual affirmative action plan update, it is important to keep a record of all affirmative action activities. Attendance at meetings and affirmative action program activities should be recorded and maintained, minutes for important meetings should be summarized. Materials, which document activities and efforts should be collected for reference and possible use as exhibits to the affirmative action plan(s) such as the following:

- organization charts
- current annual report
- brief history of the organization
- copies of relevant union agreements or contracts
- information on previous OFCCP audits (dates & disposition)
- prior affirmative action plan(s)
- employee handbook
- formal EEO policy statement
- sexual harassment and/or general harassment policy
- employee newsletters
- company and/or recruiting brochures
- booklets describing benefits
- copies of employment advertisements
- performance appraisal forms
- copy of purchase order
- memos re: company-sponsored social and community activities
- pictures of employee activities
- relevant communications: (attach documentation, outlines, copies of letters, minutes, etc.)
- relevant meeting notices and materials
- employee orientation information
- supervisory orientation information
- training programs to help unemployed or underemployed

- relevant employment recruiting and outreach resources: newspapers, trade associations, trade journals, civic or community groups, public agencies, private agencies, minority organizations, women's groups, organizations for the disabled, veterans groups, secondary schools, technical schools, community colleges, colleges and universities, other schools
- policies or procedures which explain procedures for: application, selection, use of arrest records, credit checks, security clearance, military records, employment physicals, required tests, job descriptions, job specifications, job costing, transfers, promotions, seniority systems, apprenticeship programs.

In addition, all accommodations made for employees and/or job applicants, including specific examples, should be documented. This will include accommodations for Vietnam Era and disabled veterans, disabled individuals and those based on religion or national origin. This information should include employee or applicant name, position held and/or requested, a description of the accommodation, and reason for the accommodation. Types of accommodations which should be documented include:

- salary continuation, benefit and leave programs
- policy and/or procedure exceptions
- development and/or use of special building and parking accessibility
- revision of work responsibilities and/or duties
- revision of schedule(s)
- development or provision of special equipment, furniture, or special tools

11.0 OFCCP AUDITS

There are three types affirmative action audits or reviews: (1) pre-award reviews; (2) reviews based upon complaints; and (3) regularly scheduled reviews.

Pre-award reviews occur prior to the award of a federal government contract of one million dollars or more. Detailed in chapter 5 of the compliance manual, a notice of a pre-award review generally gives the government contractor five days to prepare for a combined desk and on-site review. During 1993, distribution of limited OFCCP resources have severely curtailed the number of actual pre-award audits conducted.

Complaint reviews generally result from individual complaints of discrimination on the basis of disability, Vietnam Era or status as a disabled veteran. Such a complaint triggers a review and investigation of the circumstances surrounding that charge.

Regularly scheduled reviews occur when contractors are selected under the OFCCP's Equal Employment Data System (EEDS) procedures or at the discretion of the district director. Most affirmative action reviews are selected through EEDS and many contractors continue to be audited at least once every three years. Additionally, with the maturity of the compliance enforcement program, special Glass Ceiling Audits are reflecting a new initiative. Conducted as regular audits with an additional component, audit focus is placed on entry, mid- and senior-level management to determine how top positions are filled, what action-oriented recruitment strategies are employed, how people are developed and promoted through the organization, how they are identified for special assignments, etc. In addition to regular salary analyses, these audits focus on a broader look at executive compensation including stock options and other perquisites. Currently managed by the National Office of the OFCCP, it is expected that, during the next fiscal year, the authority for Glass Ceiling Audits will be given to the regions to be conducted by the district office directors. Special training will no doubt be provided.

11.1 The Review or Audit Process

Companies selected by the OFCCP for a review are notified by certified letter. The law outlines three phases of the audit process:

- Desk Audit—initial review of the AAP/support documents
- Onsite Review—in-depth review of records and facilities
- Offsite Analysis—additional analyses as needed to conclude review

11.2 Possible Review Outcomes

There are several possible outcomes to an OFCCP review. Serious enforcement action, which can normally be avoided by cooperating with the OFCCP auditor, can include termination from current contracts, or debarment from future contracts.

A conciliation agreement is required when serious violations are found, such as when back pay is ordered. Major deficiencies in compliance with the regulations also require a conciliation agreement. A formal contract between a government contractor and the OFCCP, a conciliation agreement includes a mandatory enforcement clause allowing the OFCCP to take action whenever the employer violates the conciliation agreement with 15 days' notice. Quarterly or semi-annual reporting may also be required for a period of up to two years.

Less formal than the conciliation agreement, the letter of commitment is required when minor deficiencies are identified. Signed by an official of the organization, the letter of commitment itemizes deficiencies and specifies remedies. One or two monitoring reports may also be required to allow follow-up by the OFCCP.

Finally, the best possible outcome, a letter of compliance certifies that the employer is in full compliance with the regulations. This outcome occurs most infrequently, since the OFCCP often takes the position that improvement is always possible.

12.0 A REVIEW OF CURRENT AFFIRMATIVE ACTION PRACTICES

The term "affirmative action" was conceived over a quarter of a century ago, yet people are continuing to ask just what this really means? Obviously, "taking affirmative action" means taking positive steps above and beyond routine personnel practice. The steps might include the actions taken by a contractor to create applicant pools, which include minorities or women, for job vacancies where they are underutilized as compared to their numbers in the qualified workforce. The steps must also insure that, subsequent to employment, individuals are treated without discrimination through internal dissemination of EEO information as well as through monitoring of personnel activity.

Often however, these steps result in affirmative actions that are reactive rather than proactive in nature. Today, successful affirmative action *must* be proactive, including action-oriented programs as the cornerstone of affirmative action commitment. Future success depends upon action-oriented programs which are linked to the attainment of established goals. Organizations with successful affirmative action programs must develop and execute action-oriented programs which are specific enough and result-oriented enough to accomplish the aims for which they were created.

13.0 CONCLUSION

Successful affirmative action practices will have increasing strategic importance as entrants to the U.S. workforce, predominantly women and minorities, change the face of the workplace. Government contractors must engage in affirmative action in all employment decisions and maintain written annual affirmative action plans. Although the statistical analyses are extensive and time-consuming, the heart of these plans are the identification of problem areas and action-oriented programs to address these problems.

Chapter 2

FAMILY & MEDICAL LEAVE ACT OF 1993[1]

Francis W. Palmieri
Palmieri & Eisenberg

John L. Thurman
Mason, Griffin & Pierson

1.0 INTRODUCTION

The Family & Medical Leave Act of 1993 ("FMLA" or "Act"), which takes effect on August 5, 1993, is the product of eight years of Congressional debate over an appropriate response to the changing composition of the American family and workplace. In recognition of the pressures facing today's families, the FMLA's stated purpose is:

- to balance the demands of the workplace with the needs of families, to promote the stability of

---

[1] This chapter was prepared shortly after the release of interim regulations interpreting the Family & Medical Leave Act of 1993, Pub. L. No. 103-3, 107 Stat. 6. The regulations, which will appear at 29 CFR Part 825, became effective with the Act on August 5, 1993. Final regulations will be released early in 1994. Government Institutes, Inc., is publishing a detailed Compliance Guide prepared by the authors of this chapter which will provide all forms and policies necessary for implementation of and compliance with the Act. Please contact Government Institutes, Inc., for additional information.

economic security of families, and to promote national interest in preserving family integrity;
- to entitle employees to take reasonable leave for medical reasons, for the birth or adoption of a child, and for the care of a child, spouse, or parent who has a serious health condition;
- to accomplish these goals in a manner that accommodates the legitimate interests of employers; and
- to accomplish these goals in a manner which preserves equal opportunity.[2]

The objective of this chapter is to assist employers in understanding their responsibilities and rights under the FMLA. This chapter does not address the special rules covering employees of local educational agencies or leave for civil service employees. Many states have adopted their own family leave acts. Employers should consult state laws for local compliance obligations.[3]

2.0 EMPLOYERS SUBJECT TO THE FMLA

2.1 The 50-Employee Threshold

An employer with 50 or more employees may be subject to the FMLA. To determine whether the Act applies, an employer must examine its workforce in the current, and possibly the preceding calendar year. If the employer employed at least 50

---

[2] *See* Pub. L. No. 103-3, § 2(b), 107 Stat. 6, 7.

[3] As of January 1993, the following states had adopted family leave measures affecting private and public sector employees: California, Connecticut, District of Columbia, Hawaii, Kentucky, Maine, Minnesota, Montana, New Jersey, Oregon, Rhode Island, Vermont, Washington, and Wisconsin. In addition, the following states had adopted measures affecting public sector employees only: Alaska, Arizona, Delaware, Florida, Georgia, Idaho, Illinois, Maryland, Missouri, North Dakota, Oklahoma, South Carolina, and West Virginia. Iowa, Louisiana, Massachusetts, Puerto Rico, and Tennessee have adopted laws which provide for maternity leave. Section 7.4 of this chapter addresses the coordination of the FMLA with state laws.

employees nationwide each working day during each of 20 or more calendar workweeks (they need not be consecutive workweeks) in either the current or preceding calendar year, the employer is subject to the Act.[4] For purposes of this rule, both full-time and part- time employees are taken into consideration. An employee whose name appears on the employer's payroll is considered to be employed for each working day of the calendar week the employee appears on the payroll, and must be counted whether or not any compensation was received for the week in question.[5]

Example: Last year an employer employed 40-full time employees and 10 part-time employees, all of whom appeared on the payroll for at least 20 calendar workweeks. Earlier this year the employer laid off five part-time employees, thereby reducing its workforce to 45 employees. The employer is subject to the Act based on its employment of 50 employees in the preceding year.

It should be noted, as is further addressed below,[6] that employees do not enjoy an automatic entitlement to family leave under the Act if their employer meets the 50-employee threshold for coverage.

2.2 Common Law Employees

The Act's definition of employee is drawn from the Fair Labor Standards Act which defines an employee as "any

---

[4] *See* Pub. L. No. 103-3, § 101(4), 107 Stat. 6, 8; *see also* 29 C.F.R. § 825.105(d) (Interim Regs.).

[5] *See* 29 C.F.R. § 825.105(a) (Interim Regs.).

[6] *See* Section 3.0.

individual employed by an employer."[7] The Supreme Court of the United States has interpreted similar language in an employee benefits context to *exclude* independent contractors.[8] In reaching this ruling, the Court concluded that the term "employee" should be given its common law meaning. Accordingly, the status of an individual as an employee, independent contractor, or leased employee must be carefully examined to determine whether the individual should be counted as an employee for purposes of the Act. The Interim Regulations provide that leased employees are to be counted as employees for purposes of meeting the 50-employee threshold.[9]

Example: An employer with 30 professional employees engages the services of 20 full-time clerical workers through an employment agency or employee leasing company. Under these facts, the employer is deemed the employer of all 50 individuals and therefore is subject to the FMLA.

2.3 Related Companies and Successor Employers

Separate companies will be deemed parts of a single employer and their employees will be aggregated for purposes of meeting the 50-employee threshold for FMLA coverage if they constitute an "integrated employer". Identifying separate entities as an integrated employer requires evaluation of their relationship including: (1) extent of common management, (2) interrelation between operations, (3) centralized control of labor relations, and (4) degree of common ownership/financial control.

---

[7] *See* Pub. L. No. 103-3, § 101(3), 107 Stat. 6, 8 (incorporating 29 U.S.C. § 203(e)).

[8] *See Nationwide Mutual Ins. Co. v. Darden,* —U.S.—, 112 S.Ct. 1344, 117 L.Ed.2d 581 (1992).

[9] *See* 29 C.F.R. § 825.106 (Interim Regs.).

A determination on integrated employer status can be made only after the companies' entire relationship has been reviewed.[10]

A successor in interest to a covered employer is also subject to the FMLA. Consequently, sale or transfer of a company to a successor in interest will not affect an employee's entitlement to leave. The determination of whether an employer is a "successor in interest" turns on the totality of circumstances including the following: (1) substantial continuity of the same business operations, (2) use of the same plant, (3) continuity of the workforce, (4) similarity of jobs and working conditions, (5) similarity of supervisory personnel, (6) similarity in machinery, equipment, and production methods, (7) similarity of products or services, and (8) the ability of the predecessor to provide relief.[11]

3.0 EMPLOYEES ELIGIBLE FOR FAMILY LEAVE

Employees are eligible for family leave if they:

- are employed for at least 12 months (they need not be consecutive months) by an employer who is subject to the FMLA;
- work at least 1250 hours of service (including overtime and hours worked but unpaid) in the 12-month period preceding the request for a leave;
- work for an employer who employs 50 or more employees within 75 road miles of the worksite at which the individual is employed.[12]

Because the FMLA provides separate tests for determining which employers are subject to the Act and which employees are eligible for leave, it is possible for an employer to be

---

[10] *See* 29 C.F.R. § 825.104(c)(2) (Interim Regs.).
[11] *See* 29 C.F.R. § 825.107 (Interim Regs.).
[12] *See* Pub. L. No. 103-3, § 101(2)(A) & (B), 107 Stat. 6, 7-8; *see also* 29 C.F.R. §§ 825.110 & .111 (Interim Regs.).

subject to the Act, yet have no member of its workforce who is eligible for leave.

Example: An employer employs 40 employees in Boston and 40 employees in Los Angeles. Although the employer meets the 50-employee threshold for coverage under the Act, none of the employees qualify for family leave because the employer employs fewer than 50 employees within 75 miles of either worksite. If the employer in this example employed an additional 15 employees at a site in Cambridge, the employees in Boston and Cambridge would qualify for leave, but the employees in Los Angeles would remain ineligible.

For employees with no fixed worksite such as traveling salespersons and construction workers, the "worksite," for purposes of testing the employee's eligibility for leave, is the site to which the employee is assigned as a home base, the site from which the employee's work is assigned, or the site to which the employee reports.[13] While an employer is free to reassign employees to different worksites, an employer who reshuffles its workforce solely for the purpose of evading the 50-employee threshold for a particular worksite will likely draw fire for interfering with employee rights under the Act.[14]

4.0 EMPLOYEE ENTITLEMENTS UNDER THE FMLA

If an employee satisfies the eligibility requirements described in Section 3.0 above, he or she will generally be entitled to 12 weeks of unpaid leave per year, preservation of medical benefits during the leave, and an opportunity to return to work after expiration of the leave. Before discussing the

---

[13] *See* 29 C.F.R. § 825.111(a)(2) (Interim Regs.).
[14] *See* Pub. L. No. 103-3, § 105(a)(1), 107 Stat. 6, 14 (1993).

benefits provided to employees under the Act, we will briefly discuss the circumstances in which leave may be taken.

4.1 Circumstances in Which Family Leave May Be Taken

The FMLA provides leave to permit employees to address important family events and crises. Accordingly, leave may be taken in the following circumstances:

- the birth or placement of a son or daughter with the employee ("child care leave");[15]
- the serious health condition of a spouse, son, daughter, or parent ("family care leave");[16] or
- the serious health condition of the employee ("self care leave").[17]

Terms such as "son or daughter" and "serious health condition" have special meanings under the Act which must be considered in determining whether an employee is eligible for a child care, family care, or self care leave.

For purposes of child care and family care leaves, "son or daughter" includes any biological, adopted, or foster child, stepchild, legal ward, or child of a person standing in loco parentis.[18] The child must be under 18 years of age, unless he or she is incapable of self-care because of a mental or physical disability. A child care leave must be concluded within 12 months of the birth or placement of the child.[19]

For purposes of family care and self care leaves, "serious health condition" means an illness, injury, impairment, or physical or mental condition that involves inpatient care in a hospital, hospice, or residential medical care facility, or continu-

---

[15] *See* Pub. L. No. 103-3, § 102(a)(1)(A) & (B), 107 Stat. 6, 9.
[16] *See* Pub. L. No. 103-3, § 102(a)(1)(C), 107 Stat. 6, 9.
[17] *See* Pub. L. No. 103-3, § 102(a)(1)(D), 107 Stat. 6, 9.
[18] *See* Pub. L. No. 103-3, § 101(12), 107 Stat. 6, 9.
[19] *See* Pub. L. No. 103-3, § 102(a)(2), 107 Stat. 6, 9; *see also* 29 C.F.R. § 825.201 (Interim Regs.).

ing treatment by a health care provider.[20] When inpatient care is not called for, a serious health condition will generally require continuing treatment and a period of incapacity of at least three calendar days.[21] Prenatal care and incurable health conditions qualify as serious health conditions.[22]

The Act defines a "health care provider" as a doctor of medicine or osteopathy who is authorized to practice medicine or surgery by the State in which the doctor practices, or any other person determined by the Secretary of Labor to be capable of providing health care services.[23] The interim regulations include the following individuals among the "other persons" capable of providing such services: podiatrists, dentists, clinical psychologists, optometrists, chiropractors, nurse practitioners, nurse midwives, and Christian Science practitioners.[24] In addition to establishing the existence of a serious health condition, an employee who wishes to take self care leave must be prepared to show that the condition prevents the performance of work of any kind or, in the alternative, prevents performance of the essential functions of the employee's position.[25]

The Act defines a "parent" as the biological parent of an employee or an individual who stood in loco parentis to an employee when the employee was a son or daughter.[26] In-laws are not included in this definition. The term "spouse" for purposes of the Act means any husband or wife as defined or recognized under state law for purposes of marriage, including common law marriage where recognized.[27]

---

[20] *See* Pub. L. No. 103-3, § 101(11), 107 Stat. 6, 9.
[21] 29 C.F.R. § 825.114(a)(2) (Interim Regs.).
[22] 29 C.F.R. § 825.114(a)(3) (Interim Regs.).
[23] *See* Pub. L. No. 103-3, § 101(6), 107 Stat. 6, 8-9 (1993).
[24] *See* 29 C.F.R. § 825.800 (Interim Regs.).
[25] *See* Pub. L. No. 103-3, § 102(a)(1)(D), 107 Stat. 6, 9; *see also* 29 C.F.R. § 825.306(b) (Interim Regs.).
[26] *See* Pub. L. No. 103-3, § 101(7), 107 Stat. 6, 9.
[27] Pub. L. No. 103-3, § 101(13), 107 Stat. 6, 9; *see also* 29 C.F.R. § 825.800 (Interim Regs.).

4.2 Types of Leave Available to Employees

The FMLA affords eligible employees great flexibility in the manner in which they take family leave in order to accommodate the diverse circumstances giving rise to the need for leave. Thus, the Act recognizes three types of leave schedule including continuous leave, reduced schedule leave, and intermittent leave.

Continuous leave is leave taken for a uninterrupted period of up to 12 consecutive weeks. The employer may not deny a timely request for continuous leave if the employee is otherwise eligible. Because few employees will be able to take a full 12 weeks of uninterrupted, unpaid leave, most employees will likely request a shorter period of continuous leave.

A reduced schedule leave is a leave schedule that reduces the usual number of hours per workweek, or hours per workday of an eligible employee.[28] For example, an employee who needs to take a sick parent to a physician on a weekly basis may request a reduced leave schedule in order to leave work early one day a week.

An intermittent leave is a family leave taken in separate periods of time due to a single illness or injury, rather than for one continuous period of time, and may include leave of periods from one hour or more to several weeks.[29] For example, an employee might take intermittent leave on an occasional basis for chemotherapy.

Three important features of reduced schedule and intermittent leaves distinguish them from continuous leave. First, an employer may deny requests for such leaves except where such leaves are medically necessary.[30] Thus, an employer can deny a new parent's request to reduce his or her workweek by taking reduced schedule leave (e.g., working 4 days a week). Second, if a reduced schedule or intermittent leave is foreseeably based

---

[28] Pub. L. No. 103-3, § 101(g), 107 Stat. 6, 9; *see also* 29 C.F.R. §§ 825.203(c) & .800 (Interim Regs.).

[29] *See* 29 C.F.R. §§ 825.203(b) & .800 (Interim Regs.).

[30] *See* Pub. L. No. 103-3, § 102(b)(1), 107 Stat. 6, 9-10. A family leave "approval matrix" appears at Section 8.0 of this Chapter.

on planned medical treatment, the employer may require the employee to transfer temporarily to an available alternative position for which the employee is qualified for the duration of such leaves. In these circumstances, however, the temporary position must have equivalent pay and benefits and must better accommodate the employee's recurring periods of leave than the employee's regular position.[31] Third, the legislative history of the Act makes it clear that a safe-harbor exists for employers who reduce the pay of salaried employees for working less than a full day while on a reduced schedule or intermittent leave.[32] Under the Fair Labor Standards Act's so-called "pay docking" rule, an employer may not dock the pay of a salaried employee for working less than a full day without jeopardizing the employee's status as an exempt employee and thereby exposing the employer to liability for overtime. This rule would be violated by providing a partial day of unpaid leave to a salaried employee but for the safe harbor created by the Act. Employers should note, however, that the safe harbor does not extend to deductions from an employee's pay, when the absence is due to a leave required by only state law or permitted by the employer's own leave policies, where such leave does not qualify as FMLA leave.

4.3 Notice and Certification Requirements Under the FMLA

The FMLA provides that employees shall give at least 30 days notice for all family leaves unless such notice is impracticable, or unless a collective bargaining agreement, state law, or the employer's own leave policy allows for a shorter notice period.[33] While expectant parents may be able to give at least 30

---

[31] *See* Pub. L. No. 103-3, § 102(b)(2), 107 Stat. 6, 10; *see also* 29 C.F.R. § 825.204 (Interim Regs.).

[32] *See* Pub. L. No. 103-3, § 102(c), 107 Stat. 6, 10; *see also* 29 C.F.R. § 825.206 (Interim Regs.). For legislative history, *see* House Report No. 103-8 (Additional Views of Representatives Thomas E. Petri and Robert E. Andrews).

[33] *See* Pub. L. No. 103-3, §§ 102(e)(1) & 102(e)(2)(B), 107 Stat. 6, 10-11; *see also* 29 C.F.R. §§ 825.302(g) & .701(a)(3).

days notice of their intent to take family leave, employees who need to take a family care or self care leave will often find it impracticable to provide such notice. The interim regulations provide that the employee need not expressly assert rights under the FMLA or even mention the FMLA when giving notice, but merely needs to state a factual basis for leave under the Act.[34] However, an employer who adopts formal notice requirements and notifies employees of such requirements, may, in some circumstances, delay a request for leave based on a lack of proper notice.[35]

In the event of a family care or self care leave for foreseeable medical treatment, the employee is not only expected to give advance notice but must also make a reasonable effort to schedule the treatment in a manner so as not to disrupt unduly the operations of the employer, subject, of course, to the approval of the health care provider.[36] After the leave has begun, the employer may require the employee to report periodically on his or her status and intent to return to work.[37]

The Act permits an employer to require employees to provide timely certification of their entitlement to family care or self care leave.[38] The certification is typically issued by the health care provider of the person receiving care and will be deemed sufficient to establish an employee's entitlement to family leave if it states:

- the date on which the serious health condition commenced;
- the probable duration of the condition;
- the appropriate medical facts, within the knowledge of the health care provider, regarding the condition;

---

[34] *See* 29 C.F.R. § 825.202(c).
[35] *See* 29 C.F.R. § 825.304(c).
[36] *See* Pub. L. No. 103-3, § 102(e)(2)(A), 107 Stat. 6, 11.
[37] *See* Pub. L. No. 103-3, § 104(a)(5), 107 Stat. 6, 13.
[38] *See* Pub. L. No. 103-3, § 103(a), 107 Stat. 6, 11.

- in the case of a family care leave, a statement that the employee is needed to care for the family member;
- in the case of a self care leave, a statement that the employee is unable to perform the functions of his or her position or, in the alternative, of any position;
- for leave taken on an intermittent or reduced leave schedule basis for planned medical treatments, the dates on which such treatments are to be given and their duration;
- for leave taken on an intermittent or reduced leave schedule for the employee's own care, a statement of the medical necessity for such leave and the expected duration of the leave; and
- for leave taken on an intermittent or reduced leave schedule for care of a spouse, son, daughter, or parent, a statement that the employee's leave is necessary for such care or will assist in the recovery of the family member and the expected duration and schedule of the leave.[39]

The Act permits an employer who has reason to doubt the validity of a certification, to require the eligible employee to obtain the opinion of a second health care provider designated or approved by the employer, unless a second certificate is barred by a state law providing for a similar type of leave.[40] The employer is required to pay for the cost of any second opinion and may not refer the employee to a health care provider who is employed on a regular basis by the employer.[41] Where the second opinion fails to confirm the opinion expressed in the original certification, the employer may require the employee to

---

[39] *See* Pub. L. No. 103-3, § 103(b), 107 Stat. 6, 11-12.

[40] *See* Pub. L. No. 103-3, § 103(c)(1), 107 Stat. 6, 12; *see also* 29 C.F.R. § 825.701(a)(4) (Interim Regs.).

[41] *See* Pub. L. No. 103-3, § 103(c)(1) & (2), 107 Stat. 6, 12.

obtain an opinion from a third health care provider designated or approved jointly by the employer and the employee. The opinion of the third health care provider is binding on the employer and the employee.[42]

After a family care or self care leave has commenced, the employer may require the employee to obtain subsequent recertifications on a reasonable basis, but normally no more often than every 30 days.[43] The employer may also adopt a uniformly applied policy requiring employees to submit a certification confirming their fitness to return to work before permitting them to resume their positions after a self care leave. Such a certification cannot be required, however, if it would conflict with a valid state or local law or a collective bargaining agreement governing the return of employees after medical leave.[44]

4.4 Treatment of Employee Benefits Under FMLA

During a family leave, employees are entitled to continuation of group health plan coverage on the same terms and conditions as active employees.[45] Thus, for example, if an employer subsidizes the cost of health care coverage by paying 80 percent of the cost of insurance premiums, the employee will continue to enjoy this subsidy.

If the employee does not return to work at the conclusion of a family leave, the employer is permitted to recover the cost of this subsidy, unless the employee's failure to return to work is due to a serious health condition of the employee or a family member or because of other circumstances beyond the employee's control.[46] Thus, employees who return to work obtain free subsidized medical coverage, while employees who fail to return to work may be required to reimburse the

---

[42] *See* Pub. L. No. 103-3, § 103(d)(1) & (2), 107 Stat. 6, 12.

[43] *See* Pub. L. No. 103-3, § 103(e), 107 Stat. 6, 12; *see also* 29 C.F.R. § 825.308 (Interim Regs.).

[44] *See* Pub. L. No. 103-3, § 104(a)(4), 107 Stat. 6, 13.

[45] *See* Pub. L. No. 103-3, § 104(c)(1), 107 Stat. 6, 13.

[46] *See* Pub. L. No. 103-3, § 104(c)(2), 107 Stat. 6, 13-14.

employer for the cost of coverage during leave. The interim regulations permit an employer to withhold the cost of continued coverage from any sum owed an employee who fails to return from leave, provided such withholdings do not violate state or federal wage and hour laws.[47] An employee who returns to work for at least 30 calendar days is deemed to have "returned" to work and is no longer liable to reimburse the employer for health benefit subsidies received during leave.[48]

Employers who permit employees to contribute to the cost of health care coverage with pre-tax dollars through Section 125 Plans (so-called "Cafeteria Plans") face numerous unresolved issues under the FMLA. For example, in the above illustration the employer paid 80 percent of the cost of medical coverage. If the employee paid his or her 20 percent with after-tax dollars, no difficulties are encountered since the employee will continue to make a 20 percent contribution with after-tax dollars while on leave. However, if the employee normally pays his or her 20 percent through a Cafeteria Plan, the employee will lose the benefit of making contributions with pre-tax dollars during the unpaid family leave. The interim regulations suggest prepayment at the employee's option through additional pre-leave payroll deductions.[49]

Another unresolved issue involving the interaction of family leave and medical benefits is the question of whether an employee is generally entitled to 18 months of continuation health coverage under Title X of the Consolidated Omnibus Budget Reconciliation Act of 1986 ("COBRA")[50] if the individual does not return to work upon the conclusion of leave. The legislative history of the FMLA provides that leave taken under the Act does not constitute a qualifying event for purposes of triggering an employee's entitlement to 18 months

---

[47] 29 C.F.R. § 825.213(e) (Interim Regs.).
[48] 29 C.F.R. § 825.213(b) (Interim Regs.).
[49] 29 C.F.R. § 825.210(c) (Interim Regs.).
[50] Pub. L. No. 99-272, title X, § 10002, 100 Stat. 227; 29 U.S.C. §§ 1161-1168.

of continuation of health benefits under COBRA.[51] The Act's legislative history further provides that COBRA coverage is not triggered until it becomes known that an employee is not returning from family leave. The FMLA does not, however, amend basic COBRA rules. In the absence of such amendment, a "qualifying event" under COBRA arguably occurs as soon as an employee's hours of work are reduced due to commencement of a family leave. Consequently, it is unclear whether an employee who takes 12 weeks of family leave and thereafter fails to return to work will be entitled to only 15 or to a full 18 months of COBRA continuation coverage.[52]

4.5 Coordination of Family Leave with Paid Leave

Many of the payment issues identified in Section 4.4 above would be resolved if an individual continued to receive pay during family leave. Accordingly, the FMLA provides for the coordination of paid leave with family leave by permitting employers to require, or employees to elect, the substitution of accrued paid leave for unpaid family leave as follows:

- For child care leave, substitution of an employee's accrued paid vacation, personal and family leave for unpaid family leave;[53]
- For family care leave, substitution of an employee's accrued paid vacation, personal, family, and medical or sick leave for unpaid family leave;[54]
- For self care leave, substitution of an employee's accrued paid vacation, personal, medical or sick leave for unpaid family leave.[55]

---

[51] *See, e.g.*, Senate Report No. 103-8. The qualifying events for COBRA continuation coverage are set forth at 29 U.S.C. § 1163(2).

[52] *See also* 29 C.F.R. § 825.309(b) (Interim Regs.).

[53] *See* Pub. L. No. 103-3, § 102(d)(2)(A), 107 Stat. 6, 10.

[54] *See* Pub. L. No. 103-3, § 102(d)(2)(A) & (B), 107 Stat. 6, 10.

[55] *See* Pub. L. No. 103-3, § 102(d)(2)(B), 107 Stat. 6, 10.

Paid leave provided under a plan covering temporary disability is considered sick/medical leave for purposes of substitution under the FMLA.[56] If the employer does not require the employee to substitute paid leave for unpaid family leave, the employee may nevertheless elect such a substitution.[57] An employee's entitlement to job security, discussed below, is not affected by the substitution of paid leave for unpaid leave.

4.6 Job Security Under FMLA

Upon returning from family leave, an employee is entitled to restoration to the position he or she held prior to the commencement of leave or to an equivalent position with equivalent employment benefits, pay, and other terms and conditions of employment.[58] Although a family leave does not result in the loss of any employment benefit accrued prior to leave (unless, of course, the employer requires or the employee elects to spend down accrued paid leave during family leave), an employee is not entitled to accrue additional seniority or employment benefits during family leave.[59] Nor is the employee entitled upon returning from leave to any right, benefit, or position of employment other than such right, benefit, or position to which the employee would have been entitled had the employee not taken family leave.[60] The interim regulations state that in order to ensure an employer satisfies its responsibility to provide equivalent benefits to an employee upon return from an unpaid family leave, it may be necessary for the employer to continue to pay nonhealth-related benefit premiums during the employee's absence, to prevent a lapse in coverage. In such circumstances,

---

[56] 29 C.F.R. § 825.207(c)(2) (Interim Regs.).
[57] *See* Pub. L. No. 103-3, § 102(d)(2)(A) & (B), 107 Stat. 6, 10; *see generally* 29 C.F.R. § 825.207 (Interim Regs.).
[58] *See* Pub. L. No. 103-3, § 104(a)(1)(A) & (B) 107 Stat. 6, 12.
[59] *See* Pub. L. No. 103-3, §§ 104(a)(2) & 104(a)(3)(A), 107 Stat. 6, 12-13.
[60] *See* Pub. L. No. 103-3, § 104(a)(3)(B), 107 Stat. 6, 13.

the employer may be able to recover premium payments made on the employee's behalf.[61]

If an employee is a highly compensated key employee, the employer may deny the employee restoration to his or her position, if such restoration would cause substantial and grievous economic injury to the employer's operations.[62] A "key" employee is a salaried employee who is among the highest paid 10 percent of all employees who work within 75 miles of the employer's facility.[63] The test for "substantial and grievous economic injury" cannot be precisely defined. A finding of such injury, however, can be based only on the effects of restoring the employee and not on whether the employee's absence will cause injury.[64]

Employers should note that although key employees do not enjoy unconditional job security under the Act, they are nevertheless entitled to take family leave. Further, an employer must notify a key employee of its intent to deny restoration to his or her position. This notice must be given at the time the employer makes the determination that denial of restoration is necessary to prevent substantial and grievous economic injury to its operations.[65] If this determination is made after a key employee has commenced a family leave, the employer should afford the employee a reasonable period of time to return from leave.[66] A key employee is still entitled to request reinstatement at the end of the leave period, even if the employee did not return to work in response to the employer's notice.[67]

---

[61] *See* 29 C.F.R. § 825.213(f) (Interim Regs.).
[62] *See* Pub. L. No. 103-3, § 104(b)(1)(A), 107 Stat. 6, 13.
[63] *See* Pub. L. No. 103-3, § 104(b)(2), 107 Stat. 6, 13; *see also* 29 C.F.R. § 825.217 (Interim Regs.).
[64] *See* 29 C.F.R. § 825.218 (Interim Regs.).
[65] *See* Pub. L. No. 103-3, § 104(b)(1)(B), 107 Stat. 6, 13.
[66] *See* Pub. L. No. 103-3, § 104(b)(1)(C), 107 Stat. 6, 13.
[67] 29 C.F.R. § 825.219(d) (Interim Regs.).

5.0 REASONS FOR WHICH FAMILY LEAVE MAY BE DENIED

An employer may deny a request for family leave for one or more of the following reasons:

- The employer has employed the employee for fewer than 12 months.
- The employee has provided fewer than 1250 hours of service in the 12-month period preceding the proposed commencement date of the employee's leave.
- The employee has already taken 12 weeks of family leave in the relevant 12-month period.[68]
- The employee's spouse is also employed by the employer and together they have already taken 12 weeks of child care leave and/or family care leave to care for a parent in the past 12 months, and the employee's current leave request is for such purpose.[69]
- The employee requests a child care leave extending beyond the 12-month period, beginning on the date of the birth or placement of the employee's child.
- The employer does not agree to grant the employee's request for child care leave on an intermittent or reduced schedule basis.
- The employee has requested leave in connection with the serious health condition of someone other than the employee's son, daughter, spouse, parent, or self.
- The employee's health care provider is not a health care provider recognized by the Act.

---

[68] The Interim Regulations set forth four methods for computing the 12-month period. *See* 29 C.F.R. § 825.200(b) (Interim Regs.).

[69] *See* Pub. L. No. 103-3, § 102(f), 107 Stat. 6, 11; *see also* Section 7.2, *infra*.

- The employee's health care provider has failed to certify that the employee or the employee's son, daughter, spouse, or parent suffers from a "serious health condition" as defined by the Act.
- The certification submitted by the health care provider is not sufficient under the terms of the Act.
- The employee has failed to establish the medical necessity of a family care leave or self care leave on an intermittent or reduced schedule basis.
- The employee has failed to give prior notice of the need for family leave within the time required by the Act, and has not claimed that it was not practicable to do so.

An eligible employee whose request for family leave is denied for one of the above reasons, should be invited to reapply for such leave if the employee has reason to believe that the grounds on which the employer denied the request are no longer valid.

6.0 PENALTIES FOR VIOLATIONS OF THE FMLA

The FMLA authorizes legal action against employers who interfere with, restrain, deny, or attempt to deny an employee's exercise of rights under the Act.[70] The Act also protects employees who attempt to oppose activities made unlawful by the Act as well as employees who cooperate with or participate in investigations and legal proceedings based on violations of the Act.[71]

An employee has the option of filing a complaint with the Secretary of Labor or proceeding directly against the employer in State or Federal court.[72] An employee who pursues such action against an employer who violates the Act may obtain the following damages:

---

[70] *See* Pub. L. No. 103-3, § 105(a)(1), 107 Stat. 6, 14.
[71] *See* Pub. L. No. 103-3, §§ 105(a)(2) & 105(b), 107 Stat. 6, 14.
[72] *See* Pub. L. No. 103-3, §§ 107(a)(2) & 107(b)(1), 107 Stat. 6, 16.

- Lost wages, salary, benefits, or other compensation, plus interest, denied or lost by reason of a violation.[73]
- In cases where leave is denied, employees may recover actual monetary damages such as costs incurred by hiring someone to care for a family member. These damages are capped, however, at 12 weeks of wages or salary, plus interest.[74]

An unusual feature of the Act is its provision for automatic liquidated damages (i.e., an additional sum equal to the total of all other damages) except where the employer proves it acted in good faith with reasonable grounds for believing it was in compliance with the law.[75] The Act also provides for equitable relief, such as reinstatement and promotion.[76] In addition to the preceding damages, the Act requires a losing employer to pay the employee's attorneys fees, expert fees, and costs of suit.[77]

7.0 MISCELLANEOUS

7.1 Notice to Employees

Employers subject to the FMLA are required to post and keep posted, in conspicuous places on their premises where notices to employees and applicants for employment are customarily posted, a notice in a form prepared or approved by the Secretary of Labor. This notice must set forth summaries of the pertinent provisions of the Act and information regarding the filing of charges against an employer for violations of the Act.[78] The Act imposes a $100 penalty for failure to post an appropriate notice.[79]

---

[73] See Pub. L. No. 103-3, § 107(a)(1)(A)(i) & (ii), Stat. 6, 15.
[74] See Pub. L. No. 103-3, § 107(a)(1)(A)(i)(II), Stat. 6, 15.
[75] See Pub. L. No. 103-3, § 107(a)(1)(A)(iii), 107 Stat. 6, 15.
[76] See Pub. L. No. 103-3, § 107(a)(1)(B), 107 Stat. 6, 15.
[77] See Pub. L. No. 103-3, § 107(a)(3), 107 Stat. 6, 16.
[78] See Pub. L. No. 103-3, § 109(a), 107 Stat. 6, 19.
[79] See Pub. L. No. 103-3, § 109(b), 107 Stat. 6, 19.

The Secretary of Labor has approved a form of notice (a copy appears at the conclusion of this chapter) for purposes of complying with the Act. The notice cannot be smaller than 8.5 inches by 11 inches and must be fully legible.[80]

The interim regulations provide that employee handbooks must be updated to include information on FMLA entitlements and employee obligations under the Act. If the employer does not have a handbook, separate written information on the FMLA must be provided.[81] Further, when an employee provides notice of a need for leave, the employer must provide information detailing the specific expectations and obligations of the employee and explain the consequences of failing to meet them.[82]

7.2 Spouses Employed by Same Employer

In the event an employee and his or her spouse work for the same employer, the aggregate number of work weeks of family leave to which both individuals may be entitled may be limited to 12 work weeks during any 12-month period, if leave is taken for birth or placement of a child, or for the care of a sick parent.

7.3 Clarification of Employment Status

As with all employment policies, an employer's family leave policy should be accompanied by a statement that the policy does not constitute a contract of employment, nor does it confer any rights upon employees other than those conferred by the FMLA. In most jurisdictions, such language will prevent the creation of enforceable contractual expectations in the absence of a written employment agreement or a collective bargaining agreement.

---

[80] 29 C.F.R. § 825.300(a) (Interim Regs.).
[81] 29 C.F.R. § 825.301(a) & (b) (Interim Regs.).
[82] 29 C.F.R. § 825.301(c) (Interim Regs.).

7.4 Coordination with State Family Leave Laws

When state and federal family leave laws overlap, the state law's provisions on notice take precedence where they allow a shorter notice period than the FMLA's 30-day notice provision.[83] In addition, the employer cannot require a greater number of certifications than the number permitted by State law.[84] Where State law provides for leave under circumstances not covered by the FMLA—e.g., leave to care for a grandparent or parent-in-law—leave used for that purpose does not reduce the amount of leave available under the FMLA.[85]

7.5 Effective Date of the FMLA

The effective date of the FMLA is August 5, 1993. However, in the case of a collective bargaining agreement in effect on that date, the effective date becomes the earlier of (1) the date of the termination of the collective bargaining agreement, or (2) February 5, 1994.[86]

8.0 FMLA APPROVAL MATRIX

Reason for Leave	Type of Leave	Can Deny	Cannot Deny
CHILD CARE	Continuous Leave		X
	Intermittent Leave	X	
	Reduced Schedule Leave	X	
FAMILY CARE	Continuous Leave		X
	Intermittent Leave	X*	
	Reduced Schedule Leave	X*	
SELF CARE	Continuous Leave		X
	Intermittent Leave	X*	
	Reduced Schedule Leave	X*	

* Cannot be denied in cases of medical necessity.

---

[83] 29 C.F.R. § 825.701(a)(3) (Interim Regs.).
[84] 29 C.F.R. § 825.701(a)(4) (Interim Regs.).
[85] 29 C.F.R. § 825.701(a)(5) (Interim Regs.).
[86] See Pub. L. No. 103-3, § 405(b), 107 Stat. 6, 26.

YOUR RIGHTS
FAMILY AND MEDICAL LEAVE ACT OF 1993

FMLA requires covered employers to provide up to 12 weeks of unpaid, job-protected leave to "eligible" employees for certain family and medical reasons. Employees are eligible if they have worked for a covered employer for at least one year, and for 1,250 hours over the previous 12 months, and if there are at least 50 employees within 75 miles.

REASONS FOR TAKING LEAVE: Unpaid leave must be granted for any of the following reasons:

- to care for the employee's child after birth, or placement for adoption or foster care;
- to care for the employee's spouse, son or daughter, or parent, who has a serious health condition; or
- for a serious health condition that makes the employee unable to perform the employee's job.

At the employee's or employer's option, certain kinds of paid leave may be substituted for unpaid leave.

ADVANCE NOTICE AND MEDICAL CERTIFICATION: The employee may be required to provide advance leave notice and medical certification. Taking of leave may be denied if requirements are not met.

- The employee ordinarily must provide 30 days advance notice when the leave is "foreseeable."
- An employer may require medical certification to support a request for leave because of a serious health condition, and may require second or third opinions (at the employer's expense) and a fitness for duty report to return to work.

JOB BENEFITS AND PROTECTION:

- For the duration of FMLA leave, the employer must maintain the employee's health coverage under any "group health plan."
- Upon return from FMLA leave, most employees must be restored to their original or equivalent positions with equivalent pay, benefits, and other employment terms.
- The use of FMLA leave cannot result in the loss of any employment benefit that accrued prior to the start of an employee's leave.

UNLAWFUL ACTS BY EMPLOYERS: FMLA makes it unlawful for any employer to:

- interfere with, restrain, or deny the exercise of any right provided under FMLA;
- discharge or discriminate against any person for opposing any practice made unlawful by FMLA or for involvement in any proceeding under or relating to FMLA.

ENFORCEMENT:

- The U.S. Department of Labor is authorized to investigate and resolve complaints of violations.
- An eligible employee may bring a civil action against an employer for violations.

FMLA does not affect any Federal or State law prohibiting discrimination, or supersede any State or local law or collective bargaining agreement which provides greater family or medical leave rights.

FOR ADDITIONAL INFORMATION: Contact the nearest office of the Wage and Hour Division, listed in most telephone directories under U.S. Government, Department of Labor.

U.S. Department of Labor, Employment Standards Administration
Wage and Hour Division, Washington, D.C. 20210

WH Publication 1420
June 1993

[FR Doc. 93-13028 Filed 6-3-93; 8:45 am]

Chapter 3

AMERICANS WITH DISABILITIES ACT OF 1990: EMPLOYER RESPONSIBILITIES

Michael Starr
Parker Chapin Flattau & Klimpl[*]

1.0 OVERVIEW

The Americans with Disabilities Act of 1990 ("ADA") (42 U.S.C. § 12101 *et seq.*) may be the most far reaching civil rights legislation in the last 25 years. Title I of the ADA governs employment and, in general, prohibits discrimination with regard to job application procedures, hiring, advancement, discharge, compensation, training, and all other terms, conditions and privileges of employment.[1] When fully effective on July 26, 1994, all employers with 15 or more employees will have to comply.

The ADA is more than a typical employment discrimination law, though not quite an affirmative action one. Under the concept of "reasonable accommodation," the ADA requires employers to take some affirmative steps in favor of people with

---

[*] The author gratefully acknowledges the assistance of Steven Felsenfeld in the production of this chapter.

[1] ADA § 102(a)

disabilities that are not required for people in other protected classifications. Employers must also continue to comply with federal, state or local laws that provide greater or equal protection for individuals with disabilities.[2] Among those laws are Sections 503 and 504 of the federal Rehabilitation Act of 1973 (29 U.S.C. §§ 793 and 794), which bar recipients of federal grants from discriminating against, and require federal contractors to take affirmative action in favor of, qualified individuals with disabilities.

The Equal Employment Opportunity Commission, which is charged with enforcing the ADA, has issued implementing regulations (29 CFR Part 1630), together with an extensive "Interpretive Guidance," which is published as an Appendix to the regulations. In addition, the EEOC has published *A Technical Assistance Manual on the Employment Provisions (Title I) of the Americans with Disabilities Act* (the *"EEOC Tech. Asst. Manual"*), which presents in less formal ways its views on what employers can and cannot do under the ADA.

2.0 QUALIFIED PERSONS WITH DISABILITIES

It is useful to remember that Title I of the ADA does *not* offer employment protections to people with disabilities. Rather, the statute protects only *qualified* individuals with disabilities.[3] Similarly, the obligation to make reasonable accommodation (which will be discussed below) benefits only an *otherwise qualified* individual with a disability.[4] The first questions to be asked, therefore, are who has a "disability" under the ADA, and in what sense is he or she qualified for employment.

2.1 The Definition of Disability

The ADA defines the term "disability" broadly to include any (a) physical or mental impairment that (b) substantially

---

[2] ADA § 501(b).
[3] ADA § 102(a).
[4] ADA § 102(b)(5)

limits one or more major life activities.[5] The statute brings under the definition of "individual with a disability" those who:

- have an impairment constituting a disability;
- have a record of having such an impairment; or
- are regarded as having such an impairment.

2.1.1 Physical or Mental Impairment

Conditions qualifying as an impairment include virtually any physiological disorder, cosmetic disfigurement or anatomic loss, as well as any mental or psychological disorder, such as mental retardation, mental illness, and specific learning disabilities. But only physiological or mental *disorders* count as impairments. Impairments do not include physical characteristics, such as left handedness, height or weight (provided they are within "normal" range), or characteristic predispositions to illness or disease.

For this reason, pregnancy is *not* a disability under the ADA. Though it is a distinctive physical condition, it is not a physiological disorder.

Personality traits—such as poor judgment, a quick temper or irresponsible behavior—are not themselves impairments. Neither are the "stress" or "depression" that can come from ordinary pressures at work or home; but these conditions may become impairments if they result from a documented physiological or mental disorder.

Infectious diseases, such as tuberculosis, AIDS or HIV infection, can be disabilities under the ADA if they actually impair a major life activity. For example, courts have ruled under related federal laws that AIDS is a protected disability because it impairs the major life activities of sexual relations and procreation.[6] In fact, even if AIDS or HIV infection did not actually impair a major life activity, people with those condi-

---

[5] ADA § 3(2).

[6] *See, e.g., Doe* v. *District of Columbia*, 796 F. Supp. 559 (D.D.C. 1992).

tions would be protected by the ADA if they were *regarded* as having such an impairment.[7]

Despite its breadth, the definition of disability does not include physical, psychological, environmental, cultural and economic factors, even if they dramatically impair an individual's ability to work. To put this in perspective: Illiteracy due to poverty or lack of education is not a protected impairment, but inability to read due to dyslexia (which is a learning disability) is.

2.1.2 Substantially Limits a Major Life Activity

Not all those with qualifying impairments are protected by the ADA. An impairment rises to the level of a disability under the ADA only if it substantially limits one or more major life activities. (Major life activities include functions like caring for oneself, performing manual tasks, walking, seeing, hearing, speaking, breathing, learning, and working.) The critical factor is not the name or diagnosis for any particular condition or disease, but rather the actual effect of that disease on the life of the affected individual, and this may vary from person to person with the same impairment.

The factors considered in determining whether an impairment causes a substantial limitation include:

- its nature and severity;
- its actual or expected duration; and
- its permanent or long-term impact, actual or expected.

Temporary, non-chronic conditions with little or no long-term effect—like a broken leg or a sprained back—are not disabilities under the ADA.

Special problems arise when the only major life activity limited by the impairment is work itself. The ADA would not come into play if the condition only rendered the individual unable to perform some specialized job or profession requiring

---

[7] *See School Board of Nassau County v. Arline*, 480 U.S. 273 (1987).

extraordinary skills, powers or talents—such as a major league baseball pitcher with a bad elbow.

On the other hand, there are people whose impairment prevents them from performing a "class of jobs or a broad range of jobs in various classes"—such as, the worker with a bad back who cannot perform heavy labor. These people may have disabilities protected by the ADA, and this is so (says the EEOC) even if there is another wide range of other jobs (such as, semi-skilled work), that the bad-backed laborer could still competently perform.[8]

2.1.3 Past and Suspected Impairments

The ADA protects not only those who are currently disabled, but also those who once were or are thought to be. In protecting those with a "record of impairment," the ADA aims to ban discrimination against those with a history of, but no present disability (such as, former cancer patients or those with treated mental illness). The belief that a corrected or treated condition may re-emerge and cause a future disability does not justify current discrimination.

Even those who have neither a past, present nor a future disability may be protected if the attitudes of others toward their condition (or suspected condition) is an impediment to work. For example, negative reactions of customers or co-workers to people with facial disfigurements, involuntary muscle spasms, or infectious diseases that are not currently contagious in the workplace (such as AIDS or inactive tuberculosis) would render those individuals "disabled." In fact, perfectly healthy people who are falsely rumored to be HIV infected could qualify as having a disability under the ADA.[9]

---

[8] *See* 29 C.F.R. § 1630.2(j) and Interpretive Guidance.

[9] Interpretive Guidance to 29 C.F.R. § 1630.2(l). *But see Rose City Oil Co. v. M.C.H.R.*, 832 S.W.2d 314 (Mo. Ct. App. 1992) (false AIDS rumors not "perceived" handicap under Missouri law).

2.2 Otherwise Qualified for Employment

Applicants for employment and employees with disabilities are *qualified* for the positions they hold or desire only if they (a) satisfy the requisite skill, experience, education and other job-related requirements, and (b) can perform the essential functions of the job, with or without reasonable accommodation. The first branch of this definition is sometimes referred to as the requirement that disabled employees or applicants be "otherwise qualified" for the job.

Otherwise qualified individuals must, at a minimum, possess any license, certification or other credential that is required for the job. Having the minimum level of training, education or years of work experience are also legitimate job prerequisites under the ADA. So, too, are personality traits, like good judgment and the ability to work with people.

2.3 Essential Job Functions

The ability to perform the "essential functions" of the job (with or without reasonable accommodation) is central to the concept of a *qualified* individual with a disability. Surprisingly, the ADA itself provides no definition of this key term. The EEOC says that "essential functions" means the fundamental job duties, not the marginal ones or, to put it otherwise, the duties that would fundamentally change the nature of the job, if removed.[10]

2.3.1 Criteria of Essential Functions

There are a variety of criteria for determining which job functions are essential. The three most significant are as follows:

- The position exists to perform the function;
- There are a limited number of other employees available to perform the function, or among whom it can be distributed; and

---

[10] 29 C.F.R. § 1630.2(n)(1); *EEOC Tech. Asst. Manual* at II-13.

- The function is highly specialized so that the incumbent is hired for his or her expertise or ability at that function.

The size of the work force and the fluctuating demands of the business operation are often critical to deciding what job functions are essential for which employees. For example, a clerical worker may answer telephones only a few minutes a day, but that task would still be an essential job function if no one else is available to do it.

2.3.2 Evidence of Essential Functions

The ADA mandates that consideration be given to the employer's judgment as to which job functions are essential and which are not.[11] This is primary evidence of what are essential job functions. But the employer's judgment does not end the matter. What the employer says must be borne out by the facts.

For example, if the employer says typing is essential for some job, but no incumbents have ever had to type, it is unlikely that typing is essential. On the other hand, if an employee spends most of his or her time operating a cash register, then doing so is likely an essential function of the job.

In some cases, the consequences of *failing* to require a function to be performed are more critical than the actual time spent on the task. So, for example, pulling an unconscious adult from a burning building is (hopefully) an infrequent chore for a firefighter, but it must surely be an essential function of the job.

In general, the actual work experience of past or present incumbents, the flow of work to and among employees, and the terms of the collective bargaining agreements, are all factors in determining essential job functions.

---

[11] ADA § 101(8).

2.3.3 Job Descriptions

Written job descriptions prepared *before* advertising a position or interviewing applicants for the job *must* be considered as evidence of essential job functions.[12] However, the ADA does *not* require that employers develop or maintain written job descriptions.

While a job description (and job analyses) can serve many useful human resources functions, they may not be an effective tool for ADA compliance. That a function is listed as essential on a job description may carry little weight if an actual work review shows that it is infrequently performed or otherwise marginal. On the other hand, employers may be hard pressed to explain how a job function is essential if it is omitted from the pre-existing job description. For this reason, written job descriptions must be periodically reviewed for accuracy. They should expressly state that the positions subject to a single job description might not all have precisely the same essential functions, and that those functions may change over time.

2.4 Drug and Alcohol Abusers

The ADA expressly exempts from coverage any employee or applicant who is currently engaging in the illegal use of drugs.[13] This includes the use of illicit drugs (like cocaine) and the illegal use of prescription drugs (like Valium).

In contrast, people erroneously regarded as engaged in illegal drug use are protected by the statute, as are former drug users who (a) are successfully rehabilitated or (b) are participating in a supervised rehabilitation program. This protection applies only to those who are continuing to refrain from illegal drug use, and employers may seek reasonable assurances, through drug testing and other means, that continuing use is not so recent as to be a real and ongoing problem.[14]

---

[12] ADA § 103(8); *EEOC Tech. Asst. Manual* at II-15 to II-16.
[13] ADA § 104(a).
[14] *See* ADA § 104(b); Interpretive Guidance to 29 C.F.R. § 1630.3(a)-(c).

The ADA is neutral on drug testing. Such tests are neither encouraged, authorized nor prohibited, and they are not regarded as a medical examination.[15] For this reason, the confidentiality requirements applicable to medical examinations and inquiries do not apply to drug test results. If, however, those results reveal something about a person's medical condition (other than his or her illicit use of drugs), that information should be treated as a confidential medical record.

Employers also have wide authority under the ADA to regulate both drug and alcohol abuse in the workplace. Employers may:

- prohibit alcohol and illegal drug use at work by all employees;
- require employees not to be under the influence of alcohol or illegal drugs while at work; and
- require employee compliance with the Drug-Free Workplace Act of 1988 (41 U.S.C. § 701 *et seq.*) and other federal regulations governing workplace substance abuse.

Most importantly, an employer may hold alcoholics and illegal drug users to the same qualification, performance, and behavioral standards as all other employees, even if their unsatisfactory performance or behavior results from the employee's substance abuse.[16]

2.5 Other Exceptions

A variety of conditions that are or could arguably be regarded as disabilities are expressly excluded from ADA coverage. Neither homosexuality nor bisexuality are impairments, and so are not disabilities under the ADA.[17] Also excluded are certain specific mental disorders that Congress apparently felt employers should not have to accommodate, namely:

---

[15] ADA § 104(d).
[16] ADA § 104(c).
[17] ADA § 511(a).

- transvestitism, transsexualism, pedophilia, exhibitionism, voyeurism, gender identity disorders, and other sexual behavior disorders;
- compulsive gambling, kleptomania, or pyromania; or
- psychoactive substance use disorders resulting from current illegal use of drugs.[18]

As if for double measure, Congress also stated that an individual is not disabled "solely because that individual is a transvestite."[19]

3.0 HIRING AND SELECTION REQUIREMENTS

3.1 Pre-Employment Inquiries

The ADA expressly prohibits pre-employment inquiries as to whether an applicant is an individual with a disability or as to the nature or severity of such disability, but it allows inquiries into the ability of applicants to perform job-related functions.[20] Drawing the line between permissible and impermissible pre-employment inquiries must be done with care.

3.1.1 Aptitudes and Abilities

Employers can inquire as to whether the applicant is "otherwise qualified," which means whether he or she possesses the basic prerequisites of the job. These include education, work experience, skills, licenses and so forth. Employers can also ask about more generalized aptitudes, if job-related. This may include judgment, ability to work under pressure, or interpersonal skills. In one case, for example, the court concluded that a person who, due to a nervous disorder, could not tolerate criticism of his job performance was not "otherwise qualified"

---

[18] ADA § 511(b).
[19] ADA § 508.
[20] ADA § 102(c)(2).

for the job.[21] Whether the applicant can meet the employer's stated attendance requirements is also a legitimate pre-employment inquiry.

The ADA does not bar employers from asking about an applicant's ability to perform specific job functions, as long as the questions are not phrased in terms of a disability. Extreme caution is required in framing such questions in order to avoid inadvertent violations of the ADA.[22]

Sometimes an applicant has a visible disability (*e.g.*, uses a wheelchair or has a guide dog) or voluntarily discloses disability-related information. If such a *known* disability might interfere with or prevent performance of specific job functions, the applicant may properly be asked to describe or demonstrate how these functions would be performed.

3.1.2 Nature and Severity of Disabilities

Many standardized job applications ask the question, "Do you have any disabilities or impairments which may affect your performance in the position for which you are applying?" Although this question has long been regarded as acceptable under state disability laws, it is now expressly disapproved by the EEOC under the ADA.[23]

Furthermore, even where there is an apparent connection between disability and job performance, employers should not ask job applicants about:

- the nature or severity of the disability;
- the condition causing the disability;
- any prognosis or expectation regarding the condition or disability; or
- whether the individual will need treatment or special leave because of the disability.

---

[21] *Pesterfield v. Tennessee Valley Authority*, 941 F.2d 437 (6th Cir. 1991).

[22] *See generally* Interpretive Guidance to 29 C.F.R. § 1630.14(a); *EEOC Tech. Asst. Manual* at V-5 to V-14.

[23] *See EEOC Tech. Asst. Manual* at V-7.

The ADA may also prohibit questions that might indirectly reveal a disability. These include those relating to hospitalizations, diseases, psychiatric treatment, illnesses, health-related problems, physical defects, disabilities or impairments, treatment for drug addiction or alcoholism, use of prescription drugs or prior workers' compensation claims.

3.2 Medical Examinations

The ADA prohibits any medical examination or inquiry of an applicant *prior to* an offer of employment. Employers can, however, make job offers that are conditioned on satisfactory results of a post-offer medical examination or inquiry. A post-offer examination does not have to be job-related, but all candidates who receive conditional job offers in the same job category must be required to take the same examination and/or respond to the same inquiries.[24]

3.2.1 Scope of Medical Inquiries

Any post-offer medical exam or medical inquiry made by employers should be limited to:

- determining if the individual has the physical or mental qualifications necessary to perform certain jobs;
- determining whether a person can perform a job without posing a "direct threat" to the health or safety of oneself or others; or
- complying with medical requirements of other federal laws.

Employers may also conduct voluntary medical examinations, including voluntary medical histories, which are part of an employee health program generally available to employees at the worksite.[25]

---

[24] ADA § 102(c); 29 C.F.R. § 1630.13.
[25] ADA § 102(c)(4).

3.2.2 Confidentiality Requirements

All information obtained in the course of a post-offer medical examination or inquiry must be collected and maintained in separated medical files and treated as confidential. Disclosure is permitted only in certain cases:

- Supervisors or managers may be informed of work restrictions or necessary accommodation;
- First-aid and safety personnel may be informed of anticipated emergency treatment; and
- Government officials investigating ADA compliance must be provided relevant information on request.[26]

If an individual is not hired because a post-offer medical examination or inquiry reveals a disability, the reason for not hiring must be job-related and necessary for the business. The employer may also have to show that no reasonable accommodation was available.

3.3 Employment Standards

The ADA prohibits employers from using employment standards or selection criteria that adversely affect disabled workers, even if there is no intentional discrimination. Employment tests or other selection criteria that "screen out or tend to screen out" an individual with a disability are barred unless they are job-related for the position in question and consistent with business necessity.[27] Even then, the employer must show that satisfactory performance could not be achieved even with a reasonable accommodation.[28]

---

[26] ADA § 102(c)(3).
[27] ADA § 102(b)(6).
[28] ADA § 103(a).

3.3.1 Selection Criteria

The EEOC has stated explicitly that the ADA "is not intended to second guess an employer's business judgment with regard to production standards, whether qualitative or quantitative, nor to require employers to lower such standards."[29] The EEOC gives this illustration: If an employer requires its typists to be able to accurately type 75 words per minute, it will not be called on to explain why an inaccurate work product or a typing speed of 65 words per minute would not be adequate.

As a practical matter, selection criteria should be limited to only essential job functions. After all, a disabled worker who can perform *essential* job functions is "qualified" under the ADA. Any employment standard that excluded such a person would, by definition, discriminate against an otherwise *qualified* disabled employee. Moreover, the EEOC says that no selection criteria is "consistent with business necessity" unless it relates to an essential function of the job.[30]

3.3.2 Preferences Based on Qualifications

The ADA does *not* require that employers give a preference to qualified disabled applicants over anyone else applying for the same job. In fact, employers can prefer the non-disabled individual who is better qualified. But the legality of such a preference may depend on whether the superior qualifications relate to essential job functions.

For example, if the disabled employee meets the performance standard of typing 75 words per minute and a non-disabled employee *exceeds* it, the employer may hire the higher qualified employee. But if, for example, a sighted and vision-impaired applicant can each meet the essential qualifications of the job but only the sighted individual has a driver's license, the employer cannot (according to the EEOC) prefer the sighted applicant just because he or she could occasionally run errands by car. In this example, a preference would "screen out" the

---

[29] Interpretive Guidance to 29 C.F.R. § 1630.2(n).
[30] Interpretive Guidance to 29 C.F.R. § 1630.10.

disabled individual and could not meet the job-related, business-necessity requirement (as construed by the EEOC) because the selection criterion is *not* an essential element of the job.[31]

3.3.3 Physical and Mental Qualifications

Employers may establish physical or mental qualifications that are necessary to perform specific jobs (*e.g.*, jobs in the transportation or construction industries, and police and firefighters). However, if a mental or physical qualification screens out an individual (or class of individuals) with a disability, the employer must show that the standard is job-related and consistent with business necessity and also must consider whether a reasonable accommodation would allow those persons to meet the standard.

3.3.4 Religious Preferences

The ban on selection criteria that exclude people with disabilities would not prevent religious organizations, educational institutions or societies from giving an employment preference to their co-religionists, or requiring all applicants or employees to conform to their religious tenets.[32] But they must treat qualified disabled individuals who actually satisfy these religious selection criteria the same as other applicants.

3.4 Workplace Safety

Employers may adopt workplace safety requirements. It is a lawful "qualification standard" under the ADA that individuals not pose a direct threat to the health or safety of themselves or others in the workplace that cannot be eliminated by reasonable accommodation.[33] Those safety requirements that screen out or would tend to screen out people with disabilities are lawful only if justified by a "direct threat" to workplace safety.

---

[31] Interpretive Guidance to 29 C.F.R. § 1630.15(b) & (c).
[32] ADA § 103(c).
[33] ADA § 103(b); 29 C.F.R. § 1630.15(b)(2).

3.4.1 The "Direct Threat" Standard

To satisfy the direct-threat standard, there must be a significant risk of substantial harm. This determination must be made on an *individualized* assessment of the person's *present* ability to safely perform essential job functions. Even where such a risk exists, the employer may have to make a "reasonable accommodation" if that would eliminate the risk or reduce it to an acceptable level. For example, an employer could not automatically exclude an epileptic from operating dangerous machinery if his seizures were controlled by medication or if installing safety devices would significantly reduce the risk of injury.[34]

The individualized risk assessment must be based on reasonable medical judgment which relies on the most current medical knowledge or the best available objective evidence. The actual experience of the individual in previous jobs, or documentation from doctors, rehabilitation counselors or other like professionals who have expertise in the disability and/or knowledge of the particular individual, should be given the greatest weight.

3.4.2 Food-Handling Employees

Employers cannot refuse to assign individuals with an infectious or communicable disease to food-handling positions unless (a) the disease is included on a list prepared by the Secretary of Health and Human Services as being one transmitted through handling food and (b) the risk of contagion cannot be eliminated by reasonable accommodation. Although state and local public health laws and ordinances relating to food handling continue to apply, they cannot be used to justify conduct not otherwise complying with the ADA.

3.5 Testing Abilities, Not Disabilities

It is a well-known saying that people should be judged in employment for their abilities, not their disabilities. The ADA

---

[34] *See Mantolete v. Bolger*, 767 F.2d 1416 (9th Cir. 1985).

includes an express provision requiring employers to select and administer employment tests in the "most effective manner to ensure" that they accurately reflect the skills, aptitudes, or other qualifications that the test purports to measure, rather than merely reflecting impaired sensory, manual, or speaking skills of disabled individuals (except, of course, where those are the skills being tested).[35]

Fundamentally, this requirement means that employers cannot make employment decisions based on skill or aptitude tests if the person has a disability that affects test results, but not job performance. In one case, a court found unlawful discrimination against an applicant for the job of heavy equipment operator who, due to dyslexia, could not read beyond an elementary level, and was excluded from the position for failing a written mechanical aptitude test.[36]

Adjustments in standard tests are required only if the employer *knows*, prior to giving the test, that the individual is disabled and that the disability impairs sensory, manual or speaking skills. These adjustments could include giving an oral test to a visually impaired individual, or allowing more time to complete the test. Employers need not, however, offer every applicant his or her choice of test format as long as they provide, upon advance request, an alternative, accessible test.

4.0 THE DUTY TO MAKE REASONABLE ACCOMMODATIONS

4.1 The Concept of Reasonable Accommodation

The most crucial provision of the ADA may be that which defines unlawful disability discrimination as including the failure to make *reasonable accommodations* to known physical or mental limitations of an otherwise qualified individual with a disability, unless the employer can demonstrate that the accommodation would impose an undue hardship on the

---

[35] ADA § 102(b)(7).
[36] *See Stutts v. Freeman*, 694 F.2d 666 (11th Cir. 1983).

operation of its business.[37] This means the employer must take reasonable action to remove barriers to employment of the disabled. These include both physical and social barriers based on sterotypes and mistaken assumptions about disabled persons' capabilities.

Employers are also prohibited from denying employment opportunities to an otherwise qualified individual with a disability, if the decision is based on the need to make a reasonable accommodation.[38] The purpose of this latter provision is (for example) to prohibit employers from refusing to hire an individual because a costly reasonable accommodation would be required, unless the cost was so high as to cause an undue hardship. Similarly, an employer could not select a nondisabled individual over an equally qualified individual with a disability merely because a reasonable accommodation is required. Nor can employee compensation be reduced just because the employer has made a reasonable accommodation.

4.2 The Range of Reasonable Accommodation

The employer's obligation to make a reasonable accommodation ranges over all aspects of the employment relationship. According to the EEOC, the reasonable accommodation obligation applies in three distinct areas: the job-application process, job performance, and equal benefits and privileges of employment.[39]

The core concept of reasonable accommodation is that which relates to *job performance*. In this context, "reasonable accommodation" refers to modifications or adjustments in the work environment, the way the job is customarily done, or in workplace policies such as would enable an otherwise qualified individual with a disability to perform essential job functions.

A natural corollary is reasonable accommodation in the *job-application process*, which refers to modifications or adjustments that permit otherwise qualified job applicants to be

---

[37] ADA § 102(b)(5)(A).
[38] ADA § 102(b)(5)(B).
[39] 29 C.F.R. § 1630.2(o)(1).

considered for the positions they seek. Reasonable accommodation here might include assisting a visually impaired applicant to fill out an employment application or giving assistance to a wheelchaired applicant if the employment office or interview site is not accessible.

Lastly, according to the EEOC, reasonable accommodation may also require a modification of an employer's operations and/or facilities so that employees with disabilities can enjoy *equal benefits and privileges* of employment. This aspect highlights that employers may be required, as a reasonable accommodation, to make non-work areas used by its employees (such as, lunchrooms, training rooms, restrooms, etc.) readily accessible to, and usable by, individuals with disabilities. If this posed an undue hardship, the employer might still satisfy its reasonable accommodation obligation by providing a comparable facility to the disabled employee, as long as this did not isolate him from other workers (because that would violate the ban against segregating workers with disabilities).

4.3 Accommodation and Job Performance

It is in the area of job performance that the ADA's reasonable accommodation requirement will have its most significant effect. The EEOC states succinctly: *"A reasonable accommodation must be an effective accommodation."*[40] An effective accommodation is one that provides the qualified individual with a disability with an equal employment opportunity: namely, an opportunity to attain the same level of performance as is attainable by the average similarly situated employee without a disability.

Viewed another way, an employer's proffered accommodation is "reasonable" under the ADA if it allows the individual to perform essential job functions: nothing more is required. An accommodation need not be the "best" accommodation, as long as it is adequate to meet the job-related needs of the worker being accommodated.

---

[40] *EEOC Tech. Asst. Manual* at III-3.

There are a variety of ways for employers to accommodate workers with disabilities so that they can perform essential job functions. These include job-restructuring, part-time or modified work schedules, reassignment to a vacant position, acquisition or modification of equipment or devices, provision of qualified readers or interpreters, and other similar accommodations.[41]

4.3.1 Job Restructuring

Employers are not required by the ADA to customize their jobs to the needs of workers with disabilities, but they are required to do some "tailoring" if the existing jobs do not quite fit. One kind of job restructuring is to reallocate to other workers those marginal job functions that the disabled worker cannot perform due to his or her disability. To compensate for this, the employer can then assign to the disabled worker marginal functions of other jobs that he or she can perform.

Reasonable accommodation does *not* require reallocating essential job functions; after all, a worker with a disability is not "qualified" (and thus not protected by the ADA) unless he or she can perform essential job functions.[42] However, rearranging the sequence of essential tasks may be required as a reasonable accommodation unless it creates an undue hardship. Sometimes, sharing the essential job functions with another worker in a team approach would be a reasonable accommodation.[43]

4.3.2 Modified Work Schedules

Providing a part-time position, or allowing an employee to work only certain days of the week or on an altered schedule, are also types of reasonable accommodation. However, if a particular work schedule is an essential part of the position

---

[41] ADA § 101(9)(B).
[42] *See, e.g., Paegle v. Dep't of the Interior*, 813 F. Supp. 61, 65 (D.D.C. 1993); *Dexler v. Tisch*, 660 F. Supp. 1418, 1426 (D. Conn. 1987).
[43] *See LaMott v. Apple Valley Health Care Ctr.*, 465 N.W.2d 585 (Minn. Ct. App. 1991).

sought, the individual is not "otherwise qualified" and no accommodation is required.[44]

Additionally, the EEOC says that "permitting the use of accrued paid leave or providing additional unpaid leave for *necessary* treatment" are examples of a reasonable accommodation.[45] Apparently the EEOC has in mind here primarily planned short-term leaves for specific purposes (such as repairing a prosthesis or learning to use a guide dog).

A different question is presented if a worker, because of his disability, is frequently absent. Most courts have held, under pre-existing federal law, that employers can terminate employees for poor attendance, even if the result of their disability, because "regular predictable attendance is fundamental to most jobs."[46]

4.3.3 Reassignment to a Vacant Position

At times, a current employee develops a disability that prevents performing the essential functions of his or her current job. In those cases, reassignment to a vacant position could constitute a reasonable accommodation.

If there is no vacant equivalent position that the individual is qualified to perform (with or without reasonable accommodation), the employer may reassign the individual to a lower-graded position. In that case, the employer is *not* required to pay the individual at his or her former salary, unless it does so for other reassigned employees. In one recent case, a woman claimed she was too "psychologically disabled" to handle the stress of a full caseload of food-stamp recipients. The court

---

[44] *See Guice-Mills v. Derwinski*, 967 F.2d 794 (2d Cir. 1992).

[45] Interpretive Guidance to 29 C.F.R. § 1630.2(o)(emphasis added); *see also EEOC Tech. Asst. Manual* at III-22 to III-23.

[46] *Walders v. Garrett*, 765 F. Supp. 303, 310 (E.D. Va. 1991), *aff'd*, 956 F.2d 1163 (4th Cir. 1992). *See also* Interpretive Guidance to 29 C.F.R. § 1630.14(a).

concluded that being assigned a reduced workload at full pay was *not* a reasonable accommodation.[47]

Where a labor union is involved, reassignment may conflict with the seniority provisions of an existing collective bargaining agreement. Unlike other federal anti-discrimination laws, there is no bona fide seniority-system defense under the ADA. In cases decided under the prior federal handicapped discrimination law, the courts have been reluctant to override seniority provisions of a collective bargaining agreement merely to accommodate a disabled worker.[48] But it is still too early to tell how these conflicting employer obligations will be resolved under the ADA.

4.3.4 Adaptive Equipment or Devices

Obtaining adaptive equipment or devices for the worker with a disability is often a simple, and sometimes surprisingly inexpensive, reasonable accommodation. At other times, modifying existing equipment would do just as well. For example, if an applicant for a secretarial position can meet the typing standard, but has a hearing impairment which prevents him or her from answering the telephone, the employer can provide, as a reasonable accommodation, a telephone headset with an amplifier.

The obligation to provide adaptive equipment extends *only* to items that are job-related, and not for the personal benefit of the disabled worker. Thus, employers do not generally have to provide personal-care items (like eyeglasses or wheelchairs) or amenities (like a hot plate or private refrigerator) that are not supplied to other employees.

4.3.5 Personal Assistants

Hiring other individuals to assist employees with disabilities perform their jobs is another form of reasonable accommoda-

---

[47] *Hill v. Florida Department of Health and Rehabilitative Services*, 58 Fair Empl. Prac. Cas. (BNA) 1532 (M.D. Fla. 1992).

[48] *See, e.g., Mackie v. Runyon*, 804 F. Supp. 1508 (M.D. Fla. 1992).

tion. This could include qualified readers for the visually impaired, or interpreters for the hearing impaired. It could also include a page turner for an employee with no hands, or a travel attendant to act as a sighted guide to assist a blind employee on occasional business trips.

The requirement here is to provide an assistant—not a substitute. For example, if a security guard must inspect ID cards and a blind person seeks the position, providing a sighted assistant is *not* a reasonable accommodation because the assistant would be performing the job for the individual with a disability rather than assisting the individual to perform the job.

Providing personal assistants as a reasonable accommodation is intended to help the disabled employee with specified duties related to the job. Employers are not required to provide daily care attendants to disabled employees as part of a reasonable accommodation.

4.4 The Process for Selecting a Reasonable Accommodation

While employers are understandably concerned with knowing in advance whether accommodations are reasonable or not, the reality is that each individual with a disability may seek or require a different accommodation. Often, *the process used* by the employer in attempting to find a reasonable accommodation can be more important than some preconceived notions of what adjustments are appropriate for which disabilities.

4.4.1 Identifying the Limitation

EEOC guidelines recommend "a flexible, interactive process" between the employer and the qualified individual with a disability to select a reasonable accommodation.[49] The *first* step is that the employee informs the employer of the need for some accommodation to assist in his or her job performance. This is critical because the employer's obligation under the ADA is only to accommodate the *known* limitations of an employee with a disability. While employers would not be

---

[49] Interpretive Guidance to 29 C.F.R. § 1630.9.

expected to accommodate disabilities they were unaware of, an employer may inquire as to whether an accommodation is needed if an employee with a *known* disability is having job difficulty.

Some state and local laws do not limit reasonable accommodation to *known* disabilities.[50] This puts the employer in an awkward position. While employers cannot ask if the employee has a disability, they may be liable for not having offered an accommodation. One way out of this dilemma is for the supervisor to inform the employee that there has recently been a problem with job performance (or attendance) and simply to ask whether there is anything "we" could do to help. The employer must, however, be prepared to deal with the employee's answer and make an appropriate accommodation if the employee's workplace problem is the result of a protected disability.

4.4.2 Employee Consultation

The *second* step in the "interactive process" is for the employer to consult with the individual affected for possible accommodations. At this stage, employers should find out from the employee (a) what are his or her specific abilities and limitations as they relate to essential job functions, and (b) what he or she thinks would help. The fundamental challenge here is to refrain from pigeonholing the employee based on how one characterizes his or her disability. The focus must always be on specific things he or she can or cannot do, but only as they relate to getting the job done.

Technical assistance in identifying an appropriate accommodation is available from the EEOC and other government and private agencies. However, the failure to obtain technical assistance from the EEOC does not excuse the employer from its reasonable accommodation obligation.

---

[50] *See, e.g., Kimbro v. Atlantic Richfield Co.*, 889 F.2d 869 (9th Cir. 1989), *cert. denied*, 498 U.S. 814 (1990).

4.4.3 Selecting an Accommodation

The *last* step is, of course, to select a reasonable accommodation. The EEOC advises employers to give "primary consideration" to employee preference in selecting and implementing the accommodation that is "most appropriate" for both the employee and the employer.[51] While this is certainly a prudent way to proceed, there is no doubt but that the employer has the ultimate discretion to choose between effective accommodations and may select the one that is less costly or less difficult to implement.

A person with a disability is *not* required to accept a reasonable accommodation offered by his or her employer.[52] This freedom may have its costs. Workers who reject a reasonable accommodation, and cannot perform their essential job functions without it, may lose their protection under the ADA because they cease to be a *qualified* individual with a disability.

4.5 The "Undue Hardship" Defense

After the employer has, in consultation with the employee or applicant, decided on a reasonable accommodation, the next question is whether it is achievable. In the language of the statute, the ADA's reasonable accommodation obligation does not apply to an employer who can demonstrate that the accommodation would *impose an undue hardship* on the operation of its business.[53] An undue hardship is any action requiring *significant* difficulty or expense.[54]

Refusing to make a reasonable accommodation on grounds of undue hardship can be a hazardous maneuver. If there were a dispute as to ADA compliance, it is the employer who will have to prove that the requested accommodation was too burdensome to implement. Furthermore, employers are subject

---

[51] Interpretive Guidance to 29 C.F.R. § 1630.9.
[52] ADA § 501(d).
[53] ADA § 102(b)(5)(A).
[54] ADA § 101(10)(A).

to compensatory and punitive damages under the ADA unless they can prove their good faith efforts, in consultation with the employee, to identify and provide a reasonable accommodation.[55]

Consequently, instead of merely rejecting a proposed reasonable accommodation on grounds of undue hardship, employers should try to articulate why the employee's proposed accommodation was not "reasonable" in the first place and, if at all possible, proffer their own alternative reasonable accommodation. Nonetheless, there will certainly be circumstances in which employers will feel compelled to reject a proposed accommodation based on undue hardship.

4.5.1 Disrupting Business Operations

The concept of undue hardship is *not limited to financial difficulty*. Any accommodation that would be unduly extensive, substantial, or disruptive, or fundamentally alter the nature or operation of the business, would pose an undue hardship. Among such non-financial factors are the impact of the accommodation on the ability of other employees to perform their duties, and the facility's ability to conduct business.

With respect to the issue of impact on business operations, the EEOC gives this illuminating example: If a visually impaired individual who wishes to be a waiter in a dimly lit nightclub asks for brighter lighting so he can write orders, that "would impose an undue hardship if the bright light would destroy the ambience of the nightclub and/or make it difficult for the customers to see the stage show."[56]

While the effect on other employees' ability to work is a factor, the unfounded fears and prejudices of other employees or a negative impact on their morale would *not* constitute an undue hardship. Thus, it could be undue hardship if job restructuring creates a heavier workload for other employees, but *not* if other employees complain that a disabled worker is

---

[55] 42 U.S.C. § 1981a(a)(3).
[56] Interpretive Guidance to 29 C.F.R. § 1630.2(p).

allowed additional unpaid leave or a flexible work schedule as a reasonable accommodation.

4.5.2 Excessive Cost

When it comes to reasonable accommodations that create a financial (as opposed to an operational) burden, the touchstone is excessive cost. This, in turn, is based on four factors:

- nature and net cost of the accommodation;
- overall financial resources of the affected facility;
- overall financial resources of the employer; and
- the employer's type of operation.[57]

According to the EEOC, what matters is the "final net cost" to the employer, taking into account the direct and indirect subsidies that are available for making a reasonable accommodation.[58] Funding for some accommodations—such as sophisticated computer equipment—is available from governmental or private agencies. Even without such funding, the individual should be given the option of providing the accommodation or of paying that portion of the cost which constitutes the undue hardship. Certain tax credits and deductions are available to offset the costs of accommodations for workers with disabilities, and these also may be taken into account.

It is natural for employers to think of "excessive" cost by reference to the employee's compensation. But simply comparing the cost of the accommodation to the salary of the disabled employee may not be enough to create an undue hardship under the ADA.

---

[57] *See* ADA § 101(10)(b); 29 C.F.R. § 1630.2(p)(2).
[58] Interpretive Guidance to 29 C.F.R. §§ 1630(p), 1630.15(d).

4.5.3 The Employing Unit

When the costs of an accommodation are substantial, the question arises as to whose financial resources should be considered. In some cases, the finances of the employer in its entirety will be determinative, but sometimes that may not give an accurate picture of the financial resources available to the particular facility required to provide the accommodation. Unfortunately, there is little guidance given as to when the impact on the employer as a whole or on the particular facility will control. It is useful to remember that the individual-facility factor was deliberately added to the ADA, and this indicates congressional intent that it be an important consideration.

With respect to a particular facility, consideration will be given to the number of employees at the facility, and the effect on its expenses and resources. With respect to the employer as a whole, consideration will be given to the overall size of its business, number of employees, and the number, type and location of its facilities.

Another factor that affects undue hardship is the type of operation involved, which includes: the composition, structure and functions of the workforce, the geographic separateness, and the administrative fiscal relations of the facility in question to the employer. For example, a particular accommodation may impose an undue hardship at a temporary construction worksite, even though it would not be an undue hardship for a different employer or for the same employer at a permanent worksite.

5.0 EQUAL ACCESS TO EMPLOYMENT OPPORTUNITIES

A major premise of the ADA is that employers should make special efforts not only to reasonably accommodate people with disabilities, but also to ensure that they have equal access to the full range of employment opportunities and benefits available to other workers. A variety of otherwise diverse requirements of the ADA can be understood as advancing the "equal access" goal.

5.1 Non-Segregated Facilities

The ADA prohibits limiting, segregating or classifying individuals in a way that adversely affects their opportunities or status.[59] This principle of nondiscrimination may require giving employees with disabilities *equal access* to any employment opportunity available to similarly situated individuals who are not disabled.

The prohibition against segregating on the basis of disability covers the whole range of the employment relationship. It prohibits separate lines of advancement or promotion. It also forbids employers from assigning employees with disabilities to particular work areas, or limiting them to segregated comfort facilities (such as lunch rooms, lounges, etc.). For example, if the company cafeteria is not wheelchair accessible, the employer may have to provide, as a reasonable accommodation, an equivalent facility for the employees with a disability, but that alternate facility may have to permit socializing with nondisabled co-workers.

5.2 Health Insurance

The "equal access" principles apply to all employee fringe benefits, including employer-sponsored health insurance plans. Employees with a disability must be accorded *equal access* to whatever health insurance coverage the employer provides to other employees. Nevertheless, benefit limitation provisions of a health benefit plan that adversely affect individuals with disabilities are permitted so long as they are not used as a subterfuge to evade the purposes of the ADA. Meshing these two principles is not an easy task.

5.2.1 Permissible Benefit Limitations

The ADA clearly provides that employers may provide health insurance coverage (either through an insurance carrier or self-insurance) that is in accordance with accepted principles of risk assessment and/or risk classification, as required or

---

[59] ADA § 102(b)(1).

permitted by state insurance law, even if this causes limitations in coverage for individuals with disabilities.[60]

Consistent with this principle, widely accepted provisions of many health insurance plans that do not constitute a "disability-based distinction" are valid under the ADA.[61] The permitted clauses include: blanket exclusions for pre-existing conditions; benefit limits or exclusions for experimental drugs or treatment; and coverage limits for certain medical procedures (such as elective surgery or blood transfusions). Also permitted are reduced benefits or other distinctions for certain specified conditions or services (such as mental illness or vision care), provided that they are not based on a particular disability or group of disabilities.

All of these benefit plan restrictions can adversely affect employees with a disability. For example, limiting coverage to five blood transfusions a year would adversely affect a hemophiliac employee. But they do not intentionally discriminate on the basis of a disability and so are lawful under the ADA.

5.2.2 Disability-Based Distinctions

Employers cannot deny insurance to individuals with a disability or subject them to different terms and conditions based on disability alone, if the disability does not pose increased insurance risks. Accordingly, the EEOC maintains that benefit plan distinctions based on a particular disability (*e.g.*, deafness, AIDS or schizophrenia) or a discrete group of disabilities (e.g., cancers or kidney diseases) are a form of intentional discrimination and unlawful, *if* they are a subterfuge to evade the purpose of the ADA.[62] An employer might still be able to justify those policies if based on legitimate risk clas-

---

[60] *See* ADA § 501(c); 29 C.F.R. § 1630.16(f); *EEOC Tech. Asst. Manual* at VII-8 to VII-9.

[61] *See EEOC Interim Enforcement Guidance on Application of ADA to Health Insurance*, Pt. III (June 8, 1993) (hereinafter, the *"EEOC Health-Insurance Guidance"*).

[62] *EEOC Health-Insurance Guidance*, Pt. III, B.

sifications or underwriting procedures, or as necessary for the financial solvency or continued viability of the plan.

Placing a lifetime benefits "cap" on the treatment of AIDS which is substantially below that applied for other physical illnesses is an example of one such "disability-based distinction." Whether such a limitation is lawful under the ADA is hotly debated, but presently unresolved.[63]

5.3 Leave Policies

With respect to nonhealth insurance benefits, the EEOC says that leave policies and benefit plans that are *"uniformly applied* do not violate [the ADA] *simply because they do not address the special needs* of every individual with a disability."[64] Such policies would not violate the ADA even if they had an adverse impact on employees with disabilities, who may need greater sick leave or medical coverage. On the other hand, the EEOC also says that "in appropriate circumstances," employers may have to modify certain leave policies (like those forbidding all leave in the first 6 months of employment) as a reasonable accommodation to employees with disabilities.[65]

The EEOC position seems to be that leave policies which adversely affect workers with disabilities are permissible as long as they do not operate to exclude them totally from employment. When that happens (if, for example, an employee is fired for excessive leave), employers may have to show why a reasonable accommodation could not have been made.

5.4 Contractual Arrangements

The ADA includes a unique provision making employers liable merely for *participating* in a contractual, or other arrangement or relationship, that "has the effect of" subjecting the employer's qualified disabled applicants or employees to

---

[63] *See EEOC v. Mason Tenders' District Council Welfare Fund*, No. 93-3865 (S.D.N.Y., filed 6/9/93).

[64] Interpretive Guidance to 29 C.F.R. § 1630.5.

[65] Interpretive Guidance to 29 C.F.R. § 1630.15(b) & (c).

discrimination prohibited by the ADA.[66] The arrangements or relationships encompassed by this provision include those with employment agencies, labor unions, fringe benefit organizations, and training and apprenticeship programs.

Clearly, an employer violates the ADA if it hires through an employment agency and that agency intentionally excludes qualified disabled applicants. However, since merely "participating" in an arrangement that "has the effect" of discrimination is unlawful, the ADA may virtually require employers to ensure that service contractors provide equal access to applicants or employees with disabilities. For example, if an employer holds a conference for its employees at a local hotel, it is the employer that should ascertain and ensure the accessibility of the hotel and its conference facilities.

Consequently, employers should include an ADA-compliance provision in all service contracts they make that affect their own employees or applicants. Even with such a clause, however, the employer might yet be liable under the ADA if the service supplier fails to comply.

5.5 Relationship and Association

The ADA contains another requirement unique to the federal employment discrimination statutes in that it prohibits discrimination against a *non*-disabled employee based on his or her known relationship or association to someone else who has a known disability.[67] The statute places no limit on the kind of "relationship or association" involved. While it includes family relationships (having a spouse or child with a disability), it is not limited to that and may include having a "domestic partner" with AIDS.

The protection provided to qualified, non-disabled employees by the ADA is *not* the same protection as for workers with a disability because there is no obligation to provide a reasonable accommodation. So, for example, employers cannot deny employment to a non-disabled individual

---

[66] ADA § 102(b)(2).
[67] ADA § 102(b)(4).

merely because they believe that he or she will miss work frequently to care for a disabled spouse. But employers need not provide such individuals with flexible leave or modified work schedules to actually care for a disabled spouse, if that need arises. Some such leave may be required under the Family and Medical Leave Act of 1993 (29 U.S.C. § 2601 *et seq.*), but not under the ADA.

5.6 Retaliation and Interference

Like other federal anti-discrimination laws, the ADA prohibits discrimination against an individual (disabled or not) for having opposed any act or practice made unlawful under the ADA, filed a charge, or otherwise participated in an enforcement proceeding.[68] It is also unlawful to coerce, intimidate, threaten, or interfere with those who exercise or enjoy their ADA rights, or those who encourage others to do so.[69]

---

[68] ADA § 503(a).
[69] ADA § 503(b).

Chapter 4
WAGES AND SALARIES

Eric Paltell
Piper & Marbury

1.0 INTRODUCTION

Compensation is probably the single most important part of the job for most American workers. Despite its importance, federal and state law generally give employers wide latitude to pay employees whatever the market will bear.

Federal and state "wage and hour" laws do require that employers pay covered employees a basic minimum wage and overtime for hours in excess of 40 per week. These laws also require that employers pay covered employees for all hours worked, keep detailed records of wages paid, and pay equal wages to men and women who perform jobs requiring equal skill, effort, and responsibility. Additionally, wage and hour laws regulate the employment of youths under age 18.

This chapter provides an overview of the federal Fair Labor Standards Act, the most significant law regulating employee compensation. The chapter also briefly discusses state wage and hour laws, "prevailing wage" laws, and the federal Equal Pay Act.

2.0 FAIR LABOR STANDARDS ACT

The Fair Labor Standards Act ("FLSA")[1] establishes minimum wage, overtime, child labor standards, recordkeeping, and equal pay requirements that affect more than 80 million full-time and part-time workers in the private sector and in state and local governments.

The FLSA was enacted in 1938 to help spur economic recovery from the Great Depression. Its basic purpose is to ensure that employees are paid a minimum wage and to create jobs by imposing a monetary penalty—an overtime pay premium—on employers who increase the workload of current employees instead of hiring new employees.

The FLSA *does not* impose any limit on the number of hours an employee may be required to work (except for children), nor does it give employees the right to refuse to work overtime. The statute also does not require that employees be paid for holidays, sick days, or vacations.

2.1 Covered Employees and Employers

The FLSA may apply to all employees of a business or to just certain employees of a business.

2.1.1 Employees

The FLSA applies to any employee whose duties require him or her to "engage in commerce" or the "production of goods for interstate commerce." An employee "engaged in commerce" is one whose work is related to the movement of persons or goods across state lines.[2] Persons engaged in the "production of goods for interstate commerce" are those who perform work related to the manufacture of goods which may eventually cross state lines.[3]

Domestic service workers, such as chauffeurs, cooks, and full-time babysitters are covered if they receive at least $50 in

---

[1] 29 U.S.C. §201 *et seq.*

[2] *See e.g., Overstreet v. North Shore Corp.*, 318 U.S. 125, 130 (1943).

[3] *See e.g., Bracey v. Luray*, 138 F.2d 8, 11 (4th Cir. 1943).

cash wages in a calendar quarter from their employers or work a total of more than eight hours a week for one or more employers.[4] The FLSA does not apply to independent contractors.[5]

2.1.2 Employers

The FLSA applies to *all* employees employed at a business "engaged in commerce or the production of goods for commerce." For most firms, an annual "volume of business" test of not less than $500,000 applies.[6] This means that if the annual volume of business is less than $500,000, only employees who meet the individual coverage tests described above are covered by the FLSA.

2.1.3 Public Sector Employers

In 1985, the United States Supreme Court held that all state and local governments are covered by the FLSA.[7] With the exception of overtime requirements, the FLSA imposes obligations on public sector employers very similar to those imposed on private businesses. Details of public sector coverage are beyond the scope of this chapter.

2.2 Exemptions from Coverage

Some employees are excluded from the Act's minimum wage and/or overtime pay provisions. FLSA exemptions are industry-wide or are determined by an employee's duties.

2.2.1 Employee Exemptions

Executive, administrative and professional employees (including teachers and certain skilled computer professionals)

---

[4] 29 U.S.C. §213 (b) (1); 29 CFR §552.3; U.S. Department of Labor, "Small Business Handbook", Section 1.

[5] *See, e.g. Thomas v. Brock*, 617 F. Supp. 526 (D.N.C. 1985).

[6] 29 U.S.C. §203 (s) (1) (A) (ii).

[7] *Garcia v. San Antonio Metropolitan Transit Authority*, 469 U.S. 528 (1985).

and outside salespeople are exempt from the minimum wage and overtime requirements of the FLSA, but not its equal pay provisions.[8] Whether an employee falls within these exemptions depends upon the employee's salary and duties.[9] A checklist for determining whether an employee falls within the executive, administrative or professional exemptions is included as Appendix A at the end of this chapter.

With the exception of persons working in certain computer-related occupations (primarily programmers), physicians, teachers, lawyers and employees *must* be paid a salary to be exempt.[10] An employer generally cannot "dock" an exempt employee's salary for absences of less than one full day—an exempt employee whose pay is "docked" is entitled to overtime pay for the pay period in which the deduction was made.[11] An employer is permitted to pay overtime to a salaried exempt employee without losing the exemption.[12]

2.2.2 Industry Exemptions

The FLSA establishes a number of industry-specific exemptions. These include such varied businesses as amusement parks, fishing boat operators and agricultural entities.[13] Employees subject to Department of Transportation regulations—including persons who drive vehicles across state lines—generally are exempt from the overtime requirements (but not the minimum wage requirements) of the FLSA.[14]

---

[8] 29 U.S.C. §213 (a) (1).

[9] See 29 C.F.R. §541.0 et seq.

[10] *Brock v. Claridge Hotel and Casino*, 846 F.2d 180, 184-87 (3d Cir.), cert. denied, 488 U.S. 925 (1988).

[11] *Martin v. Malcom Pirnie, Inc.*, 949 F.2d 611, 615 (2d Cir. 1991), cert. denied, 113 S. Ct. 298 (1992); 29 C.F.R. §541.118(a) (1) - (6).

[12] *Field Operations Handbook* (FOH) §22b01.

[13] 29 U.S.C. §213 (a), §213 (a)-(j).

[14] 29 U.S.C. § 213 (b) (1).

2.3 Hours Worked and Compensation

2.3.1 Minimum Wage

Employers must pay covered employees a minimum wage of $4.25 per hour.[15] Employees do not have to be paid on an hourly basis. A salary, commission, piecework rates, or any other basis is legal so long as total weekly pay divided by total hours worked is equal to or exceeds the minimum wage. Any meals or lodging the employee receives may be credited toward the employer's minimum wage obligation.[16]

2.3.2 Overtime

Non-exempt employees must be paid 1-1/2 times their "regular hourly rate" for hours worked in excess of 40 in an established seven-day workweek.[17] Overtime must be paid on a weekly basis and must be paid on the pay day covering the workweek in which the overtime was worked.[18]

Employees are entitled to overtime compensation whenever the overtime work is "suffered or permitted" by the employer. This means that if the employee's supervisor knows that the employee is working overtime hours, even if the employee was not requested to do so, the employee must be paid the premium rate for the overtime work.[19]

(a) *Overtime Must be Paid at 1½ Times the "Regular Rate"*

The regular rate is an hourly rate, regardless of whether the employee is paid a salary or hourly. It is determined by dividing the total compensation for the week by the total hours worked in the week.

---

[15] 29 U.S.C. §206(a) (1).
[16] 29 U.S.C. §203 (m).
[17] 29 U.S.C. §207 (a) (1).
[18] 29 C.F.R. §778.106.
[19] 29 C.F.R. §785.11.

If the employee is paid a salary, calculating the regular rate depends upon the hours the salary was intended to compensate. As the examples below demonstrate, it makes a difference whether the salary covers a certain number of hours per week or all hours worked. (Additional examples of overtime calculations are shown in the chart included as Appendix B at the end of this chapter).

Example 1: The employee is paid $250 per week for 40 hours of work. His regular rate is $250 divided by 40 = $6.25. Any overtime must be paid at a rate of $6.25 x 1.5 = $9.37 per overtime hour. If he works 45 hours one week, his total compensation is $250 + (5 x $9.37) = $296.85.

Example 2: The employee is paid $250 per week for all hours worked. Assume, as above, he works 45 hours one week. His regular rate is $250 divided by 45 = $5.55. Because the employee is already being paid straight time for all hours worked, including the five overtime hours, overtime compensation is calculated by determining the additional half-time due for the five overtime hours. Here, it would be (1/2 x $5.55) x 5 = $13.89. Therefore, total weekly compensation due is $250 + $13.89 = $263.89.

These examples demonstrate that an employer can reduce overtime costs by paying non-exempt employees a fixed salary for all hours worked instead of an hourly rate or a salary for a fixed number of hours per week. Employers seeking to reduce overtime costs by relying on such an arrangement should be sure to have written documentation signed by the employee which shows that the employee understands that his salary was intended to cover all hours worked.[20]

Employees who hold two different jobs for an employer, or who are paid at two different rates for the same job (because of

---

[20] 29 C.F.R. §778.114.

a shift differential, for example), have a regular rate that is the weighted average of such rates. The weighted average is determined by adding together weekly earnings and dividing the total by the total number of hours worked. Alternatively, the employer and employee may agree in advance that the regular rate used in overtime calculations will be based upon the regular rate for the type of work the employee is doing during the overtime hours.[21]

(b) *What is Included in the Regular Rate?*

All compensation received for employment is included in the regular rate, except for specified statutory exclusions.[22] The regular rate includes:

- board and lodging furnished by the employer
- "non-discretionary" bonuses, where the bonus is designed to encourage increased efforts by the employee (such as accuracy, attendance, production, or quality bonuses)
- commissions
- on-call pay
- shift differentials

Items which may be *excluded* from regular rate include:

- gifts
- paid time off, such as payments for vacation, holiday or illness
- discretionary bonuses, such as Christmas bonuses
- contributions to insurance or retirement plans

Certain premium rates are excludable because they are recognized as overtime premiums. Not only are these premiums excluded from the regular rate calculation, but they are also

---

[21] 29 C.F.R. §778.115.
[22] 29 U.S.C. §207 (e).

credited against overtime liability.[23] The three types of premiums which meet this requirement are:

- premiums paid for hours worked in any day or workweek because such hours worked exceed eight in a day or 40 in a workweek.
- premiums paid for holidays, Saturdays or Sundays if the rate is at least 1½ times the regular rate for such work on other days.
- premiums paid for work outside the regular workday or workweek as established by contract or agreement.

2.3.3 Compensable Hours Worked

Employees must be paid for all hours worked, and all hours worked must be counted in determining whether an employee is entitled to overtime. Hours worked include all time where the employee is "suffered or permitted" to work. Determining exactly what constitutes "hours worked" is *essential* to determining whether an employee is entitled to overtime pay.

(a) *Waiting Time*

If an employee is relieved of his duties long enough to use the time effectively for his own purposes, he is "waiting to be engaged" and not entitled to compensation for the waiting time. But if the employee is not free to pursue his own activities, he is "engaged to be waiting" and entitled to compensation.[24] FLSA regulations state that an employee is "not completely relieved from duty and cannot use the time effectively for his own purposes unless he is definitely told in advance that he may leave the job and that he will not have to commence work until a definitely specified hour has arrived."[25]

---

[23] 29 U.S.C. §207 (e) (5), (6) and (7).
[24] 29 C.F.R. §785.15.
[25] 29 C.F.R. §785.16.

(b) *Meal Periods*

Meal periods of less than half an hour are compensable. Longer meal periods are not compensable if the employee is relieved of his or her duties.[26] All voluntary work done during meal periods must be counted as compensable working time if the employer knows or has reason to believe work is being performed.[27]

(c) *Break Time*

Breaks of 20 minutes or less are compensable.[28] The compensability of rest periods that last longer than 20 minutes depends on the employee's freedom during the breaks.[29]

(d) *"On-Call" Time*

On-call time is compensable if the employee is required to remain on call at or near the employer's premises. It is not compensable if the employee is free to pursue own activities but must be in contact by beeper.[30]

(e) *Sleeping Time*

Sleeping time is compensable if the tour of duty is less than 24 hours. If the employee is on duty for more than 24 hours, the employer and employee may agree to exclude up to eight hours from compensable time for a sleeping period. If the employee

---

[26] 29 C.F.R. §785.19.
[27] *Baker v. United States*, 23 WH Cases 1224 (Ct. Cl. 1978).
[28] 29 C.F.R. §785.18.
[29] *Brennan v. Associated Drugs*, 22 WH Cases 64 (S.D. Tex. 1974).
[30] 29 C.F.R. §785.17; *Bright v. Houston Northwest Medical Center Survivor, Inc.*, 934 F.2d 671, 677-678 (5th Cir. 1991) (*en banc*), *cert. denied*, 112 S. Ct. 882 (1992).

cannot get at least five hours uninterrupted sleep, the period is compensable.[31]

(f) *Lectures, Meetings, & Training Programs*

Lectures, meetings, and training programs are not compensable if *all four* of the following criteria are met:

(1) attendance is outside of the employee's regular working hours,
(2) attendance is voluntary,
(3) the course, meeting or lecture is not directly related to the employee's job, and
(4) the employee does not perform any productive work while attending.[32]

(g) *Preliminary and Postliminary Activities*

Work done outside of regular working hours which is done for the employer's benefit is compensable, unless it involves such an insignificant amount of time that it is *"de minimis."*[33] Courts have held that a total of ten minutes a day of preliminary and postliminary activities is *de minimis* and need not be compensated.[34]

(h) *Travel Time*

Travel from home to work is not compensable unless payment for the time is required by contract or custom.[35] If the employee must report to an office to receive an assignment and

---

[31] 29 C.F.R. §785.22.
[32] 29 C.F.R. §785.27.
[33] *Steiner v. Mitchell*, 350 U.S. 247, 256 (1956); *Anderson v. Mt. Clemens Pottery Co.*, 328 U.S. 680, 692 (1946).
[34] *See, e.g. E.I. DuPont De Nemours & Co. v. Harrup*, 227 F.2d 133, 135-136 (4th Cir. 1955).
[35] 29 C.F.R. §785.35.

then travel to the worksite, the time spent commuting from home to the office is not compensable, but the time travelling from the office to the worksite is compensable.[36]

If the employee is called out from home, after normal working hours, to perform an emergency job for a customer, the travel time is compensable. If, however, the employee is called back into the regular workplace after hours, the travel time is not compensable.[37]

Out-of-town travel is compensable to the extent it occurs during regular working hours, even on non-working days. Travel during non-working hours is non-compensable unless the employee is required to work while travelling.[38] Therefore, it is usually to the employer's advantage to require employees to travel at night.

2.3.4 Compensatory Time

A common mistake by private employers is the use of "compensatory time" in lieu of overtime. A private employer *cannot* credit an employee with "comp time," even at a time and a half rate, for overtime hours, *unless* the comp time is taken in the *same pay period* in which the overtime hours were worked. To legally use comp time, a private employer must:

a) credit the employees with 1½ hours off for every overtime hour worked, and
b) require that the time off be taken in the same pay period in which the overtime was worked.[39]

2.4 Record-Keeping Requirements

Employers must keep records concerning an employee's position, wages, hours, sex, and other information. Records must

---

[36] 29 C.F.R. §785.38.
[37] *Field Operations Handbook* (FOH) §31c06.
[38] 29 C.F.R. §785.39.
[39] *Brennan v. New Jersey*, 21 WH Cases 327, 328-329 (D.N.J. 1973); Wage-Hour Administrator Opinion Letter No. 913 (December 27, 1968).

be kept for both exempt and non-exempt employees.[40] Most records must be kept for at least two years and pay records must be kept for three years. A list of records which must be kept under the FLSA is included as Appendix C at the end of this chapter.

2.5 Penalties

2.5.1 Civil Penalties

Employers may be liable for unpaid wages, an equal amount in liquidated damages, attorneys' fees and costs.[41] A court may deny liquidated damages if the employer can convince the court that it acted in good faith and had reasonable grounds to believe that its conduct did not violate the FLSA.[42] The FLSA provides civil penalties up to $1,000 per violation for employers who willfully or repeatedly violate the Act's minimum wage, overtime, or equal pay provisions.[43]

2.5.2 Criminal Penalties

Willful violations are punishable by a fine of up to $10,000, imprisonment of up to six months, or both.[44]

2.6 Enforcement

The Fair Labor Standards Act is enforced through suits by the Secretary of Labor to collect unpaid wages and an equal amount in liquidated damages and injunctions to restrain employers from violating the law.[45]

Employees may also bring suit to recover back wages due, an equal additional amount of liquidated damages, attorneys'

---

[40] 29 U.S.C. §211 (c); 29 C.F.R. §516.1 *et seq.*
[41] 29 U.S.C. §216 (b).
[42] 29 U.S.C. §260; *Burnley v. Short*, 730 F.2d 136, 140 (4th Cir. 1984).
[43] 29 U.S.C. §216(e).
[44] 29 U.S.C. §216 (a).
[45] 29 U.S.C. §§216 (c), 217.

fees, and costs.[46] A suit by the Secretary of Labor terminates an employee's right to sue personally.[47]

Actions for wages due under the Fair Labor Standards Act must be brought within two years of the violation.[48] If the cause of action arises out of a "willful violation," it must be commenced within three years after the cause of action instead of two years.[49] A willful violation requires a showing that an employer "knew or showed reckless disregard" as to whether its conduct was prohibited by the FLSA.[50]

Proof of "good faith" compliance with a *written* administrative regulation, order, ruling, approval, or interpretation, or any administrative practice or enforcement policy issued by Department of Labor officials, will provide a complete defense to any FLSA action.[51] Additionally, as discussed above, courts are given discretion to deny liquidated damages whenever they find that the employer's violation occurred in "good faith" and that it had reasonable grounds for believing that no violation was committed.[52]

2.7 Child Labor Prohibitions

The FLSA provides that no employer covered by the Act shall employ any "oppressive child labor." "Oppressive child labor" is defined as employment of children at ages below those set by statute or regulation for various types of occupations.[53]

Most states have laws regulating child labor as well. State laws typically limit the hours persons under age 16 may work and require age certificates or work permits for minors.

---

[46] 29 U.S.C. §216 (b).
[47] 29 U.S.C. §216 (c).
[48] 29 U.S.C. §255.
[49] *Id.*
[50] *McLaughlin v. Richland Shoe Co.*, 486 U.S. 128 (1988).
[51] 29 U.S.C. §259.
[52] 29 U.S.C. §260.
[53] 29 U.S.C. §203 (1).

2.7.1 Child Labor Standards for 16- and 17-Year-Old Youths

Youths aged 16 and 17 may work at any time for unlimited hours at all jobs not declared hazardous by the Secretary of Labor. Examples of prohibited hazardous employment include working with explosives and radioactive materials; operating certain power driver machinery, such as power saws, forklifts and cranes; logging; roofing; and wrecking, demolition, and shipbreaking operations.[54]

2.7.2 Child Labor Standards for 14- and 15-Year-Old Youths

Youths aged 14 and 15 may work in any non-agricultural occupation not deemed hazardous by the Secretary of Labor so long as the employment does not interfere with school. For example, 14- and 15-year-olds may perform office and clerical work, bag groceries, wait tables, work in kitchens, and do grounds maintenance.

The Department of Labor strictly regulates the hours of work for minors aged 14 and 15. They cannot work during school hours; more than three hours in a school day; more than 18 hours in a school week; more than eight hours in a non-school day; more than 40 hours in a non-school week; or before 7:00 a.m. or after 7:00 p.m. during the school year. Between June 1 and Labor Day, minors aged 14 and 15 may work until 9:00 p.m.[55]

Youths ages 14 and 15 may not work at any job declared hazardous by the Secretary of Labor.[56]

---

[54] 29 C.F.R. §570.50 *et seq.*; U.S. Dept. of Labor Fact Sheet No. ESA 86-3.

[55] 29 C.F.R. §570.35.

[56] 29 C.F.R. §§ 570.33 (a) - (f).

2.7.3 Penalties

Employers may be fined up to $10,000 for each child labor violation.[57]

3.0 EQUAL PAY ACT OF 1963

3.1 Requirements

The Equal Pay Act of 1963 ("EPA") is an amendment to the Fair Labor Standards Act that requires that male and female workers receive equal pay for equal work requiring equal skill, effort and responsibility and performed under similar working conditions.[58] Because the Equal Pay Act is an amendment to the FLSA, it applies to employees and employers covered by the FLSA. However, there are no "white collar" exemptions from the EPA.

The Equal Pay Act requires that an employer pay male and female employees equal wages for equal work on jobs which require equal skill, effort, and responsibility, and which are performed under similar working conditions.[59] An assessment of what constitutes "equal work" must be made on the basis of job content and not job descriptions or job titles.[60] Most courts have rejected the argument that the EPA requires employers to pay equal pay for work that is of "comparable worth or value," but does not require equal skill, effort and responsibility.[61]

The Equal Pay Act allows an employer to pay different wages to men and women who hold substantially equal jobs if the employer can prove that the difference in wages is due to:

(1) a seniority system;
(2) a merit system;

---

[57] 29 U.S.C. §216 (e).
[58] 29 U.S.C. §206 (d) (1).
[59] Id.
[60] *Strecker v. Grand Forks Country Social Service Board*, 640 F.2d 96, 100 (8th Cir. 1980); 29 C.F.R. § 1620.13 (e).
[61] See e.g., *State of Washington v. AFSCME*, 770 F.2d 1401 (9th Cir. 1985).

(3) a system which measures earnings by quantity or quality of production; or

(4) "any factor other than sex".[62]

3.2 Enforcement

The Equal Employment Opportunity Commission ("EEOC") is responsible for enforcing the Equal Pay Act. A person may file a charge alleging an EPA violation with the EEOC, or may file suit in federal court without first filing a charge. Additionally, the EEOC may sue on behalf of the employee.

As an amendment to the FLSA, the EPA has the same penalty provisions as does the FLSA. These penalties include backpay, an equal amount of liquidated damages, attorneys' fees, and costs.[63] The EPA has the same statute of limitations as does the FLSA. This means that actions must be brought within two years of the date the violation occurred. In the event of willful violation, the action must be brought within three years.[64]

4.0 PREVAILING WAGE LAWS

Several federal laws require that employers who contract with the federal government pay employees "prevailing wages and benefits." These laws include the Davis-Bacon Act,[65] which applies to public construction projects; the Service Contract Act,[66] which applies to businesses that contract with the government to provide services such as food service, transportation, and grounds maintenance; the Walsh-Healey Government Contracts Act,[67] which applies to companies that contract with the federal government to supply material, supplies, articles, or equipment; the Anti-Kickback Act of 1986,[68] which provides for

---

[62] 29 U.S.C. §206 (d).
[63] 29 U.S.C. §216.
[64] 29 U.S.C. §255.
[65] 40 U.S.C. §276a, *et seq.*
[66] 41 U.S.C. §351, *et seq.*
[67] 41 U.S.C. §35 *et seq.*
[68] 41 U.S.C. §51, *et seq.*

a fine or imprisonment of any person who induces a laborer on a construction contract to "kick back" part of his wage; and the Contract Work Hours and Safety Standards Act,[69] which requires payment of time and one-half for all hours in excess of 40 per week for laborers and mechanics on public construction contracts. Many states also have prevailing wage law which require employers to provide a certain level of wages and benefits to employees working on public works projects.

5.0 STATE WAGE AND HOUR LAWS

5.1 Overtime, Minimum Wage, and Child Labor Laws

Most states have laws regulating the payment of minimum wages, overtime, and child labor. Many of these laws provide greater protection than the federal Fair Labor Standards Act. For example, several states and the District of Columbia require that employees be paid a minimum wage higher than the $4.25 per hour federal requirement. Other states require that overtime be paid for work in excess of eight hours a day. Where federal and state law conflict, the employer generally must comply with the law that gives the employee greater protection. Because an employer's wage and hour obligations vary from state to state, employers should consult the local office of the state labor department about state law requirements.

5.2 "Payment of Wages" Laws

Federal law is generally silent on when wages must be paid. However, many state laws require that employees be paid no less frequently than every two weeks.[70] State law may also limit an employer's ability to make deductions from an employee's pay (other than tax withholding) without the employee's consent.[71] Such laws effectively prohibit an employer from "docking" an employee's pay for such things as discrepancies in

---

[69] 40 U.S.C. §327, *et seq.*
[70] *See* Md. Lab. & Emp. Code Ann., §3-502 (1992 Supp.).
[71] *See* Md. Lab. & Emp. Code Ann., §3-503 (1992 Supp.).

cash register receipts, a customer's refusal to pay a bill, or an employee's failure to return company property.

Most states also have laws requiring that employees receive their final paycheck within a specific time period—usually no later than the next regular pay day following termination.[72] Employers who violate such laws are subject to substantial penalties—usually two or three times the wages due the employee, plus attorneys' fees.[73]

6.0 WHITE COLLAR EXEMPTION CHECKLIST (APPENDIX A)

6.1 Executive Employees

A. *Long Test* (for persons paid more than $155 but less than $250 per week).

1. Primarily (50 percent or more of time) manages a department.
2. Regularly supervises two or more employees.
3. Has the authority to hire, fire, promote, or effectively recommend such actions.
4. Exercises discretion on a day-to-day basis (regularly makes independent decisions with minimal guidance from superiors).
5. Spends no more than 20 percent of weekly time in non-managerial work.
6. Paid a salary of at least $155 per week.

B. *Short Test* (for persons paid $250 or more per week).

1. Primarily manages a department.
2. Regularly supervises two or more employees.
3. Paid a salary of at least $250 per week.

---

[72] *See* Md. Lab. & Emp. Code Ann., §3-505 (1992 Supp.).
[73] *See* Md. Lab. & Emp. Code Ann., §3-507 (b).

6.2 Administrative Employees

A. *Long Test* (for persons paid more than $155 but less than $250 per week)
1. Primarily consist of either:
   (a) non-manual or office work directly related to management policies or general business operations; or
   (b) performance of administrative functions in an educational establishment in work related to academic instruction or training.
2. Exercises discretion and independent judgment on day-to-day basis (regularly makes independent decisions with little guidance from superiors)
3. Meets one of the following three requirements:
   (a) regularly and directly assists a person employed in an executive or administrative capacity; or
   (b) performs under general supervision work requiring special training, experience, or knowledge; or
   (c) executes, under only general supervision, special assignments or tasks.
4. Spends no more than 20 percent of weekly work time in non-administrative work.
5. Paid a salary of at least $155 per week.

B. *Short Test* (for persons paid more than $250 per week).
1. Primarily:
   (a) performance of office or non-manual work directly related to management policies or general business operations, or
   (b) performance of administrative functions in an educational establishment in work related to academic instruction or training.
2. Exercises discretion and independent judgment on a day-to-day basis.

3. Paid a salary of at least $250 per week.

6.3 Professional Employees

A. *Long Test* (for persons paid more than $170 but less than $250 per week)
1. Primarily work requiring:
   (a) advanced learning typically acquired through prolonged intellectual study. Usually requires advanced academic degree (for example, accounting, engineering, law, medicine, nursing, pharmacology, teaching, and science); or
   (b) original or creative work depending primarily on invention, imagination, or talent; or
   (c) teaching, tutoring, instructing, or lecturing for a school system or educational institutions.
2. Exercises discretion and independent judgment on day-to-day basis (regularly makes independent decisions with minimal guidance from superiors).
3. Performs work predominantly intellectual and varied in character.
4. Spends no more than 20 percent of his weekly time in non-professional work.
5. Paid a salary of at least $170 per week. However, doctors, lawyers, and teachers employed by schools may be paid on hourly basis.

B. *Short Test*
1. Primarily does work requiring advanced learning (typically a degree) or works as a teacher.
2. Exercises discretion and independent judgment on day-to-day basis, or consistently does work requiring invention, imagination, or talent in a recognized field or artistic endeavor.
3. Paid a salary of at least $250 per week.

7.0 OVERTIME CALCULATION CHART (APPENDIX B)

Compensation Method	Regular Rate	Overtime
Hourly rate	Hourly rate + all other includable compensation	1.5 x regular rate for hours in excess of 40
Salaried with fixed 40-hour workweek	Salary + all other includable compensation divided by 40	1.5 x regular rate for hours in excess of 40
Salaried, with salary representing payment for all hours worked	Salary + all other includable compensation divided by total hours in the week	0.5 x regular rate for hours in excess of 40[74]
Salaried, with salary representing payment for 45 hours of work in the week	Salary + all other includable compensation divided by 45	0.5 x regular rate for 5 hours; 1.5 x regular rate for hours worked in excess of 45
Salaried, paid semi-monthly for all hours worked	(Salary + all other includable compensation) x 24 divided by 52 divided by number of hours worked	0.5 x regular rate for hours worked in excess of 40

8.0 FLSA RECORDKEEPING CHECKLIST (APPENDIX C)

The FLSA requires that employers keep records of wages, hours, and other personnel data. Records must be kept for exempt as well as non-exempt employees. Records of exempt employees need not be as detailed as records for non-exempt employees (for example, you need not keep records of hours

---

[74] Overtime calculation requires that you multiply 0.5 x regular rate for all hours in excess of 40, not 1.5 x regular rate, because the employee has already been paid straight-time for the hours in excess of 40.

worked), but they should be sufficient to prove that the employee really is exempt.

An employer must keep the following records for non-exempt employees for a three-year period.

1. Employee's full name, home address, and social security number.
2. Date of birth, if under 19.
3. Sex.
4. Position (occupation).
5. Time and day on which work week begins.
6. Regular hourly rate of pay, basis for payment (salary, hourly, commission, etc.), and exclusions from regular rate.
7. Hours worked each workday and total hours worked each workweek.
8. Total daily or weekly straight time earnings or wages.
9. Total overtime compensation for each week.
10. Total additions to our deductions from wages paid in each pay period.
11. Total wages paid each pay period.
12. Date of payment of wages and pay period covered by payment.

Chapter 5
EMPLOYEE BENEFIT COMPLIANCE MATTERS

Frank Palmieri
Palmieri & Eisenberg

1.0 OVERVIEW

Human resource professionals are frequently required to assist their employers in addressing employee benefit matters. The employee benefit issues they may encounter may generally be divided into several components. These components include employee benefit planning to reduce costs and streamline operations, employee benefit compliance matters which are required by statute and must be satisfied in order to avoid liability, and employee benefit communications which are critical to the success of any program. The readers of this book are uniquely qualified to address the communications aspects of employee benefits, and planning concepts are beyond the scope of this chapter. The purpose of this chapter will be to provide a basic overview of some of the legal requirements which employers must satisfy to avoid liability for qualified retirement plans, nonqualified retirement programs, and certain welfare benefit plans.

2.0 RETIREMENT PLANS

2.1 Qualified Retirement Plans

When reviewing retirement plans the first step is to identify whether a retirement plan is a "qualified" retirement plan, or if the plan is a "nonqualified" retirement plan. The primary distinction between these two types of programs relates to the preferential tax treatment granted to qualified retirement plans. Under a qualified plan an employer is entitled to a deduction when a contribution is made to a plan, and employees are not taxed on the employer's contribution until it is distributed from the plan upon retirement, termination of employment or the occurrence of another distributable event. This preferential treatment creates the opportunity to provide employees with a current benefit, to delay taxation until employees are in a lower tax bracket after retirement, and also permits contributions to a qualified plan to grow on a tax-free basis. Typical types of qualified retirement plans include defined benefit plans, various types of defined contribution plans and "hybrid" plans which combine the concept of both types of retirement plans.

2.2 Defined Benefit Plans

Defined benefit plans were the traditional plans established for union employees. Under a defined benefit plan an employer establishes a benefit formula which promises a future retirement benefit. For example, the formula may provide a benefit equal to 50 percent of an employee's average compensation over a 5-year period, which is equal to $500 a month beginning at age 65. After this type of plan is established, employees accrue benefits each year and vest in their benefits as they continue to perform service for an employer. It is the obligation of the employer to make sufficient contributions to the plan each year in order to "fund" the actuarial value of all promised benefits. If the earnings attributable to a plan's assets are favorable, an employer's contributions to a plan are reduced. However, if less favorable earnings are achieved, employers are obligated to increase contributions to fund past and current benefit obligations. It is the obligation to fund benefits and make quarterly contributions which have caused many employers to be reluctant to establish defined benefit plans in recent years.

Defined benefit plans are governed by both the Internal Revenue Code[1] (the "Code") and the Employee Retirement Income Security Act of 1974 ("ERISA")[2]. In addition, defined benefit plans must pay certain annual premiums to the Pension Benefit Guarantee Corporation (the "PBGC") each year. These premiums are used by the PBGC to provide benefits to employees if a plan is terminated without sufficient assets to pay all benefits promised under the plan.

2.3 Defined Contribution Plans

By contrast to defined benefit plans, defined contribution plans simply permit an employer to make annual contributions to the individual accounts of participants on either a mandatory or discretionary basis. The ultimate retirement benefit received by any participant is equal to the amount of contributions made to the participant's account, plus any earnings or losses associated with such contributions. No specific retirement benefit is promised. Thus, retirement benefits may grow rapidly or disappear, depending upon the investment performance of a plan or a participant's individual account.

Defined contribution plans include discretionary profit sharing plans; Section 401(k) savings plans which permit employees to elect to reduce their salaries to make contributions to save for retirement on a pre-tax basis; money purchase pension plans which combine defined benefit and defined contribution plan concepts by obligating an employer to make annual contributions, (such as 5 percent of participant compensation) while determining the ultimate benefit by the amount in a participant's account;

---

[1] *See* Title 26 of the U.S. Code.
[2] *See* Title 29 of the U.S. Code.

and employee stock ownership plans ("ESOPs"). Defined contribution plans are not required to pay premiums to the PBGC, nor are they required to make quarterly contributions. As previously indicated, a discussion of the appropriate circumstances in which to establish each type of plan is beyond the scope of this chapter. However, employers are encouraged to thoroughly research all qualified retirement plan alternatives before designing and establishing a retirement program to satisfy the specific needs of each of its employees.

2.4 Nonqualified Retirement Programs

Due to the limitations which exist in structuring qualified retirement plans, such as some of the nondiscrimination rules which are outlined below, employers frequently establish "nonqualified" retirement programs. These plans are often referred to as nonqualified plans, supplemental executive retirement program ("SERPs"), or top-hat plans for a select group of senior management employees. In general, these plans are established to permit employees to reduce their salaries and to obtain additional nonqualified retirement benefits on a tax-deferred basis, or use employer funds to provide supplemental retirement benefits in addition to or in lieu of benefits provided under a qualified retirement plan.

The basic rule governing nonqualifed programs is the "constructive receipt" rule. Under the constructive receipt rule, if an employee is able to obtain compensation, the employee is taxed on such compensation whether or not it is received. In order for employees to avoid taxation on nonqualified benefits, employees must not have any right to receive employer contributions, nor receive any property which is not subject to a substantial risk of forfeiture.[3] Therefore, employees only receive an unfunded unsecured promise by an employer to pay a future benefit under a

---

[3] *See* Section 83 of the Code regarding the taxation of property transferred in connection with the performance of services.

nonqualified plan, delaying taxation until benefits are actually paid.[4]

If employee contributions are anticipated under a nonqualified plan the employees must generally elect to defer their compensation before it is earned, before the amount is determinable, and before the amount is payable. The best scenario in which to further examine the constructive receipt rule is to review the desire of an executive to defer a year-end bonus. If services have already been performed by the executive, the amount is payable, and the due date to pay the bonus has arrived, any efforts to defer such compensation will not be effective to defer taxation. Similarly, if an employee attempts to defer compensation under a nonqualified retirement program until the individual retires or otherwise terminates employment, the necessary deferral requirements must be satisfied or current taxation will exist.

Less difficulty is encountered if an employer simply establishes a supplemental retirement plan for senior executives. For example, an employer may decide to provide senior-management employees with an additional lump sum benefit equal to $5,000 for each year of employment upon retirement. Under this approach if senior-management employees do not have any opportunity to obtain current cash compensation, no taxation exists under the constructive receipt rule. Obviously, use of employer rather than employee funds will result in economic decisions for an employer. Contributing to this decision process is the fact that employers are not entitled to any tax deduction for benefits promised under nonqualified programs until benefits are paid. Since employer deductions are delayed, and nonqualified benefits must remain unsecured promises to pay benefits to avoid taxation, they are useful tax

---

[4] Treas. Reg. Section 1.83-3(e) confirms that no taxation exists for unfunded and unsecured promises to pay money or property in the future. The vehicles to attempt to secure nonqualified benefit, such as "rabbi trusts," will not be addressed in this chapter.

planning tools for senior executives but do not work well in other contexts.

2.5 ERISA Retirement Plans

In addition to satisfying the basic tax rules consideration must be given to the ERISA rules which apply to retirement plans. In general, ERISA defines a pension benefit plan to include any plan, fund, or program which is established or maintained by an employer or an employee organization which provides retirement income to employees or results in the deferral of income by employees until after a termination of employment or a later date.[5] Accordingly, both qualified and nonqualified plans are pension plans for purposes of ERISA. The ERISA rules applicable to retirement plans are further discussed below under the reporting and disclosure rules.

3.0 WELFARE BENEFIT PLANS

After an employer has identified whether it maintains any pension plans for purposes of the Code and ERISA, consideration must be given to whether any welfare benefit plans exist. In general, ERISA defines a welfare benefit plan to include any plan, fund or program which is maintained or established by an employer or by an employee organization for the purpose of providing for its participants and beneficiaries, through the purchase of insurance or otherwise, medical, surgical, or hospital care benefits or benefits in the event of sickness, accident, disability, death, or other defined benefits.[6] The most common type of welfare benefit plan is an employer-sponsored medical program.

Employers are encouraged to identify all employee benefit plans and categorize them as pension or welfare plans, or plans which are outside the scope of ERISA. This

---

[5] ERISA Section 3(2)(A).
[6] ERISA Section 3(1).

determination is important to determine whether each plan is subject to the ERISA reporting and disclosure rules as outlined below, and any nondiscrimination rules under the Code.

4.0 REPORTING AND DISCLOSURE RULES

ERISA established specific reporting and disclosure rules for both pension and welfare benefit plans. Various reports must be prepared and filed with the Internal Revenue Service ("IRS"), and others must be furnished to plan participants and beneficiaries, the Department of Labor ("DOL"), and the PBGC. The plan administrator is required to file an initial summary plan description ("SPD") with the DOL (for most pension and welfare plans), supplemented by periodic amended descriptions. Most plans must also file an Annual Report/Form 5500 with the IRS that includes financial statements and schedules, an actuarial statement certified by an enrolled actuary (for defined benefit plans), and other information. A copy of this form is also provided to the DOL by the IRS.

This chapter does not provide an exhaustive summary of all reporting and disclosure requirements, but it does outline the general Form 5500, audit and financial statement requirements.

4.1 Form 5500 Requirements

An annual Form 5500 must be filed with the IRS by the administrators of all plans covered by ERISA (i.e., defined benefit, defined contribution, and welfare benefit plans). For plans with 100 or more participants, the Form 5500 must contain, with certain exceptions, financial statements, separate schedules which include notes disclosing a full and fair presentation of the financial position of the plan, and an independent public accountant's report. Plans with fewer than 100 participants at the beginning of the plan year are permitted to file a simplified annual return using Form 5500-C/R. Audited financial statements are not required to be included with a Form 5500-C/R filing. Generally, Form 5500-C/R must be filed as Form "C," which is a little longer than Form "R," at least once every three years by each pension benefit plan or welfare benefit plan with fewer than 100 participants. Form 5500-C/R should be filed as Form "R" for plan years when it is not required to file a Form "C." For certain plans with only one participant, an even simpler annual return may be filed using Form 5500EZ. The instructions to each Form 5500 provide details regarding the types of plans to which they apply.

4.2 Exemptions from Filing

- *Welfare Plans.* Welfare benefit plans with fewer than 100 participants at the beginning of the plan year are exempt from filing a Form 5500 if benefits are paid (1) as needed from the general assets of an employer or employee organization sponsoring the plan; (2) exclusively from insurance contracts or policies issued by an insurance company or similar organizations authorized to do business in any state; or (3) through a combination of the methods described in (1) and (2).[7] However, it should be noted that certain "fringe benefit" plans (e.g., cafeteria plans under Section 125 of the Code, and Section 127[8] educational assistance plans), must separately file an annual return under Section 6039D of the Code and may not rely on the ERISA small welfare plan exemption to avoid filing a Form 5500 under the tax rules.

---

[7] DOL Reg. Section 2520.104-20.

[8] As of May, 1993, the special tax treatment provided under Section 127 educational plans (i.e., tax free benefits of up to $5,250 each year, even if a course, if not job related) expired as of June 30, 1992. Legislative proposals may retroactively reinstate such plans in the future.

- *Other Excluded Plans.* Certain other types of pension benefit plans and welfare benefit plans are also excluded from the filing requirements. These plans include (1) unfunded pension benefit plans and unfunded or insured welfare plans maintained by an employer to provide benefits to a select group of management or highly compensated employees (these plans must meet certain requirements set forth by DOL regulations and, as previously indicated, are often referred to as "top-hat" plans)[9]; (2) plans maintained solely to comply with workers' compensation, unemployment compensation, or disability insurance laws; and (3) unfunded excess benefit plans that will provide benefits in excess of the Section 415 limitations identified below.
- *Limited Exemption.* Certain plans covering 100 or more participants have been granted a limited exemption from *some* types of reporting. This limited exemption exempts unfunded welfare plans, fully insured welfare plans, combined unfunded and fully insured welfare plans, and certain fully insured pension plans from filing financial statements, schedules, and the accountant's report.[10] This limited exclusion does not eliminate the necessity for the plan administrator to file a Form 5500 or Schedules A and B, if applicable.

---

[9] DOL Reg. Section 2520.104-23.
[10] DOL Reg. Section 2520.104-44.

4.3 When and Where To File

Form 5500 reports must be filed with the IRS within 7 months after each plan's year end. For example, a plan with a December 31 year end must file a Form 5500 with the IRS not later than July 31 of the following year. An extension of this due date of up to 2 1/2 months may be obtained by filing Form 5558, "Application for Extension of Time to File Certain Employee Plan Returns," with the IRS.

4.4 Audit Requirements

ERISA requires that independent auditors audit the financial statements of certain pension and welfare plans, and that they submit a report of the results of their examination with the annual return. DOL regulations generally do not require the accountant's opinion to encompass information pertaining to both custodial accounts and discretionary trust accounts that are certified by certain financial institutions (e.g., banks and insurance companies). This provision, however, does not eliminate the need for an audit. An independent audit must be made of other transactions and information included in the financial statements of the plan. As previously indicated, DOL regulations waive the auditor's report requirement for employee pension and welfare benefit plans with fewer than 100 participants and do not require an auditor's report from certain pension plans funded through allocated insurance contracts if the benefit payments are guaranteed by the insurance company.

4.5 Sanctions for Failure to Obtain Audit

If a plan is required to have an audit and no audit is obtained, the DOL may reject the plan's annual report. If a satisfactory revised report is not submitted within 45 days after such rejection, the DOL may take either of the following actions:

- Retain an independent qualified public accountant on behalf of the participants to perform an adequate audit.
- Bring a civil suit for appropriate relief.

4.6 Penalties for Failure to File

Plan administrators are subject to a penalty of $25 a day, up to a maximum of $15,000 for failing timely to file returns with the IRS, unless reasonable cause for delinquency is shown. The DOL may also impose a penalty of up to $1,000 per day for late returns. In addition, ERISA provides for criminal and civil actions for violation of DOL regulations.

5.0 DISCLOSURES TO PARTICIPANTS

In addition to filing reports with the federal government, a plan is required to provide certain information to participants. This information includes a Summary Plan Description ("SPD") and a Summary Annual Report ("SAR").

5.1 Summary Plan Description

ERISA requires that an SPD be published and distributed to each participant, and each beneficiary receiving benefits under the plan, within 90 days after he or she becomes a participant or, in the case of a beneficiary, within 90 days after he or she first receives benefits.[11] Alternatively, if later, an SPD may be distributed within 120 days after a plan becomes subject to ERISA.

The SPD must contain the following information:

- The name and type of administration of the plan.

---

[11] ERISA Section 104(b).

- The name and address of the person designated as agent for service of legal process.
- The name and address of the administrator, or names, titles, and addresses of any trustee or trustees if they are different than the administrator.
- A description of the relevant portions of any collective bargaining agreement.
- The plan's requirement regarding eligibility for participation and benefits.
- The circumstances that may result in disqualification, ineligibility, or denial or loss of benefits.
- The date and end of the plan year and whether the records of the plan are kept on a calendar or fiscal year basis.
- The process to be followed in presenting claims for benefits under the plan and any remedies for redress of claims that are denied.

Every fifth year, the administrator must furnish each participant and each beneficiary receiving benefits under the plan with the updated SPD that integrates all plan amendments made within the five-year period. If any modifications are made to the plan, a summary description of such changes must be furnished to participants and beneficiaries not later than 210 days after the end of the plan year in which the modification was made.

5.2 Summary of Annual Report

Administrators of plans that are required to file annual reports must also generally distribute SARs to each plans' participants. The summary report includes a summary of plan assets and liabilities, income and expense, and a notice that the complete annual report is available upon request for a reasonable charge and is available for examination at the plan's administrative offices as well as at other specified locations.

6.0 TAX QUALIFICATION REQUIREMENTS

A review of all the tax rules which apply to qualified retirement plans is beyond the scope of this chapter. However, human resource professionals should be familiar with the general tax qualification requirements. The most important provisions that relate to qualified retirement plans include:

- Eligibility requirements
- Minimum coverage rules
- General nondiscrimination rules
- Minimum participation requirements
- Vesting rules
- Funding requirements
- Limitations on benefits and contributions
- 401(k) plans testing

6.1 Eligibility Requirements

The tax rules establish certain eligibility requirements which must be followed to determine when an employee will begin to participate in an employee benefit plan. A plan may exclude an employee from participation if the employee has not attained age 21 or completed a year of service with an employer. As a result of these provisions most qualified plans commence employee participation upon attaining age 21 *and* the completion of a year of service. In applying these eligibility requirements, a year of service is generally defined as the completion of 1,000 hours of work during a 12-month period measured from either an employees date of hire or using each plan year.

6.2 Minimum Coverage Rules

Section 410(b) of the Code requires a plan to cover a minimum number of nonhighly compensated employees in order to be qualified and receive the preferential tax treatment outlined above. These rules exist to ensure that highly compensated employees do not receive benefits which discriminate in their favor. To satisfy this rule either a percentage test, a ratio test, or an average benefits test must be met. These tests are as follows:

- *Percentage test*—70 percent of all nonhighly compensated employees must be covered by the plan.
- *Ratio test*—The percentage of nonhighly compensated employees covered by the plan must equal at least 70 percent of the percentage of highly compensated employees covered.
- *Average benefits test*—Both of the following conditions are satisfied.
  A plan covers a "classification" of employees that does not discriminate in favor of highly compensated employees (A plan satisfies the classification test if the plan covers a classification of employees that is both "reasonable" and "nondiscriminatory." To be considered reasonable, the classification must be reasonable and established under objective business criteria that identify the category of employees who benefit under the plan. A reasonable classification includes geographic locations. A classification is considered nondiscriminatory if the group of employees included in the classification satisfies either a safe harbor percentage or a facts and circumstance test.); and
  The average benefit percentage (calculated separately with respect to each employee) under all qualified plans maintained by an employer for

nonhighly compensated employees is at least 70 percent of the average for highly compensated employees.

To calculate the percentage test and the ratio test above, a determination of which employees benefit under the plan must be made. An employee is treated as "benefiting" under a Section 401(k) if the employee is *eligible* to make a cash or deferred election under the plan (regardless if contributions are actually made). An employee is treated as benefiting under the portion of a Section 401(k) plan attributable to matching contributions if the employee is eligible to make an employee contribution or to receive an allocation of matching contributions (including forfeitures of matching contributions).

Applying the above tests requires examination of the participation level of a plan. In applying these tests, however, the following individuals do not have to be taken into account:

- Employees who have not satisfied the plan's minimum age and service requirements (age 21 and a year of service); and
- Union employees (if the retirement benefits were the subject of a good-faith bargaining and the collective bargaining agreement does not provide for participation).

If a plan does not meet the coverage requirements the trust of such a plan will be treated as remaining tax-exempt for all nonhighly compensated employees. Highly compensated employees, however, will be subject to tax on their vested accrued benefit (other than employee contributions) as of the close of the employer's taxable year that ends with or within a taxable year of the trust for which the trust is not tax-exempt. Thus, highly compensated employees could suddenly become subject to taxation on very large vested benefits that they may have accumulated over many years. Plans should be periodically tested for compliance with the coverage rules because of the sanctions for noncompliance.

As is apparent, a quick answer on whether a plan satisfies the minimum coverage rules will often be unavailable. However, human resource professionals are encouraged to ask if such tests have been considered to ensure that this and the other tax requirements are being met.

6.3 General Nondiscrimination Rules

Section 401(a)(4) of the Code provides that contributions and benefits under a plan may not discriminate in favor of highly compensated employees. A plan will be considered to provide nondiscriminatory benefits or contributions under Section 401(a)(4) if it meets *each* of the following three requirements:

- *Amount Test*—A plan may not discriminate in favor of highly compensated employees ("HCEs") in the *amount* of the benefits provided or contributions made under the plan;
- *Benefits, Rights, and Feature Test*—Every option, subsidy or other right or feature under a plan (e.g., a lump sum benefit distribution option) must be available to a nondiscriminatory group of employees (*i.e.*, a group that satisfies the nondiscriminatory classification test under Code Section 410(b) coverage rules); and
- *Nondiscriminatory Plan Amendments Test*—Any plan amendment and/or plan termination may not significantly discriminate in favor of HCEs.

Although simple in intent, the final Treasury regulations are extremely technical and beyond the scope of this chapter. Human resource professionals are encouraged to determine if their qualified plans satisfy any safe-harbor rules contained in the final regulations or if the general rules must be applied in any instances. Thereafter, both the safe-harbor and general tests should be monitored, because additional changes regarding these rules are anticipated.

6.4 Minimum Participation Requirements

The minimum participation rule generally provides that a plan is not a qualified plan unless it benefits the lesser of 50 employees of the employer, or 40 percent of all employees of the employer. For purposes of applying this rule, employers who are covered by a collective bargaining agreement or who have not satisfied a plan's eligibility requirements may be excluded from consideration. This test may *not* be satisfied by aggregating plans, and the separate line of business exception addressed below is not available to satisfy this requirement.

6.5 Vesting Rules

Vested benefits are those retirement benefits to which an employee is entitled whether or not he continues in the service of an employer. Accrued benefits derived from an employee's contributions to a qualified plan are always nonforfeitable whether such contribution is made on a pre-tax basis (as in a Section 401(k) salary reduction contribution) or an after-tax basis. Employers may always provide for faster vesting than required by law. The longest vesting schedules which are permitted for non-top-heavy plans are as follows:

- A 5-year vesting schedule which requires 100 percent vesting upon the completion of 5 years of service.

- A 7-year graduated vesting schedule under which employees will be 20 percent vested in their retirement benefits derived from employer contributions after 3 years of service, and will be 100 percent vested after 7 years of service, as follows:

Years of Service	Nonforfeitable Percentage
3	20
4	40
5	60
6	80
7 or more	100

6.6 Funding Requirements

Defined benefit and money purchase plans must satisfy certain funding requirements. These requirements are imposed to assure that sufficient assets will be available to pay promised benefits. Defined contribution plans, other than money purchase plans, are not subject to these rules.

For most defined benefit plans, an employer's (or plan sponsor's) annual contribution to the plan must be sufficient to cover the normal cost for the period, annual interest on unfunded amounts, amortization of past service liability, increases or decreases in past service liability resulting from plan amendments, and experience gains or losses and actuarial gains or losses from changes in actuarial assumptions. An actuary should annually compute amortization on a level payment basis, including interest and principal needed to comply with the minimum funding requirements.

6.7 Section 415 Limitations on Benefits and Contributions

Specific limitations exist on the amount of benefits that can be paid to a participant under a defined benefit plan and the amount of contributions that can be made to the individual account of a participant is a defined contribution plan under Section 415 of the Code. Additional limitations exist for employers that maintain more than one qualified plan. If these rules are violated, a plan will not be qualified for tax purposes.

- *Defined Benefit Plan Limits.* In general, the annual benefit a participant may achieve under a defined plan may not exceed the lesser of $90,000 or 100 percent of a participant's average compensation for the participant's high three years.
- *Adjustments.* The $90,000 limitation, but not the 100 percent of compensation limit, is actuarially reduced if benefits commence before a participant's Social Security retirement age and is increased if benefits commence after this age. The $90,000 limitation is annually adjusted for inflation and is $115,641 in 1993. See Exhibit A for a summary of IRS inflation adjusted limitations for 1991 through 1993.

6.8 401(k) Plan Testing

The most popular type of retirement plan being adopted by employers today is the Section 401(k) plan. Under a Section 401(k) plan employees are permitted to elect to receive either their cash compensation, or to defer their compensation up to established limits into the Section 401(k) plan on a *pre-tax* basis. Thus, Section 401(k) plans permit employees to save for their retirement using pre-tax dollars.[12] However, to the extent non-highly compensated employees do not contribute to a plan, highly compensated employees will often not be permitted to achieve the maximum permitted savings allowed under the Code. To encourage employees to save for their retirement, employers

---

[12] It should be noted that not all states recognize the federal tax consequences of Section 401(k) plans.

frequently agree to "match" a certain amount of employee contributions. This action provides additional retirement benefits to employees who value retirement benefits and elect to reduce their salaries by execution of individual salary reduction election forms. Matching contributions are also helpful in permitting highly compensated employees to contribute up to the maximum levels permitted.

The rules regarding Section 401(k) plans which are important for human resource professionals to be familiar with are as follows:

- *Calendar-Year Limit.* Participants in a Section 401(k) plan may not contribute in excess of $7,000 to such a plan in any calendar year. The amount is indexed for inflation and is $8,994 in 1993. Amounts contributed in excess of this calendar limit are referred to as "excess deferrals." Excess deferrals should generally be distributed to participants by April 15 of the year following the excess deferral.
- *Nondiscrimination Testing for Pre-tax Salary Reduction Contributions.* In order for a Section 401(k) plan to be qualified, employee pre-tax salary reduction contributions must not be provided to highly compensated employees in an amount greater than permitted under the tax rules. Under these rules one of the following tests must be satisfied:

    The actual deferral percentage ("ADP") test applicable to salary reduction contributions for the highly compensated employees is not greater than the ADP of all other eligible employees multiplied by 1.25; or
    The excess of the ADP for the group of highly compensated employees over the ADP for all other eligible employees is not more than 2

percentage points, and the ADP for the group of highly compensated employees is not more than the ADP of all other eligible employees multiplied by 200 percent.

In applying these tests, the following rules apply:

The ADP for either group is the average of the ratio (calculated separately for each employee in such group) of (1) the employer contribution actually paid to a plan under a salary reduction election on behalf of an employee to (2) the employee's compensation. Thus, if an employee earns $40,000 and contributes $2,000 to the plan through a salary reduction election on a pre-tax basis, the employee's ADP is 5 percent. The computation of the employer contribution will include (1) all salary reduction contributions and (2) at the election of the employer, certain employer matching contributions and nonelective contributions.

If the contribution is made to a 401(k) plan in excess of the ADP limitations, "excess contributions" exist and the plan may be disqualified. To avoid this result, the excess contribution, plus earnings, must be distributed before the close of the plan year following the year in which such excess contribution occurs.

- *Rules for Matching and After-Tax Employee Contributions.* This provision establishes a nondiscrimination requirement for employer matching contributions and employee after-tax contributions. In essence, Section 401(m) establishes a rule that a plan will not be deemed to satisfy the general nondiscrimination rules of Section 401(a)(4) unless it complies with an actual contribution percentage ("ACP") requirement. A plan meets the ACP requirement if the contribution percentage for eligible highly compensated employees does not exceed the *greater* of 125 percent of the contribution percentage for all other eligible employees; or the lesser of (1) 200 percent of the contribution percentage for all other eligible or (2) the contribution percentage for all other eligible employees plus 2 percentage points.

Similar to the ADP test for 401(k) plans, the ACP is the average of the average of the ratios for each member of either group, as separately calculated. The result of this test is that higher-paid employees are generally limited as to the amount of employee contributions they can make to a plan. This rule requires annual testing because it can also trigger plan disqualification. A plan will not be disqualified for failure to satisfy this test, however, if any excess aggregate contributions for a plan year are distributed before the end of the plan year following the year in which the excess aggregate contribution was made. Excess aggregate contributions must generally be distributed in the same manner as excess contributions, discussed previously.

- *Multiple-Use Test.* In addition to the ADP and the ACP tests, a "multiple-use test" also exists. The purpose of the rule is to preclude employers from relying on the 200 percent/2 percentage point test under both the ADP and ACP tests. If a human resource professional identifies that both the ADP and ACP tests rely on the 200 percent/2 percentage point test, the Section 401(k) plan must be further examined to comply with this additional requirement.

6.9 Separate Line of Business Rules

As outlined above, all qualified retirement plans are subject to the minimum coverage standards under Sections 410 and 401(a)(4) of the Code which require that a plan not discriminate in favor of highly compensated employee, and to the Section 401(a)(26) minimum participation rules which require all plans to cover the lesser of 50 employees or 40% of all non-highly compensated employee. These rules generally apply on the basis of a controlled group of corporations. If a corporation is a member of a controlled group of corporations, then all companies are treated as a "single employer" for purposes of Sections 410 and 401(a)(26) of the Code.

When the nondiscrimination rules are applied on a controlled group basis, difficulties may be encountered due to the existence of different benefit structures in different geographic regions and markets. To provide some relief, the separate line of business ("SLOB") rules were enacted. The SLOB rules permit the coverage rules to be applied separately to the plans of each *qualified* SLOB.

Employers seeking to test some plans on a SLOB basis must divide all business operations into SLOB's. In applying the SLOB rules an employer must first determine its line(s) of business, then which lines of business may be treated as "separate," and finally, which separate lines of business may treated as "qualified."

- *Separate Line of Business.* The following four criteria must be satisfied to determine that the line of business is adequately "separate" from all other lines of business.
  Separate organizational unit: The line of business must be formally organized as

a separate organization unit (i.e., corporation, partnership, division) on every day of the testing year.

Separate financial accountability: The line of business must be a separate profit center on every day of the testing year. In addition, the line of business must maintain books and records that provide separate revenue and expense information that is used for internal planning and control.

Separate employee workforce: The line of business must have its own separate employee workforce. This requirement is satisfied if at least 90% of the employees who provide services to the line of business are "substantial-service" employees with respect to the line of business.

Separate management: The line of business must have its own separate management. This requirement is satisfied if at least 80% of the employees who are top-paid employees, with respect to the line of business are "substantial-service" employee's, with respect to the line of business.

- *Qualified Separate Line Of Business.* Once a line of business is determined to be separate, or a SLOB, each SLOB must pass the following requirements in order to be *qualified* separate line of business (a "QSLOB"):

    Each SLOB must have at least *50 employees.*

    The employer must notify the IRS that it is treating itself as a SLOB. No rules have been issued to date explaining how the notice is to be given.

A SLOB must satisfy an administrative scrutiny determination under either a general rule or a safe harbor rule.

A further examination of the separate line of business rules is beyond the scope of this chapter. However, as with the other qualification issues addressed in this chapter, a sensitivity to these rules and periodic consideration of these issues is important.

7.0 MISCELLANEOUS AND TAX-RELATED ISSUES

The following miscellaneous topics are also of importance to many employers.

7.1 Highly Compensated Employees

In applying all of the discrimination tests described above, the starting point in each instance is to identify the highly compensated employees. The definition of highly compensated employees includes any employee, who during the year to be tested or the prior year meets any of the following conditions:

- Owned 5 percent or more of the employer at any time.
- Earned more than $75,000 from the employer, as indexed for inflation.
- Earned more than $50,000, (as indexed for inflation), and was among the top-paid 20 percent groups of employees when ranked on the basis of compensation.
- Was an officer of the employer and received compensation greater than 50 percent of the annual benefit limitation for defined benefit plans (i.e., $90,000, as indexed, x 50 percent = $45,000 as adjusted). For purposes of this definition, no more than 50 employees or, if lesser, the greater of 3 employees or 10

percent of the employees shall be treated as officers. If for any year no officer earns in excess of this limitation, the highest paid officer will be treated as satisfying this test.

7.2 Rules for Top-Heavy Plans

As a result of tax changes implemented in the early 1980's, certain provisions were added to the Code that apply to plans that are determined to be "top-heavy." A defined benefit plan is top-heavy if, as of their applicable determination date, the present value of accrued benefits of all key employees exceeds 60 percent of the value of the accrued benefits of all employees. A defined contribution plan is top-heavy if, as of an applicable determination date, the total of the accounts of all key employees exceeds 60 percent of the total of the accounts of all participants. In applying these tests a key employee must be distinguished from the definition of highly compensated employee that is utilized for purposes of applying the coverage tests.

A key employee generally includes any employee who, at any time during the plan year being tested or any of the 4 preceding plan years, is in one of the following categories:

- An officer of the employer having annual compensation in excess of 50 percent of the defined benefit plan dollar limitation, as indexed;
- One of the 10 employees having annual compensation in excess of the defined contribution plan dollar limitation and owning the largest interest in the employer;
- A 5 percent owner of the employer; and
- A 1 percent owner of the employer having an annual compensation from the employer of more than $150,000, as indexed.

To determine if a plan is top-heavy, consideration must be given to whether certain companies will be treated as a single employer for purposes of applying the top-heavy rules and which plans of such employers are required or permitted to be aggregated. The top-heavy rules generally must be applied to all plans of related employers if the related employers are treated as a single employer for pension plan purposes under Section 414 of the Code. In this event, all plans of such employers that are required to be aggregated include (1) each plan in which a key employee is a participant and (2) each other plan that enables any plan to satisfy the coverage and nondiscrimination rules. An employer may further elect to aggregate any plan that is not required to be aggregated if such aggregation of plans will continue to satisfy the coverage and discrimination rules.

Once a plan or group of plans is determined to be top-heavy, certain special qualification requirements must be satisfied for such plans to retain their qualified status. The special top-heavy provisions include:

- *Minimum vesting.* A top-heavy plan must utilize either a 3-year vesting schedule or a 6-year graded vesting schedule. Under the three-year vesting schedule, employees who complete at least 3 years of service must be eligible to participate in a plan and are 100 percent vested in their benefit. The 6-year graded vesting schedule provides that employees must become vested as follows:

Years of Service	Vested Percentage
2	20
3	40
4	60
5	80
6	100

- *Minimum Benefits.* Under a top-heavy defined benefit plan, the annual retirement benefit for a non-key employee must be less than the employee's average compensation multiplied by the lesser of (1) 2 percent multiplied by the employee's years of service or (2) 20 percent. For a top-heavy defined contribution plan, the employer's contribution for each non-key employee must not be less than 3 percent of the employee's compensation. If the highest contribution percentage rate for key employees is less than 3 percent of compensation, however, the 3 percent minimum contribution rate is reduced to the rate that applied to the key employees.

7.3 Compensation Limitation

Beginning in 1989 employers have not been able to consider compensation in excess of $200,000, as indexed for inflation, in computing participants benefits. This limitation curtails the benefits highly compensated employees may receive and often results in consideration of nonqualified retirement plans to replace lost benefits. It should be noted that President Clinton is currently proposing to reduce this limitation, which is $235,840 in 1993, to $150,000. This action would force employers to further reduce retirement benefits for highly compensated employees or to increase benefits for nonhighly compensated employees, which may be cost prohibitive.

7.4 Pension Benefit Guaranty Corporation Premiums

The Omnibus Budget Reconciliation Act of 1990 raised the PBGC premium to $19 (from $16) per participant for plan years beginning after December 31, 1990. The premium for unfunded vested benefits has been increased to $9 for each $1,000 of unfunded vested benefits, up to a maximum additional premium of $53 per participant. Form PBGC-1 is filed with the PBGC by plans with fewer than 500 participants and is due by the fifteenth day of the ninth month of such plan year. Plans with more than 500 participants must file Form PBGC-1ES and Form PBGC-a with the PBGC. Form PBGC-1ES is used to pay the flat-rate portion of the premium and is due by the end of the second month of such plan year. Form PBGC-1 is used to pay the variable-rate portion of the premium and is due by the fifteenth day of the ninth month of such plan year.

7.5 Antialienation Provisions and Qualified Domestic Relations Orders

For a plan to be qualified, it must provide that benefits may not be assigned or alienated. A major exception to this general rule is provided for qualified domestic relations orders ("QDROs"). A QDRO is a domestic relations order that creates or recognizes the existence of a spouse or other alternate payee's right to receive all or a portion of the benefits payable to a plan participant. This rule permits a qualified plan to direct payment of benefits, to a former spouse in the context of a divorce.

Upon receipt by a plan of a domestic relations order a plan administrator is required to notify the participant and each alternate payee of the receipt of such order and of the plan's procedures for determining if an order satisfies all the statutory requirements to be a QDRO. A plan must therefore have procedures to handle this occurrence.

8.0 COBRA REQUIREMENTS

The requirement to provide continuation health coverage under the Consolidated Omnibus Reconciliation Act of 1985 ("COBRA") has existed since 1986. The purpose of this portion of the chapter is to review the fundamental COBRA requirements.

8.1 Purpose

Pre-COBRA, a medical plan could automatically terminate coverage when certain events occurred. For example, plans typically stopped covering an employee's spouse upon divorce, or an employee's child when the child reached a designated age. Coverage of an employee was also generally terminated in the month the employee ceased employment. Under COBRA, "qualified beneficiaries" must be given the opportunity to "elect," within specific election periods, to extend coverage under a "group health plan" after the occurrence of certain "qualifying events" that would have previously terminated their coverage. If elected, the premiums for continued medical coverage are paid for by the electing individuals. The intent of this law was to avoid the loss of medical benefits where other coverage might not be available.

8.2 Effective Date

The provisions of COBRA generally applied to the first "plan year" of a health plan beginning on or after July 1, 1986.

8.3 Employers Subject to COBRA

For purposes of COBRA, the term employer generally includes all entities which are treated as a single employer under Section 414 of the Code, and their successors. The COBRA rules do not, however, apply to "small-employer plans." A small employer plan is a group health plan maintained by an employer which employs fewer than 20 employees on at least 50 percent of its working days during the preceding calendar year. All full-time and part-time employees are counted for this test. In addition, agents, independent contractors, leased employees and directors are treated as employees if eligible for coverage. If a small employer grows to 20 or more employees, it becomes subject to COBRA on the following January 1.

8.4 Definitional Considerations

- *Group Health Plans.* A group health plan is *any plan* maintained by an employer to provide "medical care" to employees, former employees and dependents. Both insured and uninsured plans are group health plans subject to COBRA, whether provided directly or through use of a Section 125 cafeteria plan. Medical care encompasses the diagnosis, cure, mitigation, treatment, or prevention of disease. Medical care will not be deemed to include an exercise/fitness program available for general use.

- *Qualified Beneficiaries.* A qualified beneficiary is generally any individual who on the day before a qualifying event is covered under an employer's plan and includes a "covered employee," the spouse of a covered employee, or the dependent child of the covered employee. Eligibility for coverage is not relevant, *actual coverage* must exist in order for COBRA rights to be extended. It is important to note that the group of qualified beneficiaries entitled to elect COBRA coverage as a result of a qualifying event is "closed" as of the day before such event. Thus, new spouses and children may later be covered by a plan, but will not qualify as qualified beneficiaries.
- *Qualifying Events.* The qualifying events triggering entitlement to COBRA rights if they result in an immediate or deferred loss of coverage include:

    The death of the covered employee;

    The termination of employment (other than by reason of an employee's gross misconduct), or reduction of hours of a covered employee's employment, regardless if voluntary;

    The divorce or legal separation of the covered employee from his or her spouse;

    The entitlement of the covered employee to benefits under Medicare;

The end of a child's status as a dependent child under the requirements of a plan; and

The commencement of certain proceedings in bankruptcy.

8.5 COBRA Coverage

Upon the occurrence of a qualifying event, a qualified beneficiary must be given an opportunity to elect to continue the group health plan he or she was receiving immediately before the qualifying event. If the coverage offered varies in any regard, COBRA coverage is not extended and the compliance requirements are not satisfied unless otherwise permitted. For example, no evidence of insurability may be required for the extension of coverage after a qualifying event.

Variances in benefits are permitted in the following instances:

- If an employer changes or eliminates coverage for similarly situated active employees, but continues one or more group health plans, the employer must permit qualified beneficiaries receiving COBRA to elect to be covered under any remaining plan.
- If an employer offers "core medical coverage" and "non-core coverage" (i.e., vision and dental benefits), qualified beneficiaries must generally be permitted to elect to receive either the core coverage alone, or the combined coverage previously received. The ability of qualified beneficiaries to elect core and non-core coverages will depend upon the facts of each situation.

8.6 Election

A qualified beneficiary must be given at least *60 days* in which to elect continued coverage. The election period must begin on or before the date coverage will terminate, and must not end before 60 days after the *later* of: the date the individual would lose coverage; or the date notice is sent of the right to elect benefits. Unless the election states otherwise, the election of one qualified beneficiary to continue coverage will serve as an election by all qualified beneficiaries who would otherwise lose coverage under a plan. If benefits are elected within the 60 day period, coverage must be provided from the date it would have otherwise lapsed.

8.7 Period of Coverage

In general, the extension of coverage must be made available for at least *36 months* after a qualifying event occurs. In the case of a termination or reduction of hours of an employee, however, coverage need only be extended for a period of *18 months*. If coverage of a qualified beneficiary expires at the end of the period, the plan must provide the qualified beneficiary the opportunity to convert the group health plan coverage to individual plan coverage on the terms generally available to other beneficiaries. These periods are outlined in Exhibit B.

The 18-month period may be extended for certain disabled individuals. If a qualified beneficiary is disabled under the Social Security Act at the time of a qualifying event triggered by a termination or reduction in hours, the 18-month period is extended to 29 months. This change continues medical coverage for the 29-month period before Medicare benefits commence. The new 29-month rule is effective for plan years beginning on or after November 22, 1989, the date of enactment of this legislation. To be entitled to this relief, however, a disabled individual must notify the plan administrator of the disability status within 60 days of such determination. The individual is also responsible for notifying the plan administrator within 30 days after any disability ceases to exist. An employer may increase the cost of this increased coverage as further addressed below.

8.8 Termination of Coverage

Under certain circumstances, an employer may terminate the extended coverage before the end of either the 36-, 29- or 18-month periods. Specifically, an employer need only provide coverage until the earlier of:

- The last day of the appropriate 36-, 29- or 18-month coverage period;
- The first day benefits may be terminated for non-payment;
- The date an employer ceases to maintain any group health plan (including successor plans);
- The first day a qualified beneficiary is actually covered (not merely eligible) under another group health plan which does not exclude any preexisting conditions;
- The date the qualified beneficiary becomes entitled (not eligible) to Medicare benefits;
- The first day of the month more than 30 days after a disability ceases, if 29 months were extended.

8.9 Notifications

All employees must initially receive *written* notification of their COBRA rights *upon enrollment* in a medical plan. All employers are encouraged to review their employee communications or handbooks to ensure that they contain an explanation of COBRA. If a qualifying event occurs because an employee dies, is terminated, has his hours reduced, becomes entitled to Medicare benefits, or if a bankruptcy proceeding is commenced, the employer must generally notify the plan administrator of the qualifying event within *30* days. If no specific plan administrator is appointed by the employer, this notice is not necessary.

With regard to a child ceasing to be dependent or a divorce, the responsibility of notifying an employer or the plan administrator, if any, rests with the *covered employee* or *qualified beneficiary*. If notice is not given to an employer or plan administrator within *60* days after the later of a qualifying event or loss of coverage, a plan does *not* have to offer an opportunity to elect COBRA benefits. Additional notice requirements also exist for certain disabled individuals, as previously discussed.

No later than *14* days after receiving either notice from an employee or becoming aware of any other qualifying event, an employer must notify any qualified beneficiaries of their right to elect continuation coverage under the health plan. Notification to the spouse of an employee will be treated as notification to all other qualified beneficiaries residing with the spouse.

8.10 Premium

An employer may require the payment of a premium for any period of continued coverage. This premium may generally not exceed 102 percent of the costs of the plan of coverage for other beneficiaries. For individuals who receive continued coverage due to a disability, however, an employer may charge 150 percent of its cost for providing coverage in the 19th to 29th months. Whoever pays the premium (generally the qualified beneficiary or covered employee) may elect to make payments in monthly installments and has 45 days after continuation of coverage is elected to pay the premium for the period that preceded the election.

8.11 Sanctions

The COBRA rules are contained in both ERISA and the Internal Revenue Code. Under ERISA, a qualified beneficiary who does not receive appropriate notice may sue to recover benefits that he would have received if he had been notified of his continuation rights and elected a continuation of coverage. In addition, a plan administrator may be liable for up to $100 per day to *each participant or beneficiary* who fails to receive appropriate notice (in the same manner the $100 per day penalty applies for failure to furnish a summary plan description under ERISA, etc.).

Under the Internal Revenue Code, the following sanctions and rules apply:

- *Excise Tax.* Failure to satisfy the COBRA rules results in an *excise tax* equal to $100 per day for each qualified beneficiary during the period of noncompliance, with a maximum penalty of $200 per day for any family.
- *Noncompliance Period.* A noncompliance period begins on the date a failure occurs and ends on the earlier of:
  - (a) the date the failure is corrected; or
  - (b) 6 months after the last date on which an employer could have been required to provide continuation coverage.
- *Grace Period.* No excise tax is imposed if a failure is due to "reasonable cause" and not willful neglect, if the failure is corrected within 30 days from its occurrence.
- *Audit Rule.* If a failure is not corrected by the date a "Notice of Examination of Income Tax Liability" is sent to an employer, and the failure occurred or continued during the period under review, the excise tax will not be less than the lesser of: (i) $2,500; or (ii) the tax computed without the reasonable diligence exception or 30-day grace period. Furthermore, if the failure is more than de minimis, the minimum dollar penalty is $15,000.
- *Maximum Penalty for Single Employers.* A maximum penalty exists for unintentional failures by employers equal to the lesser of: (i) 10 percent of an employer's medical expense for the preceding tax year; or (ii) $500,000. The penalties for nonemployers, such as insurance carriers, may be as high as $2,000,000. TAMRA also provides, however,

that the IRS may *waive* all or part of the penalties if they would be excessive.
- *Reasonable Diligence.* The COBRA penalties may be *excused* if none of the responsible parties knew, or had reason to know of the failure. Penalties may also be *waived* if due to reasonable cause and corrected within 30 days of learning of a failure. Under these circumstances a failure is considered corrected if: (i) the rules are retroactively satisfied to the extent possible; and (ii) a qualified beneficiary is put in the same position he or she would have been in but for the failure.

This summary of COBRA is not a comprehensive discussion of all issues which might arise under the statute and the provisions of an employer's plan. We hope it is helpful in alerting employers to some of the major issues concerning COBRA. We recommend that all COBRA forms and procedures be periodically reviewed for compliance with current laws, legislative and judicial changes.

Exhibit A

INTERNAL REVENUE SERVICE
COST-OF-LIVING CHART

The 1991 through 1993 values for various cost-of-living adjusted dollar amounts are outlined below for your convenience.

Description of Limit	Code Section	1991 Value	1992 Value	1993 Value
Dollar limit on annual benefit in a defined benefit plan	415(b)(1)(A)	$108,963	$112,221	$115,641
Dollar limit on annual additions under a defined contribution plan	415(c)(1)(A)	$30,000	$30,000	$30,000
Maximum 401(k) deferral	402(g)(1)	$8,475	$8,728	$8,994
Limits used in definition of highly compensated employees	50% of 415(b)(1)(A) 414(q) 414(q)	$54,481 $60,535 $90,803	$56,110 $62,345 $93,518	$57,820 $64,245 $96,368
Annual $200,000 compensation limit	401(a)(17) 404(1) 408(k)(3)(C)	$222,220 $222,220 $222,220	$228,860 $228,860 $228,860	$ 235,840 $ 235,840 $ 235,840

Exhibit B

COBRA Coverage

Qualifying Event	Beneficiaries Who Must be Notified	Period of Coverage
1. Covered employee's death	Spouse Dependent child not residing with spouse[1]	36 months
2. Termination or reduction of hours of covered employee	Covered employee Spouse Dependent child not residing with spouse	18 months[2]
3. Divorce or legal separation of covered employee from spouse	Spouse Dependent child not residing with spouse	36 months
4. Covered employee's eligibility for Medicare	Spouse Dependent child not residing with spouse	36 months
5. Dependent child ceasing to be dependent	Spouse Dependent child not residing with spouse	36 months
6. Bankruptcy of employer	Retired employee Spouse or surviving spouse Dependent child not residing with spouse	36 months

[1] Notification to spouse is considered notice to beneficiaries residing with spouse.

[2] Coverage is extended for 29 months if a qualified beneficiary is permanently and totally disabled as defined under the Social Security Act at the time of a qualifying event, if certain notice requirements are satisfied.

Employee Benefit Checklist for Pension and Welfare Plans

	Defined Benefit Plans	*Defined Contributions Plans*	*Nonqualified Retirement Plans*	*Welfare Plans*
Plan Documents				
Summary Plan Descriptions				
Summary Annual Reports				
Form 5500s				
PBGC Premiums				
PBGC Termination Filings				

Employee Benefit Comp. Matters (EBCM-Article)

Chapter 6
OSHA CONCERNS

Andrew C. Peterson
Martin C. Mead
Paul, Hastings, Janofsky & Walker

1.0 INTRODUCTION

In 1970, Congress passed the Occupational Safety and Health Act (the "Act"), the purpose of which was to "assure as far as possible every working man and woman in the nation safe and healthful working conditions."[1] The Act, which is administered by the Occupational Safety and Health Administration ("OSHA"), requires the employer to comply with safety and health standards covering conditions and operations in the workplace and to maintain a workplace that is free from recognized hazards.

This chapter summarizes the principal obligations of employers under the Occupational Safety and Health Act. Section One addresses OSHA's general industry safety and health standards. Section Two discusses the employer's duties under the Act's general duty clause. Section Three deals with recordkeeping and reporting regulations. Section Four addresses the Act's prohibition against unlawful discrimination. Section Five deals with variances. Finally, Section Six analyzes certain defenses employers can raise when cited for violations of OSHA standards.

---

[1] 29 U.S.C. § 651(b).

2.0 GENERAL INDUSTRY SAFETY AND HEALTH STANDARDS

OSHA's General Industry Safety and Health Standards apply to most private businesses involved in interstate commerce in the United States and its territories.[2]

The General Industry Standards can be categorized into three types. First, there are standards of universal application, or standards which apply to some extent to every employer, regardless of the specific conditions in that employer's workplace. Second, there are specific safety standards, or standards that only apply to workplaces containing specific potential safety hazards. Finally, there are specific health standards, or standards that only apply to workplaces containing specific potential health hazards.

2.1 Standards of Universal Application

Every employer must be aware of certain universally applicable General Industry Standards. For example, employers must provide and properly maintain approved personal protective equipment for the eyes, face, head and extremities. They may have to provide protective clothing, shields and/or barriers, and must provide and require the use of respirators selected under the National Standard Practices for Respiratory Protection whenever it is "necessary" to protect employees from hazards.[3] Employers must provide approved first aid supplies and personnel where a hospital or clinic is not in "near proximity" to the workplace.[4]

---

[2] Industries such as construction, agriculture, longshoring, and shipping are also subject to standards addressing industry-specific safety problems. For specific industry standards, see, e.g., 29 C.F.R. pt. 1926 (standards for construction), 29 C.F.R. pt. 1928 (standards for agriculture), 29 C.F.R. pt. 1918 (standards for longshore operations), 29 C.F.R. pts. 1501-1503 (standards for shipping).

[3] 29 C.F.R. §§ 1910.132-1910.140.

[4] 29 C.F.R. §§ 1910.151-1910.153.

Employers also must provide employees with access to relevant exposure and medical records.[5] "Exposure" refers to situations where employees are subjected to toxic substances or harmful physical agents in the course of employment.[6] Employers must preserve and maintain employee exposure and medical records for 30 years after the termination of employment.[7] They must respond to employee requests for access to exposure and medical records within 15 working days of the request.[8]

The Hazard Communication Standard ("HCS"),[9] requires that employers inform employees about the hazardous chemicals to which they may be exposed under normal operating conditions or in foreseeable emergencies.[10]

The principal component of the HCS is the Material Safety Data Sheet ("MSDS"). Employers are responsible for having an MSDS for each hazardous chemical found in the workplace.[11] The MSDS must provide the common name and chemical identity of a substance,[12] and its physical and chemical characteristics.[13] The MSDS must describe the chemical's physical and health hazards, along with any medical conditions which it might aggravate.[14] Precautions for safe handling, procedures for the clean-up of spills and leaks, and proper first aid procedures must be included.[15] The MSDS must provide the name, address, and telephone number of someone who can

---

[5] 29 C.F.R. § 1910.20.
[6] 29 C.F.R. § 1910.20(c)(8).
[7] 29 C.F.R. § 1910.20(d).
[8] 29 C.F.R. § 1910.20(e).
[9] 15 U.S.C. § 1681 (1976).
[10] 29 C.F.R. § 1910.1200(b)(2).
[11] 29 C.F.R. § 1910.1200(g)(8).
[12] 29 C.F.R. § 1910.1200(g)(2)(i)(A).
[13] 29 C.F.R. § 1910.1200(g)(2)(ii).
[14] 29 C.F.R. § 1910.1200(g)(2)(iii)-(iv).
[15] 29 C.F.R. § 1910.1200(g)(2)(viii)-(x).

provide additional information and appropriate emergency procedures.[16]

Employers must label containers of hazardous substances used in the workplace, identifying the chemicals contained and their hazardous properties. These labels must be legible, in English,[17] and displayed prominently.[18] Substances must be labeled "hazardous" if they are dangerous in any concentration and under any circumstances.[19]

The HCS requires employers to establish a written hazard communication program outlining how compliance will be attained, describing employee training, specifying where MSDS's are to be maintained, and establishing procedures by which employees can obtain them.[20] The program also should establish a consistent labeling system and the persons responsible for ensuring the labeling of in-plant and shipped containers.

The HCS also requires employers to institute formal employee training.[21] Employers must include both procedures for training new employees and for training employees when a new hazard is introduced into the workplace.[22] Employees must be trained to observe and detect the presence of hazardous chemicals, and should be taught to recognize their visual appearances and odors.[23] They also are to be trained to recognize the physical and health hazards posed by the substances with which they work.[24] Finally, employees should be shown how to take protective measures and how to react to emergency situations.[25]

---

[16] 29 C.F.R. § 1910.1200(g)(2)(xii).
[17] 29 C.F.R. § 1910.1200(f)(9).
[18] 29 C.F.R. § 1910.1200(f)(5).
[19] *See General Carbon Co. v. OSHRC*, 860 F.2d 479 (D.C. Cir. 1988).
[20] 29 C.F.R. § 1910.1200(e).
[21] 29 C.F.R. § 1910.1200(h)(1)(i).
[22] OSHA Instruction CPL 2-2.38C, at A-34 (Oct. 22, 1990).
[23] 29 C.F.R. § 1910.1200(h)(2)(i).
[24] 29 C.F.R. § 1910.1200(h)(2)(ii).
[25] 29 C.F.R. § 1910.1200(h)(2)(iii).

Although there is no specific standard compelling employee training, there are standards, a number of which have been noted in this Chapter, that include training requirements. Nonetheless, it goes without saying that employees must be trained with respect to safe and healthful work practices generally, and with respect to how they can safely perform their particular job assignments.[26]

2.2 Specific Safety Standards

The General Industry Standards also include a number of specific safety standards which deal with structural conditions in the workplace, machinery, the handling and storage of hazardous materials, and fire protection.

2.2.1 Structural Conditions

Employers must ensure that structural conditions comply with OSHA's specific safety standards. Walking and working surfaces in permanent places of employment, including floor and wall openings, stairs, ladders and scaffolds, must meet OSHA criteria, which are designed to protect employees from trip and fall hazards.[27] All buildings and structures must have clearly marked and illuminated safety exits that permit the prompt escape of occupants in case of a fire or other emergency.[28] If the employer uses powered platforms, manlifts, or vehicle-mounted work platforms, those platforms must meet specific requirements.[29] Finally, regulations that incorporate the National Electric Code ensure electrical safety in the workplace through electrical systems design, work and maintenance practices, and safety requirements for special equipment.[30]

---

[26] Employers have been held criminally liable for a failure to train their employees. *See, People v. Reliance Steel & Aluminum Co.*, Ca. Muni. Ct. No. S 34359 (April 5, 1988).
[27] 29 C.F.R. §§ 1910.21-1910.32.
[28] 29 C.F.R. §§ 1910.35-1910.40.
[29] 29 C.F.R. §§ 1910.66-1910.70.
[30] 29 C.F.R. §§ 1910.301-1910.398.

In addition, OSHA has proposed criteria for personal fall protection systems, including fall arrest systems, work positioning systems, travel restricting systems, and systems for climbing.[31] The rules on personal protective equipment and on walking and working surfaces would be amended to incorporate the new criteria.

2.2.2 Machinery

Employers also must ensure that workplace machinery complies with OSHA's specific safety standards.

The standards are intended to ensure that machinery is operated safely and that machine operators and nearby employees are protected from hazards, such as rotating parts, hazards at the point of operation, flying chips, and sparks.[32] The power tool standard requires safe design, operation, and guarding of hand and portable power tools used by employees, including saws, drills, mowers, and jacks.[33] The machinery standards also cover the operation of air receivers and other equipment used in providing and utilizing compressed air for cleaning, drilling, hoisting, and chipping.[34] Employers whose workers perform welding, cutting, and brazing activities must use approved torches and manifolds for these activities.[35] The standards also include requirements for using and storing materials handling equipment, including derricks, cranes, and helicopters.[36] Finally, the lockout/tagout rule[37] requires employers to disable machinery that is being serviced or that is undergoing maintenance so that it cannot be inadvertently energized, placing nearby employees at risk.

---

[31] 55 Fed. Reg. 13,360; 13,423 (Apr. 10, 1990) are concurrent proposals to amend 29 C.F.R. Part 1910, subparts D (walking and working surfaces) and I (personal protective equipment), respectively.
[32] 29 C.F.R. §§ 1910.211-1910.222.
[33] 29 C.F.R. §§ 1910.241-1910.245.
[34] 29 C.F.R. § 1910.169.
[35] 29 C.F.R. §§ 1910.251-1910.254.
[36] 29 C.F.R. §§ 1910.176-1910.190.
[37] 29 C.F.R. § 1910.147.

2.2.3 Hazardous Materials

The General Industry Standards also include procedures for the safe handling and storage of hazardous materials, including hydrogen, oxygen, nitrous oxide, compressed gases, and other flammable and combustible materials.[38] Additionally, the "HAZWOPER" standard regulates hazardous waste operations and emergency responses to releases of, or substantial threats of releases of hazardous substances.[39]

2.2.4 Fire Protection

OSHA's fire protection standards set forth a number of requirements.[40] Employers who establish employee fire brigades must meet OSHA requirements for the organization, training, and personal protective equipment of those brigades.[41] The standards also set forth requirements for the placement, use, maintenance, and testing of portable fire extinguishers provided for the use of employees.[42] Stand pipes and hoses,[43] automatic sprinkler systems,[44] fixed extinguishing systems,[45] and fire detection systems[46] all must meet OSHA requirements as well.

2.3 Specific Health Standards

The General Industry Standards also include specific health standards requiring the employer to institute environmental controls and protect workers from exposure to toxic and hazardous substances.

---

[38] 29 C.F.R. §§ 1910.101-1910.116.
[39] 29 C.F.R. § 1910.120.
[40] 29 C.F.R. §§ 1910.155-1910.165.
[41] 29 C.F.R. § 1910.156.
[42] 29 C.F.R. § 1910.157.
[43] 29 C.F.R. § 1910.158.
[44] 29 C.F.R. § 1910.159.
[45] 29 C.F.R. §§ 1910.160-1910.163.
[46] 29 C.F.R. § 1910.164.

2.3.1 Environmental Controls

The General Industry Standards require environmental controls pertaining to ventilation, noise, radiation, and sanitation. Employers who engage in abrasive blasting, grinding, polishing, buffing, spray-finishing, electroplating, pickling, dying, dipping, and tanning must comply with the ventilation standard, which requires employers to ensure the quality of air flow in the work area and to provide employees with respiratory protective equipment.[47] The noise standard specifies maximum noise exposure levels, including a permissible exposure limit of ninety decibels over an eight-hour time-weighted average.[48] Employees can be protected against excess exposure to occupational noise through the use of hearing protection and engineering controls.[49] The radiation standards restrict employee exposure to ionizing radiation, such as x-rays, and non-ionizing radiation, such as electromagnetic radiation.[50] Finally, OSHA's grain dust standard requires employers to clean up mills and elevators when more than one eighth of an inch of grain dust has accumulated.[51]

2.3.2 Toxic and Hazardous Substances

OSHA has promulgated a number of specific substance standards, which regulate employee exposure to substances such as asbestos, vinyl chloride, cadmium, benzene, and lead.[52] Those standards set forth permissible exposure and action levels, and mandate monitoring requirements, personal protective equipment, and employee training. The employer must implement administrative or engineering controls to achieve compliance with specified exposure levels. Where these controls are not feasible,

---

[47] 29 C.F.R. § 1910.94.
[48] 29 C.F.R. § 1910.95.
[49] 29 C.F.R. § 1910.95.
[50] 29 C.F.R. §§ 1910.96-1910.97.
[51] *National Grain & Feed Ass'n Inc. v. OSHA*, 903 F.2d 308 (5th Cir. 1990).
[52] 29 C.F.R. §§ 1910.1000-1910.1047.

the employer must provide appropriate personal protective equipment, such as respirators.

In early 1989, OSHA published a new air contaminants standard, which adopted more restrictive permissible exposure levels for 212 substances, and established limits for 164 substances that were not previously regulated.[53] In July 1992, the U.S. Court of Appeals for the Eleventh Circuit struck down these exposure limits.[54] OSHA, therefore, is currently enforcing the exposure limits in effect before the 1989 air contaminants standard went into effect.[55]

2.3.3 Blood-Borne Diseases

OSHA's Blood-Borne Pathogens Standard is intended to reduce occupational exposure to the hepatitis B virus, the human immunodeficiency virus (HIV), and other blood-borne pathogens. The Blood-Borne Pathogens Standard calls for a combination of engineering and work practice controls, personal protective clothing and equipment, training, medical follow-up of exposure incidents, vaccination, and other approaches.[56] The standard applies to businesses as diverse as health care, law enforcement, corrections facilities, research laboratories, blood banks, the funeral industry, and fire and rescue squads. It may apply to any business, in any industry, depending upon anticipated incidence of employee exposure to body fluids.

2.3.4 Process Safety

OSHA's Process Safety Standard requires employers to analyze potential hazards in each step of chemical processes and take any necessary action to avoid and prevent chemical

---

[53] 54 Fed. Reg. 2332 (Jan. 19, 1989), amending 29 CFR § 1910.1000.
[54] *AFL-CIO v. OSHA*, 965 F.2d 962 (11th Cir. 1992).
[55] 22 O.S.H. Rep. (BNA) 1754 (Mar. 24, 1993).
[56] 29 C.F.R. § 1910.1030.

releases and explosions. The rule primarily affects the petrochemical and chemical industries.[57]

2.3.5 Confined Spaces

OSHA's confined-space standard went into effect on April 15, 1993.[58] It requires employers to provide training programs for workers who enter storage tanks and other confined spaces. It is intended to protect these workers from toxic fumes, lack of oxygen, or other hazards.

2.3.6 Special Industries

The General Industry Standards, subparts R and T, contain special provisions concerning the following industries: pulp, paper and paperboard mills, sawmills, pulpwood logging, textiles, bakeries, laundries, agriculture, laboratories, telecommunications, and commercial diving operations. Special obligations are imposed on employers in these industries. Employers in these fields should consult the applicable standards to determine their duties.

3.0 GENERAL DUTY CLAUSE

The Occupational Safety and Health Act contains a general duty clause, which states:

> Each employer . . . shall furnish to each of his employees employment and a place of employment which are free from recognized hazards that are causing or are likely to cause death or serious physical harm to his employees.[59]

---

[57] *See* 55 Fed. Reg. 14,072 (Apr. 13, 1990), correcting 29 CFR Part 1910.120, as amended by 54 Fed. Reg. 9294 (Mar. 6, 1989).
[58] 58 Fed. Reg. 4462 (Jan. 14, 1993), promulgating 29 C.F.R. § 1910.146.
[59] 29 U.S.C. § 654(a).

This broad clause is meant to reach those hazards for which no specific standards have been established, but which nevertheless present a threat of serious injury or death.

OSHA must establish several elements in order to issue a citation for a violation of the general duty clause. First, a hazard must be "recognized."[60] Recognized dangers include hazards that are detectable by human senses or through the use of technical devices. Furthermore, a hazard that has been recognized by the industry will be cited even if the employer has not realized its danger, because the employer is deemed to have "constructive knowledge" of hazards identified by the industry.[61] Second, the condition must be "causing or likely to cause death or serious physical harm to [the employer's] employees."[62] Finally, OSHA must establish the particular steps the employer should have taken to avoid the violation, and must demonstrate the feasibility and utility of those measures.[63]

Despite its breadth, the general duty clause does not impose absolute liability on an employer. For instance, unforeseeable hazards are not considered "recognized" under the clause. Courts take a narrow view of this defense, however, and employers are expected to anticipate actions of employees that can cause serious injury or death.

Other defenses to a general duty clause citation include arguments that a specific-industry standard applies and that feasible measures are not available to correct the violation.

If a specific standard is applicable, the general duty clause may not be used to increase the penalty. OSHA has successfully used the general duty clause, however, as an alternative sanction when a specific standard violation was alleged but could not be proven.[64] OSHA must also show that measures to correct a

---

[60] *Id.*

[61] *OSHA Field Operations Man.* § IV A.2.b.(2)(1991).

[62] 29 U.S.C. § 654(a).

[63] *National Realty & Constr. Co. v. OSHRC*, 489 F.2d 1257 (D.C. Cir. 1973).

[64] *UAW v. General Dynamics Land Systems Div.*, 815 F.2d 1570 (D.C. Cir. 1987), *cert. denied* 484 U.S. 976 (1987).

hazardous situation could have been taken.[65] However, if the proposed measure would simply maintain or actually decrease the protection, the citation will not stand.[66]

For several years OSHA pursued cumulative trauma syndrome cases and other ergonomics matters under its general duty clause. This approach enabled OSHA to impose very large fines on cited employers. However, in *Secretary of Labor v. Pepperidge Farm, Inc.*,[67] an administrative law judge preliminarily ruled that OSHA cannot use the general-duty clause to force abatement of repetitive stress hazards in the absence of a federal ergonomic standard.[68]

From a practical standpoint, the employer must be sensitive to any area in which work practices pose hazards to employees, and must be prepared to improve safety and health practices, even if no occupational safety or health standards mandate action. If the employer takes reasonably prudent steps to detect and to guard against such conditions, it will be in a better position to defend itself from citation for a violation of the general duty clause.

4.0 RECORDKEEPING AND REPORTING REGULATIONS

4.1 General Requirements

In addition to record keeping requirements found in the General Industry Standards and Industry-Specific Standards, private sector employers are obligated to maintain specific records of occupational illnesses, injuries, and fatalities.

There are two types of OSHA recordkeeping and reporting requirements. First, employers must maintain records of reports of employee accidents and illnesses in the workplace. Second, employers must keep additional records required by OSHA

---

[65] *National Realty and Construction Co. v. OSHRC*, 489 F.2d 1257 (D.C. Cir. 1973).
[66] *Id.*
[67] O.S.H. Cas. No. 89-265 (Mar. 26, 1993).
[68] 22 O.S.H. Rep. (BNA) 1897 (Mar. 31, 1993).

addressing specific issues, such as asbestos,[69] lead,[70] and personal respiratory equipment.[71] Also, access to employee exposure and medical records is regulated under the General Industry Standards.

OSHA's general recordkeeping requirements apply to all employers subject to OSHA, except those having ten employees or less, those subject to job injury and illness recordkeeping and reporting requirements of other federal agencies, and those exempted because of low illness and injury rates.[72] Even those employers who are generally exempt from the recordkeeping and reporting requirements must still comply with other applicable OSHA standards and report to OSHA within forty-eight hours[73] any accident that results in one or more fatalities or the hospitalization of five or more employees.

The form used for recording occupational injuries and illnesses is the OSHA Form 200 log and summary, or its equivalent. The last section of the log, which shows the injury and illness totals for the year, must be posted annually between February 1 and March 1.[74] The employer must then retain the log for five years.[75] Employers also must keep supplementary records that contain additional information about each injury or illness. The OSHA Form 101 is used for this purpose but equivalent forms, such as workers' compensation or insurance forms, are acceptable.[76] Any employer who desires to maintain

---

[69] 29 C.F.R. § 1910.1001(m) (includes requirement that employers subject to the asbestos standard maintain personal, environmental, and medical records for thirty years).

[70] 29 C.F.R. § 1910.1025(n) (includes requirement for maintenance of lead monitoring and medical records of employees for at least forty years, or for the duration of employment plus twenty years, which ever is longer).

[71] 29 C.F.R. § 1910.134(f)(iv) (includes requirement for maintenance of records of inspection dates and findings regarding respirators maintained for emergency use for an unspecified period of time).

[72] 29 C.F.R. §§ 1904.15-1904.16.

[73] 29 C.F.R. § 1904.8.

[74] 29 C.F.R. § 1904.5(d)(1).

[75] 29 C.F.R. § 1904.6.

[76] 29 C.F.R. § 1904.4.

records in a manner different from that is required by the recordkeeping regulation may submit a petition stating the reasons relief is sought with the appropriate regional commission of the Bureau of Labor Statistics.[77]

The employer must retain records in each establishment for five years following the end of the year to which they relate.[78] If the employer has more than one establishment, it must maintain a separate set of records for each one. An establishment is defined as a "single physical location where business is conducted or where services or industrial operations are performed."[79] Distinctly separate activities performed at the same physical location are treated as separate "establishments" for recordkeeping purposes.[80]

Where an employer has more than one establishment, and thus keeps separate records for each, the employer must ensure that actual copies of the OSHA Form 200 are available at each establishment. The Review Commission has held that "available" means "present or ready for immediate use." Under the Review Commission's interpretation, an employer can comply with this requirement by making the OSHA Form 200 available by telecopier. However, a delay of two days between an employee's request and receipt of the form is clearly impermissible.[81]

4.2 Fatalities or Multiple Hospitalizations

The employer must report within forty-eight hours any work-related fatality or hospitalization of five or more employees to the office of the nearest area director of OSHA. The report may be oral or in writing and must state the circumstances of the accident, the number of fatalities, and the

---

[77] 29 C.F.R. § 1904.13.
[78] 29 C.F.R. § 1904.6.
[79] 29 C.F.R. § 1904.12(g)(1).
[80] 29 C.F.R. § 1904.12(g)(1).
[81] *Secretary of Labor v. Price Chopper Supermarkets*, 15 O.S.H. Cas. (BNA) 1518 (1992).

extent of any injuries.[82] The 48 hours runs from the time of the accident, not from the time of the employee's death.[83] "Hospitalization" is defined as admission of the employee to a hospital on an overnight basis.[84]

"Work-related" is broadly interpreted by OSHA.[85] If the employer is uncertain whether a fatality is work-related, it should nevertheless report it. If the employer does not do so, it may later be subject to a penalty for failure to maintain proper records. There may be some question, for example, as to whether the death of an employee who had contracted an illness was due to the workplace environment.[86] In those cases, the employer should record the illness. The employer may later amend the record if the fatality should be attributable to another cause. It should be noted that fatalities involving accidents at work or workplace exposure to hazardous substances must be reported despite the length of time between the injury or illness and death.[87]

4.3 Injuries and Illnesses

An occupational injury is any injury that is caused by a work-related accident or from exposure to a single incident in the workplace. Examples of occupational injuries are cuts, sprains, amputations, and fractures.[88] An occupational illness is any abnormal condition or disorder, other than one resulting from an occupational injury, caused by environmental factors in

---

[82] C.F.R. § 1904.8.

[83] *William Edwin Reitz*, O.S.H. Dec. (CCH) ¶ 19,373 (1975).

[84] *Simplex Time Recorder Co. v. Secretary of Labor*, 766 F.2d 575 (D.C. Cir. 1985).

[85] Recordkeeping Guidelines For Occupational Injuries and Illnesses (September 1986).

[86] *See General Motors Corp. (Inland Div.)*, O.S.H. Dec. (CCH) ¶ 24,743 (1980).

[87] Recordkeeping Guidelines For Occupational Injuries and Illnesses. (September 1986).

[88] Instructions to OSHA Form 200 (1990).

the workplace.[89] Therefore, injuries are generally caused by instantaneous events in the work environment, while incidents resulting from anything other than instantaneous events are generally considered illnesses.

The employer must record all work-related illnesses. However, injuries must be recorded only when they require medical treatment (other than first aid), involve loss of consciousness, restriction of work or motion, or transfer to another job.[90] The distinction between injuries and illnesses, therefore, has significant recordkeeping implications. Whether an incident involves an injury or an illness is determined by the nature of the original event or exposure that caused the incident, not the resulting condition of the affected employee.

4.4 Enforcement of Recordkeeping and Reporting Requirements

OSHA has recently focused its efforts on issuing citations for recordkeeping and reporting violations as one method of monitoring the safety and health status of covered employees. This, in turn, has led to the imposition of a record number of penalties on employers.

Failure to maintain, file, or keep required detailed records according to the recordkeeping regulations may result in the issuance of citations and civil penalties under the Act.[91] Citations may be issued to employers who, without knowingly falsifying any records, nevertheless fail to maintain the log and summary of injuries and illnesses or supplementary records properly, or who fail to file a survey report or a fatality or multiple hospitalization report. Generally, an honest error in evaluating whether an injury or illness is recordable will not constitute a violation.[92] If the employer is in doubt, however, it should record the incident.

---

[89] Id.
[90] Id.
[91] 29 C.F.R. § 1904.9(b).
[92] *Amoco Chemicals Corp.*, O.S.H. Dec. (CCH) ¶ 27,621 (1986).

Criminal sanctions of up to $10,000 or six months imprisonment, or both, can be ordered for knowingly making "any false statement, representation, or certification in any application, record, report plan or other document filed or required to be maintained pursuant to [the] Act."[93] The criminal sanctions may be imposed on anyone or any entity convicted of such offense, not just on the employer.

5.0 UNLAWFUL DISCRIMINATION

Employers may not discriminate against employees who have exercised rights accorded them by the Occupational Safety and Health Act. Specifically, Section 11(c)(1) states:

> No person shall discharge or in any manner discriminate against any employee because such an employee has filed any complaint instituted or caused to be instituted any proceeding under or relating to this Act or has testified or is about to testify in any such proceeding or because of the exercise by such employee on behalf of himself or others of any rights afforded by this Act.[94]

OSHA has issued interpretations that have extended Section 11(c) protection.[95] One of the more important gives an employee the right to refuse to work in certain situations. An employee may be protected against discipline or discharge if the employee is confronted with the choice of not performing assigned tasks or being subject to injury or death arising from the hazardous condition. If the employee reasonably refuses in good faith to be subjected to the dangerous situation, the employee is protected from later discrimination by the employer.[96]

This right is not unqualified, however. If possible, the employee must first seek correction of the hazard. In addition,

---

[93] 29 U.S.C. § 666(g).
[94] 29 U.S.C. § 660(c).
[95] 29 C.F.R. pt. 1977.
[96] *Whirlpool Corp. v. Marshall*, 445 U.S. 1 (1980).

if the employee's refusal to work is later determined to have been unreasonable, the employee will be subject to any disciplinary action taken by the employer, including dismissal.[97]

6.0 VARIANCES

Under Sections 6 and 16 of the Occupational Safety and Health Act, the Secretary of Labor has the discretion to issue a rule or order for a variance that temporarily or permanently excuses the employer's compliance from an OSHA standard.[98] Three types of variances are available. A temporary variance may be granted where the employer is unable to timely comply with an OSHA standard. A permanent variance may be granted where the employer can prove that alternative measures will provide the same safe and healthful workplace that would exist through compliance with the standard. Finally, a variance may be granted where it is necessary to avoid serious impairment of national defense.[99]

7.0 EMPLOYER DEFENSES TO CITATIONS FOR VIOLATION OF OSHA STANDARDS

Employers may raise a number of affirmative defenses to citations for violation of OSHA standards. These defenses can be divided into two groups: those of a procedural nature and those that involve substantive or factual issues. Some of the procedural defenses include jurisdictional objections to OSHA coverage, statute of limitations, lack of reasonable promptness in issuing a citation, improper service, failure to forward in a timely manner a notice of contest, improper amendment of the citation, lack of commerce clause jurisdiction, preemption by another federal agency, and lack of an employment relationship.

---

[97] *Id.*

[98] 29 U.S.C. §§ 655(d), 665.

[99] Specific requirements and procedures for obtaining variances, including procedures for variance hearings, are contained in 29 C.F.R. § 1905.

The more significant substantive defenses are discussed in the following sections.

7.1 The Infeasibility of Compliance Defense

The infeasibility of compliance defense was formerly known as the "impossibility of compliance defense." To establish this defense, the employer must show that compliance with the cited standard is infeasible, and it must offer proof of alternative protection for employees.

A recent case illustrates its application. In *Dun-Par Engineered Form Co.*, it was possible for the employer to construct guardrails on the sixth floor of a construction site. However, to do so would have been infeasible because some employees would have been forced to work outside the guardrails to perform their duties, the railing would have interfered with the pouring of concrete, and only one employee who rarely worked near the perimeter would have been "protected" by the rails. The Occupational Safety and Health Review Commission, therefore, excused the employer's failure to comply with the cited standard.[100]

7.2 The Isolated Incident Defense

The isolated incident defense, also referred to as the "unpreventable employee misconduct" defense, is frequently asserted. Employers are not expected to constantly monitor every employee on the job, and even the most complete safety program will not prevent all employee misbehavior. Thus, this defense precludes employer responsibility for violations that cannot be prevented with reasonable diligence.

In order to establish the isolated incident defense, the employer must show that the violation resulted from employee misconduct that violated a company work rule that was effec-

---

[100] *Brock v. Dun-Par Engineered Form Co.*, 843 F.2d 1135 (8th Cir. 1988).

tively communicated and uniformly enforced.[101] The employer can avoid liability for employee misconduct only if it maintains an effective safety program designed to achieve compliance with OSHA standards.[102] Infrequency of violations is strong evidence of an effective safety program.[103] On the other hand, if the employer has a record of violations over a period of time, its safety program will be found inadequate and the isolated incident defense will fail.[104]

7.3 The Greater Hazard Defense

An employer is excused from strict compliance with a standard if compliance would result in a greater hazard to its employees than noncompliance. Three elements of this defense must be proven: (1) the hazards of compliance are greater than the hazards of noncompliance; (2) alternative means of protecting employees are not available; and (3) a Section 6(d) variance application would be inappropriate.[105]

As with the infeasibility defense, an employer may be required to change its procedures in order to avoid the hazard that compliance would cause. Thus, if the greater hazard envisioned by the employer can be avoided by changes in the employer's work practices, the defense will fail.[106]

7.4 The Multi-Employer Work Site Defense

When employees of more than one employer occupy the same worksite, it may become necessary to apportion liability.

---

[101] *Texland Drilling Corp.*, 9 O.S.H. Cas. (BNA) 1023 (1980); *H.B. Zachary Company*, 70 O.S.H. Cas. (BNA) 202 (1980), *aff'd*, 638 F.2d 812 (5th Cir. 1981).

[102] *Capital Elec. Line Builders v. Marshall*, 678 F.2d 128 (10th Cir. 1982).

[103] *Texland Drilling Corp., supra* n. 100.

[104] *Jensen Constr. Co.*, 7 O.S.H. Cas. (BNA) 1477 (1979).

[105] *General Elec. Co. v. Secretary of Labor*, 676 F.2d 558 (3d Cir. 1978).

[106] *Voegele Co. v. OSHRC*, 625 F.2d 1075 (3d Cir. 1980).

Multi-employer worksites are most common in the construction industry.

At multi-employer worksites, OSHA normally will issue citations to the employer whose employees are exposed to hazards (the "exposing employer").[107] However, there are exceptions to this general rule. The Occupational Safety and Health Review Commission's decisions in *Anning-Johnson Co.* and *Grossman Steel & Aluminum Corp.* provide further guidelines for responsibility at multiple employer worksites. Those decisions hold:

1. The employer that creates or controls a hazardous condition is responsible for correcting the violation even if its own employees are not in the zone of danger;
2. The employer that neither creates nor controls a hazard to which its employees are exposed will not be cited if it has taken realistic measures to protect its employees; and
3. A general contractor is responsible for violations it could reasonably prevent or abate because of its supervisory capacity.[108]

OSHA will not cite an exposing employer for violations if the employer did not have the responsibility, authority, or ability to have the hazard corrected,[109] or if the employer has instructed its employees to recognize the hazard and on how to avoid the dangers associated with it.[110]

---

[107] *OSHA Field Operations Man.* § V F.1 (1991).

[108] *See Anning-Johnson Co.*, O.S.H. Dec. (CCH) ¶ 20,690 (1976), 516 F.2d 1081 (7th Cir. 1975); *Grossman Steel & Aluminum Corp.*, O.S.H. Dec. (CCH) ¶ 20,691 (1976).

[109] *OSHA Field Operations Man.* § V F.2.B-C (1991).

[110] *OSHA Field Operations Man.* § V F.2.E (1991).

Chapter 7

WORKPLACE DRUG TESTING PROGRAMS

Stephen L. Berry
Paul, Hastings, Janofsky & Walker

1.0 INTRODUCTION

It is estimated that some three to seven percent of the employee population use illicit drugs daily, and that five to ten percent of all employees are likely to have a problem with alcohol. Workers suffering from alcoholism or drug addiction are, according to experts, at least 25 percent less productive than their co-workers, and cost their employers one-quarter of their salaries in absenteeism, tardiness, spoiled materials, reduced efficiency and effectiveness, and higher medical premiums due to an increased number of on- and off-duty accidents. In addition, drug abusers are more likely to embezzle or steal company property to support their habits.

Faced with the significant security and financial risks associated with employees who abuse alcohol and/or drugs, many employers feel compelled to implement a program of testing for drug and/or alcohol abuse by employees.

While a well-drafted drug and alcohol prevention policy, including a provision for testing of applicants or employees, can be an effective deterrent and detection strategy, employers must proceed cautiously, taking into account the relevant provisions of the Americans With Disabilities Act ("ADA"), as well as other federal, state and local laws or regulations with which the employer must comply in implementing its drug and alcohol testing program.¹

2.0 DRUG TESTING UNDER THE ADA

The provisions of the ADA concerning the status of current and former drug users are complex and, unless carefully examined and applied on a case-by-case basis, can present a liability trap for the unwary.

Although a drug test is not a "medical examination" under the ADA and, therefore, is theoretically permissible at any time, the ADA does not articulate a standard which employers can use to verify the accuracy or validity of a drug test. Further, the ADA limits an employer's ability to question individuals concerning their use of prescription drugs. For this reason, the ADA's limitations on an employer's right to ask medical questions and conduct medical examinations must be considered in connection with establishing a drug testing program.

2.1 Pre-Employment Medical Inquiries and Examinations

The ADA's protection extends to pre-employment inquiries. While an employer may ask whether an applicant is currently using illegal drugs or abusing alcohol, an employer may *not* ask whether an applicant is addicted to illegal drugs or abuses alcohol, or inquire whether the applicant has ever been in a drug rehabilitation program, until *after* extending a conditional offer of employment.² The employer may then exclude an individual based on past illegal drug use or alcohol abuse, but only if it can demonstrate the exclusion is job-related and consistent with business necessity, and that legitimate job criteria cannot be met with a reasonable accommodation.³

---

¹ This chapter provides a synopsis of federal laws, including the ADA, which relate to workplace drug testing. Users of this Handbook should consult with local counsel to determine what, if any, state and local laws or regulations also apply.

² *Technical Assistance Manual* at VIII-6.

³ *Technical Assistance Manual* at VIII-6-7.

Similarly, the ADA permits pre-employment medical examinations only *after* an offer of employment has been extended. However, it does not require that the medical examination be job-related or consistent with business necessity, nor must the employer justify its decision to require a pre-employment medical examination.[4] However, if the applicant is not hired because a post-offer medical examination or inquiry reveals a disability, all of the ADA's protections come into play. In other words, the employer must show that the reason(s) for the adverse hiring decision are job-related and consistent with business necessity,[5] or that the applicant posed a direct threat to health or safety.[6]

2.2 Medical Examinations of Current Employees

Under the ADA, an employer may not require a medical examination of a current employee unless it is job-related and consistent with business necessity. A medical examination or inquiry will meet these criteria if, for example, (1) the employer has evidence that an employee's job performance is hindered by his or her medical condition, or that the employee's condition poses a direct threat to others, (2) applicable laws or regulations (such as Department of Transportation regulations) compel the employer to conduct the examinations, or (3) the employer needs to determine an employee's fitness for a particular job (*e.g.*, where the employee is having difficulty performing the job or becomes disabled).[7]

2.3 Employer Conduct Allowed by the ADA

As a general matter, an employer may:

- Require an applicant to take a drug test prior to a conditional offer of employment or require an

---

[4] *Technical Assistance Manual* at VI-5.
[5] *Technical Assistance Manual* at VI-1.
[6] *Technical Assistance Manual* at VI-7.
[7] *Technical Assistance Manual* at VI-2, VI-5, VI-12-13.

employee to take a drug test (but not a blood alcohol test) though the test is not job-related or consistent with business necessity.

Note: For purposes of the ADA, a drug test is not a medical examination[8] and does not entitle the person giving the test to ask questions regarding the applicant's or employee' s use of legal prescription drugs. Without this information many drug tests cannot accurately distinguish between illegal and legal drug use. Worse yet, many licensed drug testing laboratories have substantial error rates, including false positives. Any disciplinary or unfavorable action against an applicant or employee legally using drugs would subject the employer to liability under the ADA.

Caution: Many drug tests will reveal information about the subject's medical condition. It is not enough for the testing laboratory to treat such information as a confidential medical record and withhold from disclosure to the employer any information about the applicant's "medical condition." Indeed, if the drug test reveals any information besides the applicant's use of *illegal* drugs, the test will be a medical examination and hence subject to the ADA's requirements.

Hint: A better strategy is to condition a job offer on the applicant successfully passing a drug test. The employer could then properly ask the applicant about *legal* drugs the applicant was using before conducting the drug test so the drug testing laboratory can accurately determine *illegal* drug use. Since current users of illegal drugs are not protected by the ADA, the employer could withdraw its job offer if the applicant tested positive for illegal drug use.

---

[8] 42 U.S.C. § 12114(d)(1); *Technical Assistance Manual* at VIII-7.

- Use reasonable procedures to verify that a rehabilitated or rehabilitating illegal drug user is no longer engaging in illegal drug use. Such verification may include drug testing.
- Prohibit the illegal use of drugs and the use of alcohol at work and require that employees not be under the influence of illegal drugs or alcohol while at work.
- Hold users of alcohol or illegal drugs to the same standards of performance and behavior as other employees, even where the unsatisfactory performance or behavior is directly related to the alcohol or illegal drug use.
- Require that employees comply with the Drug-Free Workplace Act of 1988.[9]
- If the employer can demonstrate that its decision to not hire an individual with a past history of illegal drug use is job-related and consistent with business necessity, such as in law enforcement, the employer may terminate or refuse to hire a person with such a past history.
- If the employer is subject to regulations regarding the use of alcohol or illegal drugs promulgated by the Department of Defense, the Department of Transportation, or the Nuclear Regulatory Commission, it can require that employees comply with such regulations.[10]

Although Congress stated explicitly that an employer may employ drug testing and that such testing is not subject to the same requirements as medical testing, Congress also made clear that *it does not encourage or authorize* the use of drug tests for

---

[9] 42 U.S.C. § 12114(c)(3). The Act applies to federal contractors and recipients of federal grants. Among other things, the Act requires that the contractor or grantee adopt and publish for employees a written anti-drug policy and take action against employees who violate the policy.

[10] 42 U.S.C. § 12114(c)(5).

job applicants or employees.[11] Thus, employers must still comply with federal, state and local laws and regulations in adopting a drug testing program.

3.0 DRUG TESTING UNDER THE U.S. CONSTITUTION

Workplace drug testing programs must comply with the protections afforded by the U.S. Constitution only if "state action" is involved, *i.e.*, the program is required by some federal law or regulation. However, some state constitutions have provisions which would prohibit such programs adopted by non-government, private employers as well. In such jurisdictions, the courts are guided by the approach used in the federal courts.

3.1 Balancing Test Applied

The United States Supreme Court has evaluated and upheld workplace drug testing programs in two cases: *Skinner v. Railway Labor Executives' Ass'n*,[12] and *National Treasury Employees Union v. Von Raab*[13]. In each of the cases the Court applied a balancing test to determine whether an employer's drug testing program violated the Fourth Amendment,[14] weighing the employer's need for the program against the employee's reasonable expectation of privacy. These cases teach that, absent individualized suspicion of drug use or impairment, a program will pass constitutional muster only if the employer is able to advance a valid, and in some cases a "compelling," governmental interest which outweighs the individual's privacy interests.

In its decisions, the Supreme Court identified three valid interests which will support a workplace drug testing program where employees have a diminished expectation of privacy:

---

[11] 42 U.S.C. § 12114(d)(2).

[12] 489 U.S. 602 (1989). *Skinner* involved the drug testing procedures applied by railroad employers pursuant to regulations issued by the Federal Railroad Administration.

[13] 489 U.S. 656 (1989). *Von Raab* involved the drug testing procedures adopted by the United States Customs Service for its employees.

[14] Among other things, the Fourth Amendment provides protection from unreasonable searches.

- Maintaining public safety,
- Protecting truly sensitive information, and
- Ensuring the integrity and physical fitness of certain employees.

3.2 Application of the Legal Test to Specific Workplace Drug Testing Programs

For the most part, the lower federal courts have narrowly construed the Supreme Court's balancing test, particularly when identifying which interests will outweigh an individual's right to personal privacy. Thus, the governmental interests identified by the Supreme Court in *Skinner* and *Von Raab* may be the only permissible reasons for drug testing.

The lower federal courts also carefully scrutinize employer drug testing programs to determine whether the employer has adopted procedures which minimize the intrusiveness of the drug test. An otherwise constitutional program likely will be ruled invalid if the testing procedures are careless and not solicitous of employees' privacy concerns. However, to satisfy the Fourth Amendment's reasonableness requirement, a drug testing program need not involve the least intrusive method available for detecting drug use.[15]

3.2.1 Applicant Testing

Von Raab authorized the drug testing of employees who were seeking promotion or transfer to certain sensitive job categories. The Supreme Court's analysis suggests that an employer will have to show a *compelling interest* before requiring drug tests of current employees seeking promotion. Unless the job sought is safety-sensitive, involves drug interdiction, the use of firearms, or access to sensitive information, mandatory drug testing of current employees seeking promotion likely is proscribed.

---

[15] *See, e.g., International Bhd. of Teamsters v. Dept. of Transp.*, 932 F.2d 1292, 1304-05 (9th Cir. 1991) (upholding random drug testing of commercial drivers by private employers under authority of regulations issued by Federal Highway Administration).

The same is not true for an applicant for employment. The court cases make it clear that an applicant has a "diminished expectation" of privacy. Thus, for example, in *Willner v. Thornburgh*,[16] the District of Columbia Circuit upheld the Department of Justice's drug testing of applicants seeking attorney positions. The court relied on the following factors:

(a) The agency used procedures which minimized the invasiveness of the test;
(b) The applicants could control whether or not they would be tested by simply choosing not to apply for a position;
(c) The applicants were required to fill out questionnaires inquiring into several personally sensitive areas showing they had a reduced expectation of privacy in seeking employment with the agency; and
(d) The employer had a strong interest in gathering information as to an individual's suitability for employment.[17]

Similarly, in *Teamsters*, the Ninth Circuit upheld the Federal Highway Administration's drug testing regulations requiring motor carriers to administer drug tests to all prospective employees. The court reasoned that the privacy expectations of motor carriers are diminished since "[t]hey have voluntarily chosen to enter a highly regulated profession that already requires periodic extensive physical examinations and urinalysis to determine the qualifications of its members."[18] The important public policy of highway safety was held to justify the intrusion into an applicant's privacy.

---

[16] 928 F.2d 1185 (D.D.C. 1991), *cert. denied*, 112 S. Ct. 669 (1991).
[17] *Id.* at 1192.
[18] *Teamsters*, 932 F.2d at 1307.

3.2.2 Current Employees

There is a significant risk that drug testing of current employees will be deemed to violate an employee's right to be free from "unreasonable searches," and any right of "privacy" afforded by state law, *unless* either (a) the employer has reason to believe that an employee has used illegal drugs at work or is drug impaired at work, *or* (b) the necessity for periodic testing because of a public safety risk overrides the employee's right of privacy (applicable to employment categories such as airline pilots, bus drivers, truck drivers, etc.) *and* the employer conducts such testing by the least intrusive method reasonably available.

3.2.3 Fitness-for-Duty Testing

In *Teamsters*, the Ninth Circuit also upheld the Highway Administration's requirement that drivers be tested for drugs during their biennial fitness-for-duty medical examinations. The Court noted that the periodic drug test constituted a minimal intrusion upon employee privacy since the employees were already asked to submit to medical examinations, including urinalysis, as a condition of continuing employment. Indeed, the only increase in the intrusiveness of the test involved the employee submitting two specimens rather than one.

Because there exists a reduced expectation of privacy where an employee's job requires a fitness-for-duty medical examination, it is likely that most courts would follow the Ninth Circuit and permit employers to test for drugs as part of such examinations.

3.2.4 Reasonable Suspicion Testing

Employers may require drug tests where they have formed a reasonable suspicion that the employee is working while drug-impaired. Such programs will likely withstand constitutional scrutiny if the procedures for detecting impairment are reasonable and employees have been forewarned of the policy. However, courts have held that employers *may not* ordinarily test employees holding nonsafety-sensitive jobs if the employee presents indicia of *off-duty* drug use or impairment.[19]

The critical issue in determining the constitutionality of a reasonable suspicion drug test is whether the criteria used to spot impairment are "reasonable." Criteria are reasonable if they are based upon specific objective facts and the rational inferences that may be drawn from those facts. Thus, courts have struck down programs which allow testing based on vague, amorphous indicators of on-the-job drug use or impairment.[20]

Although reasonable suspicion may be formed by reference to workplace rumors, the rumor must permit a reasonable inference that the employee actually used drugs.[21]

Some courts have upheld drug testing programs which consider workplace accidents as indicia of drug use.[22] However, because such an approach allows the employer to circumvent the stringent standards otherwise imposed on post-accident

---

[19] *See, e.g., National Treasury Employees Union v. Yeutter*, 918 F.2d 968, 974 (D.D.C. Cir. 1990) (employer has no legitimate reason for detecting off-duty drug use) *National Fed'n of Fed. Employees v. Cheney*, 742 F. Supp. 4, 8 (D.D.C. 1990) (employee may not be tested based on an off-duty arrest or conviction for a drug-related offense); *but see Von Raab*, 489 U.S. at 674 ("the almost unique mission of the [Customs] Service gives the government a compelling interest in insuring that many of these covered employees do not use drugs, even off-duty, for such use creates risks of bribery and blackmail against which the government is entitled to guard").

[20] *See, e.g., Yeutter*, 918 F.2d at 968 (the "reasonableness of a suspicion of drug use formed solely on basis of 'abnormal conduct' is not self-evident"); *Burka v. New York City Transit Auth.*, 739 F. Supp. 814 (S.D.N.Y. 1990) (employee may not be tested on "reasonable suspicion" after returning to work from an extended absence or suspension); *Cheney*, 742 F. Supp. at 7-8 (absent careful observation by a supervisor trained in detection of drug-impairment, employer may not rely on symptoms, such as an elevated heart rate and drowsiness, which could easily be attributed to nondrug-related causes).

[21] *See Ford v. Dowd*, 931 F.2d 1286 (8th Cir. 1991) (police officer could not be asked to submit to drug testing based solely on unsubstantiated rumor that he associated with drug dealers).

[22] *See, e.g., Burka*, 739 F. Supp. at 829 (a "reasonable suspicion of drug use arises from the rational inference of a causal connection between an employee's impairment and an incident or accident").

testing (discussed below), it is likely that many courts would conclude that the occurrence of an accident alone does not provide reasonable suspicion.

3.2.5 Post-Accident Testing

The prevailing view concerning post-accident testing is that it is a form of "suspicionless" testing and, therefore, that it is subject to a stricter scrutiny. Post-accident drug tests should be conducted primarily in two situations:

- Where the employee occupies a safety-sensitive position, or
- Where the accident is serious.

Courts have invalidated programs where the policy provides for testing of nonsafety-sensitive employees following a minor mishap or authorizes testing of employees only peripherally involved in the accident.[23]

3.2.6 Random Testing

The federal courts balance the countervailing interests, adhering strictly to the parameters established in *Von Raab* and *Skinner*. Thus, random testing has only been upheld where:

- The employee has a diminished expectation of privacy; and

---

[23] *See, e.g., Teamsters*, 932 F.2d at 1308 (upholding the validity of regulations requiring an employee to submit to testing if an accident involves (1) a fatality, (2) an injury demanding immediate medical treatment away from the scene of the accident or (3) at least $4,400 in property damage); *American Fed'n of Gov't Employees v. Derwinski*, 777 F. Supp. 1493, 1502 (N.D. Cal. 1991) (striking down drug testing program where the standard for "seriousness" of accident was not sufficiently certain and supervisors were given sole discretion to determine whether a test was warranted); *American Fed'n of Gov't Employees v. Sullivan*, 744 F. Supp. 294 (D.D.C. 1990) (striking down testing following accidents involving as little as $1,000 in property damage).

- There is a compelling interest in safety and/or national security which outweighs the employee's diminished privacy expectation.

Thus, before implementing a random testing program, employers must meet the compelling interests articulated in *Von Raab* and *Skinner*, enhancing safety, protecting confidential information, and/or ensuring worker integrity. Additionally, a random testing scheme should include the procedural protections of notice, non-arbitrary standards for selecting subjects, and methodology which respects an individual's privacy concerns to the fullest extent possible.

(1) *Safety*

Safety interests become compelling when an employee's job duties are such that drug impairment could result in substantial harm to the employee or others. The courts have recognized a compelling interest supporting random drug testing in a variety of safety-sensitive jobs, such as vehicle, boat or aircraft operators and related positions; handlers of dangerous equipment, including firearms; employees in inherently dangerous positions, including those who handle hazardous materials; and health care workers who would pose a risk to their patients if they attempted to perform their duties drug-impaired.

(2) *National Security*

Random drug testing has been upheld where the employees at issue possess security clearances or either directly handle or have access to "secret" or "top secret" information on the ground that these employees pose a risk to national security. However, courts have had difficulty determining which employees are covered by this test.

While a person with top secret security clearance generates a sufficiently grave potential risk to national security to make random testing reasonable regardless of any other attendant circumstances, an employer probably cannot randomly test employees who handle confidential information which is neither "top secret" nor "secret." Similarly, it is doubtful that employees who simply have *access* to confidential information may be selected for random testing.

(3) *Employee Integrity*

Courts have upheld random drug testing where testing is necessary to ensure the drug-free integrity of certain employees and where drug use would be irreconcilable with the goals of a particular job. Employees falling under this category include law enforcement officials charged with the duty of stopping illegal drug sale and use, and prison guards having direct contact with drug offenders.[24]

If the position does not involve law enforcement or drug interdiction, the courts have been unwilling to recognize a compelling interest for random testing based on employee integrity.[25]

(4) *"Due Process" Protection*

It has been held that the element of surprise in random testing is constitutionally suspect and, in a close case, might "tip the scales" against such testing. Therefore, it is important that the employer use a reasonable method for selecting employee-subjects. For example, the Highway Administration's random testing regulations were held to be valid by the Ninth Circuit in *Teamsters*, in part, because they provided for selection of subjects in a "scientifically accepted" manner which allowed the administrators "no discretion to target individual employees for excessive testing."[26]

Again, an otherwise valid random drug testing program must ensure that the tests are conducted in the least intrusive fashion and with respect for an individual's privacy.

---

[24] *See, e.g., Penny v. Kennedy*, 915 F.2d 1065 (6th Cir. 1990) (upholding testing of police officers).
[25] *See Taylor v. O'Grady*, 888 F.2d 1189, 1196 (7th Cir. 1989) (interest in the integrity of its *entire workforce* is insufficient to overcome privacy interest of certain Department of Corrections employees).
[26] *Teamsters*, 932 F.2d at 1300.

4.0 MINIMIZING THE RISK OF LIABILITY

4.1 Determine the Company's Need for an Alcohol and Drug Abuse Program

- Base need on specific facts at your company, not merely because "everyone is doing it!"
- Draft a carefully conceived position paper which specifies the facts on which the perceived need is based (*e.g.*, increase in absenteeism or accident rate; decrease in productivity).

4.2 Design an Alcohol and Drug Policy which Fits Your Company's Needs

- Seek input from a variety of sources, including human resources staff, supervisors, company medical personnel and legal counsel.
- Gather relevant data on known drug and alcohol incidents, absenteeism, tardiness, productivity, health care usage, accidents and workers' compensation claims within the company's work force. Take necessary steps to cover analyses by the attorney-client privilege.
- Evaluate the nature and extent of the perceived problem, the actual or potential impact on the company's business and the cost of and legal risk associated with alternative policies and programs.
- Decide whether to emphasize rehabilitation, discipline or both. Most employers will want to establish a program which combines the rehabilitation and discipline approaches.[27]

---

[27] In this regard, the employer must comply with the ADA and applicable state or local laws.

4.3 Draft a Comprehensive Company Policy Concerning Drugs, Alcohol, Controlled Substances and Searches

- State in writing what conduct is prohibited on company property or during working hours (*e.g.*, trafficking, possession, use, being under the influence). Indicate what disciplinary action will be taken against employees who violate the policy.
- Cover situations in which an employee is taking over-the-counter or prescribed medication. An employee who is under the influence of a medication may present the same production and safety problems as one using illegal drugs.
- Identify the circumstances under which testing or searches may be conducted (*see* next section). An employer will be limited within the parameters of its policy. Provide in the policy that employee refusal to submit to a test or search may result in termination for violation of the policy.

4.4 Establish and Follow Proper Guidelines for Conducting Substance or Other Medical Tests

- Make sure any testing program takes into account and complies with the requirements of the ADA.
- Before an applicant or employee is tested, have the individual sign a consent form authorizing the test and communication of the test results to the company. Do not use threats or force to obtain consent.
- If pre-employment tests for the presence of alcohol, drugs or controlled substances are given, administer them to all applicants who reach a given stage of the selection process for the classification(s) covered by the policy. Give notice to job applicants on either the job application form or pre-employment medical forms

indicating that testing will be conducted as a part of the employment process.
- The most prudent course is to limit testing of current employees to those cases where there is reason to believe the employee is "under the influence" of alcohol, drugs or controlled substances. Any company which requires all employees to submit to a test whenever they compile a record of excessive absences or when they contribute to an on-the-job injury or accident, etc., should document the factual, statistical and other information which the company believes establishes a "reason to believe" such an employee is likely to be under the influence. Remember, random testing of employees is very risky and likely to be challenged in court; it should be limited to employees in positions that are highly safety or security sensitive. Employers who require periodic physical examinations, particularly for jobs where a safety risk is involved, may be able to successfully defend a drug screen as a part of such periodic physical examination, if conducted pursuant to an established written policy.
- Where practicable, use an outside medical facility which is experienced in collecting urine and/or blood samples for drug and alcohol testing.

4.5 Inquiries which Employers Should Make of Prospective Laboratories

- Is the facility licensed by the Center for Disease Control? Is the facility licensed to perform toxicology, forensic or industrial testing by the state and federal governments? Other licenses?
- What experience does the facility have in testing contraband substances and in testing for the

presence of alcohol, drugs or other controlled substances in the system?
- For which other employers does the laboratory perform such testing? Check these references. Select only a reputable laboratory which specializes in these tests.
- What applicable qualitative and quantitative tests does the laboratory run? EMIT screening? Gas chromatography-mass spectrometry?
- What is the error rate on each test, *i.e.*, false positive results, false negative results? Has the laboratory established a threshold level for positive readings that is sufficiently high to eliminate questionable test results based on trace amounts of drugs which might result from indirect exposure (e.g., employee's presence in a smoke-filled room)?
- What procedures are used to double-check results? Courts have held that a second test using a gas chromatography-mass spectrometry procedure is sufficiently reliable to make an employment decision on the basis of the results.
- Does the laboratory have toxicologists who could testify on matters such as the type of test used, its accuracy, the testing process followed, and the interpretation of the test results? What are the credentials of these individuals?
- Will the laboratory indemnify the employer if the employer is sued as a result of action it takes on false positive results?
- What system does the laboratory use to maintain a documented chain of custody to establish the identity of the specimen and protect its integrity throughout the process of collection, transportation and testing?
- What system does the laboratory use to ensure that samples are retained and preserved for possible future checking by the employee or his or her representative? How long are samples

retained? How are they stored? What labeling process is used?

4.6 Clearly Articulate Company Policy to Employees

- Communicate the new policy and program well in advance of its institution.
- State company's anti-drug/alcohol/controlled substance philosophy in as many written forms as possible: employment application, employee handbook, employee rules, memorandum on new policy, bulletin board notices and signs in employment office and locker rooms. Consider requiring the employee to sign an acknowledgment of the testing requirement on the employment application or other pre-hire form.
- If feasible, organize a meeting of current employees before instituting the policy. At the meeting, explain the company policy and have all employees sign a statement indicating that they are aware of and have received a copy of the policy. If the employee refuses to sign, a supervisor should document in writing that the statement was provided.
- Explain the policy to new employees at orientation programs and have them sign a statement indicating that they are aware of and have received a copy of the policy.

4.7 Train Supervisors to Deal Effectively and Appropriately with Employees Who Appear to be Under the Influence of or Abusing Drugs, Alcohol or other Controlled Substances

- Supervisors should receive training on the provisions of the company's policy, including search and test procedures; the physical appearance of various illegal substances; the physical and psychological symptoms of someone who is under the influence of alcohol, drugs, or other

controlled substances; the subtle changes in personality and actions which are characteristic of an abuser, as well as the following potential performance indicators: procrastination, poor judgment, performance variability between a.m. and p.m., tardiness and absenteeism, irritability, and long breaks; and the importance of developing and articulating performance standards, assessing performance against those standards, and identifying, documenting, and counseling or disciplining employees for *specific* problems with work performance.
- If an employee is suspected to be under the influence of alcohol, drugs, or other controlled substances, *two or more supervisors* should observe the employee, if possible.

4.8 Establish and Follow Appropriate Procedures for Conducting Searches

- Limit searches of employees to cases where the employer has reason to believe that the employee is in violation of company policy. However, if an employer acts pursuant to a published rule which allows random searches, unintrusive searches of lockers, work stations and personal belongings may be defensible if the employer has a generalized suspicion that employees are violating the rule. A "reason to believe" or "suspicion" may be based on the physical appearance of the employee, the employee's observed inability to perform work in a safe and productive manner, and/or any detectable evidence of alcohol, drugs or controlled substances in the workplace.
- Develop and require supervisors to comply with specific procedures in conducting searches, such as:
    - Absent an emergency, notify and obtain approval of the personnel department or

a designated management official before conducting a search.
- After receiving approval for the search, have a second supervisor or management official present to witness the investigation and search.
- Explain the purpose and scope of the search to the employee in a reasonable, quiet and courteous manner. Force should *not* be used under any circumstance.
- Inform any employee who refuses to submit to the search that refusal will require immediate suspension of the employee pending investigation, and will further require the company to make determinations concerning discipline of that employee, up to and including discharge, on the basis of the evidence then available to the company, any reasonable inferences which the company draws from that evidence and the refusal to consent to the search. If the employee still refuses, complete the investigatory interview, suspend the employee pending further investigation and submit a full report to the personnel department. After review, appropriate disciplinary action should be taken based upon the available evidence.
- Conduct searches of lockers or other personal possessions in the presence of the employee. Avoid conducting searches in a circus-like atmosphere (e.g., dramatic thrusting open of lockers, rummaging through contents).
- Take possession of any suspected contraband in plain view. If the employee refuses to turn over the suspected contraband, the supervisor should not use

force, but should inform the employee that refusal to surrender the material may be grounds for discharge. Care should be taken to ensure that the employee does not dispose of the suspected contraband, if at all possible.

- Place any suspected contraband which is seized into a sealed container and mark for future identification and testing.
- Conduct an interview with the employee about the suspected violation and give the employee a chance to explain his or her version of the situation in the presence of a second management representative.
- Deliver the contraband seized to a qualified laboratory for testing and indefinite retention.
- Arrange for and obtain a written report of the laboratory's test results.
- After the test results are received, two representatives of management should meet with the employee. A bargaining unit employee should be permitted to have a union representative present, if requested. If the test results on the samples are negative, the employee should be returned to work and assured that the investigation is over, that no report will be placed in his or her personnel file and that the incident will not affect his or her employment with the company. If the test results are positive, the results should be explained to the employee, he or she should be asked for any further explanation or information that management should consider, and the company should discharge or otherwise

discipline in accordance with company policy.
- With advice of counsel or some other qualified expert, prepare a detailed written report about the incident, including all facts which indicated a reason to believe the employee had violated company policy and steps taken to comply with procedural safeguards. Obtain written statements from witnesses.
• Use special procedures for searches of the body or personal effects in the employee's possession as follows:
  - If the search is of the employee or personal effects in the employee's possession, such as his or her lunch box or wallet, escort the employee from the workplace to a private room for the search.
  - If at all possible, obtain the employee's signed written consent to a search of the body or personal effects in the employee's possession.
  - Search any employee who refuses to sign the consent form but is willing to submit to the search. Two witnesses should document on the consent form that the employee verbally agreed to the search in their presence.

4.9 Keep Information Confidential

• Communicate information relative to investigations, possible employee rule violations, medical tests, and discipline only to those few individuals who "need to know" the information in order to perform their job function.
• Place information about suspected substance abuse and testing results in locked files separate

from the routine personnel file of the person involved.

4.10 If the Company is Unionized, Involve the Union

- Unless the union has clearly and unmistakably waived its right to bargain over the matter, the employer has an obligation under the National Labor Relations Act to bargain over "terms and conditions of employment," including disciplinary rules.
- In any event, implementation of any program will go more smoothly if the union cooperates. Inform the union of the proposed policy and program and then seek its input and support.

Chapter 8
IMMIGRATION AND VISAS FOR WORKERS

Ann L. Lamdin
Piper & Marbury

1.0 OVERVIEW OF THE UNITED STATES IMMIGRATION SYSTEM

1.1 Determining Immigration Status

One of the first issues which must be addressed in connection with any immigration problem is to determine the immigration status of the person in question. Every person in the United States falls into one of the following categories:

1.1.1 United States Citizen

Citizenship in the United States can be acquired in many ways, including through birth in the United States,[1] birth to United States citizen parents abroad,[2] or through a legal procedure known as naturalization.[3] Generally, in order to become a United States citizen through naturalization, an alien[4]

---

[1] U.S. Const. Amend XIV, § 1; 8 U.S.C. § 1401.
[2] 8 U.S.C. §§ 1401(c)-(g), 1409.
[3] 8 U.S.C. §§ 1421, 1427, 1431, 1432.
[4] "Alien" is a term used in the immigration field to describe ". . . any person not a citizen or national of the United States." 8 U.S.C. § 1101(a)(3).

must, among other things, already be a permanent resident of the United States.[5]

Citizens of the United States have the right to reside permanently and to engage in any lawful employment in the United States. They must pay United States income taxes. Only United States citizens have the right to vote.

United States citizenship can be renounced by a knowing and voluntary expatriating act.[6] Naturalized United States citizens can be denaturalized for certain offenses, including the concealment of a material fact or a willful misrepresentation in connection with a naturalization application or the establishment of a foreign residence within one year after naturalization.[7]

1.1.2 Permanent Resident of the United States

A permanent resident of the United States is an alien who has permission from the United States government to reside permanently in the United States.[8] A permanent resident of the United States has the right to engage in any lawful employment in the United States and the obligation to pay United States income taxes.

Some permanent residents are admitted to the United States on a conditional basis for a limited period of time and must comply with certain requirements in order to have the condition removed.[9]

A lawful permanent resident of the United States may lose his/her status in any of a number of ways. For example, if a lawful permanent resident remains outside of the United States for an extended period of time, the government may presume

---

[5] 8 U.S.C. § 1429. An exception to this general rule may be found in 8 U.S.C. § 1440(a) which authorizes the naturalization of a person who has served honorably in the U.S. Armed Forces in times of war or other declared hostilities and enlisted or was inducted within the U.S. or certain U.S. territories.

[6] 8 U.S.C. § 1481.

[7] 8 U.S.C. § 1451.

[8] 8 U.S.C. § 1101(a)(20).

[9] 8 U.S.C. §§ 1186a, 1186b.

that he/she intends to abandon or relinquish his/her lawful permanent residence status. A lawful permanent resident may also lose his/her status by engaging in certain types of criminal conduct in the United States.

A person who holds a "green card" (also known as an "alien registration receipt card") is a lawful permanent resident of the United States.[10]

1.1.3 Temporary Resident

This category includes persons who applied for legalization or amnesty under any of several programs offered by the United States government.[11] Temporary residents may ultimately become permanent residents of the United States. A temporary resident is entitled to reside in the United States for a limited amount of time and to work in the United States.

1.1.4 Asylee

An asylee is an individual who has been granted political asylum, but who has not yet become a permanent resident of the United States. Generally, an individual must have been an asylee for a one year period before he/she is eligible to become a permanent resident.[12]

1.1.5 Holder of Temporary Protected Status

Persons from certain countries designated by the Attorney General of the United States are permitted to reside and work in the United States for a limited amount of time.[13] Countries whose nationals are eligible for temporary protected status are selected by the Attorney General because of ongoing armed

---

[10] Interestingly, the "green card" has been issued by the U.S. government in a variety of colors over the course of history. The "green card" currently issued by the U.S. government is a combination of colors: pink, blue, and white.

[11] *See, e.g.,* 8 U.S.C. §§ 1161, 1255a.

[12] 8 U.S.C. § 1159.

[13] 8 U.S.C. § 1254a.

conflicts, natural disasters, or other extraordinary circumstances of a temporary nature extant in the country.[14]

1.1.6 Nonimmigrant

An alien who comes to the United States temporarily for a specific purpose is known as a nonimmigrant. Some of the more common reasons for nonimmigrants to come to the United States include: to study at a United States college or university; to work for a particular employer in a particular and usually specialized or high-level job; to travel for business or pleasure within the United States; to participate in international cultural exchange programs; or to work for certain international organizations.[15]

Nonimmigrants are entitled to reside in the United States for a limited amount of time and, in some circumstances, are allowed to work in the United States. Nonimmigrants can, in some circumstances, become permanent residents of the United States.

1.1.7 Illegal Aliens

This category encompasses anyone in the United States without the permission of the United States government. An illegal alien can be an alien who previously had lawful nonimmigrant status but has violated the terms or conditions of that status or has overstayed his/her period of authorized admission. An illegal alien also can be an individual who has entered the United States illegally, without the required entry documentation or on the basis of a misrepresentation.

1.2 Determining an Individual's Entitlement to Lawful Status in the United States

In general, in order to obtain lawful status in the United States, an alien must fall within one of the numerous categories of persons entitled to such a benefit. Many of these categories

---

[14] 8 U.S.C. § 1254a(b).
[15] 8 U.S.C. § 1184.

require some type of family or business connection to the United States, while others depend on the nationality of the alien and/or the conditions in his/her home country. Some categories are extremely backlogged and impose long waiting periods before visa issuance; other categories have no backlogs. Some categories are subject to overall limits on the number of individuals who can be admitted in the category per year and per country; other categories are not subject to any numerical limitation. Extreme caution should be exercised in choosing between the variety of alternatives which may be available to any particular alien desiring to come to the United States, as dire consequences can result from the failure to select the best alternative.

The focus of this chapter is employment-related visa options. Therefore, the discussion below will be limited to such options, and will exclude the variety of family-based and non-employment based immigration options which may be available to an alien. However, readers should be aware that these other options may be more attractive or viable in a particular case[16] and competent immigration counsel should be consulted prior to selecting any course of action.

2.0 OBTAINING PERMANENT RESIDENCE IN THE UNITED STATES THROUGH EMPLOYMENT

Current United States immigration law divides employment-based immigrants into the following five basic categories: priority workers, professionals holding advanced degrees or aliens of exceptional ability, other workers, special immigrants, and investors.[17]

---

[16] For example, an unskilled worker will generally become a permanent resident faster as the beneficiary of a family-sponsored immigrant visa petition than as the beneficiary of an employer-sponsored visa petition.

[17] 8 U.S.C. § 1153(b).

2.1 Priority Workers

This category includes aliens of extraordinary ability in the arts, sciences, education, business or athletics; outstanding professors and researchers; and certain multinational executives and managers.[18] Significantly, no labor certification (see discussion below) is required for priority workers. Given the relatively large number of visas available to priority workers, there is currently no backlog in this category and individuals who can meet the requirements of the priority worker category can expect to become lawful permanent residents in a relatively short period of time.

2.1.1 Aliens of Extraordinary Ability in the Arts, Sciences, Education, Business or Athletics[19]

Aliens of "extraordinary ability" are those who possess a level of expertise indicating that they have risen to the very top of their field of endeavor.[20] The Immigration and Naturalization Service requires an alien seeking this classification to show that he/she has received sustained national or international acclaim, which can be evidenced by the alien's recognition for a one-time achievement (such as receipt of the Nobel Prize) or by documentation of at least three of the following criteria:

1. The alien's receipt of nationally or internationally recognized prizes or awards for excellence in the field;
2. The alien's membership in associations in the alien's field of expertise which require outstanding achievements;
3. Published material about the alien in professional or major trade publications or other major media;
4. The alien's participation as a judge of other's work in the field;

---

[18] 8 U.S.C. § 1153(b)(1).
[19] 8 U.S.C. § 1153(b)(1)(A).
[20] 8 C.F.R. § 204.5(h)(2).

5. The alien's original contributions of major significance to the field;
6. The alien's authorship of scholarly articles in the field;
7. The display of the alien's work at artistic exhibitions;
8. The alien's performance of a leading or critical role for organizations or establishments with a distinguished reputation;
9. The alien's commercial success in the performing arts; or
10. The alien's ability to command a high salary in the field.[21]

Significantly, an alien seeking this classification does not need to have a job offer in the United States nor does he need a labor certification.[22]

2.1.2 Outstanding Professors and Researchers[23]

To qualify as an outstanding professor or researcher, an alien must (1) be internationally recognized as outstanding in a specific academic area; (2) have a minimum of three years of experience teaching or researching in that area; and (3) be entering the United States to work in (1) a tenured or tenure-track teaching position or a permanent research position at a university or other institution of higher education or (2) as a permanent researcher with a private employer who already employs three full-time researchers and has documented accomplishments in the field.[24]

In order to establish that the alien is internationally recognized as outstanding, evidence showing at least two of the following must be submitted:

---

[21] 8 C.F.R. § 204.5(h)(3).
[22] 8 C.F.R. § 204.5(h)(5).
[23] 8 U.S.C. § 1153(b)(1)(B).
[24] 8 C.F.R. § 204.5(i).

1. The alien's receipt of major prizes or awards for outstanding achievement in the academic field;
2. The alien's membership in associations in the academic field which require outstanding achievements of their members;
3. Published material in professional publications written by others about the alien's work in the academic field;
4. The alien's participation as the judge of the work of others in the field;
5. The alien's original scientific or scholarly research contributions in the field;
6. The alien's authorship of scholarly books or articles, in scholarly journals with international circulation, in the academic field.[25]

2.1.3 Multinational Executives or Managers[26]

This category is available to aliens who have been employed outside the United States in a managerial or executive capacity for at least one of the three years preceding the filing of the visa petition (or in the case of an alien presently in the United States as a nonimmigrant, one of the three years preceding entry into the United States). These aliens must have been employed by the same firm, corporation, or other entity, or its affiliate or subsidiary, which seeks to employ the alien in the United States.[27] The United States employer must have been doing business for at least one year before the visa petition is filed and must seek to employ the alien in a managerial or executive capacity in the United States.[28]

In order to be classified as a managerial employee, an employee must, among other things, primarily manage the organization, or a department, subdivision, function, or component of the organization. In order to be classified as an

---

[25] 8 C.F.R. § 204.5(i)(3).
[26] 8 U.S.C. § 1153(b)(1)(C).
[27] 8 C.F.R. § 204.5(j).
[28] 8 C.F.R. § 204.5(j)(3).

executive employee, an employee must: primarily direct the management of the organization or a major component or function of the organization; establish the goals and policies of the organization, component, or function; exercise wide latitude in discretionary decisionmaking; and receive only general supervision or direction from higher-level executives, the board of directors, or the stockholders of the organization.[29]

2.2 Professionals Holding Advanced Degrees or Aliens of Exceptional Ability[30]

As its name suggests, this category is available to members of the professions who have advanced degrees (meaning something more than a bachelor's degree) and to workers of exceptional ability (meaning workers whose employment will "prospectively substantially benefit the United States"). In general, a labor certification (see discussion below) is required for this category, although the requirement can be waived in cases where such a waiver is deemed by the Attorney General to be in the national interest.[31]

2.2.1 Professionals Holding Advanced Degrees[32]

In order to fall within this classification, an alien must possess an advanced degree and must, in most cases, have a job offer from a United States employer for a position which requires such a degree. In some cases, a bachelor's degree plus five years of experience can be substituted for an advanced degree.[33]

---

[29] 8 C.F.R. § 204.5(j)(2).
[30] 8 U.S.C. § 1153(b)(2).
[31] 8 U.S.C. § 1153(b)(2)(B).
[32] 8 U.S.C. § 1153(b)(2).
[33] 8 C.F.R. § 204.5(k).

2.2.2 Aliens of Exceptional Ability in the Sciences, Arts, and Business[34]

In order to demonstrate exceptional ability, an alien must submit at least three of the following types of documentation:

1. An official academic record showing that the alien has a degree, diploma, certificate, or similar award from an institution of learning relating to the area of exceptional ability;
2. Letters from current or former employers showing that the alien has at least 10 years of full-time experience in the occupation for which he/she is being sought;
3. A license to practice the profession or certification for a particular profession or occupation;
4. Evidence that the alien has commanded a salary or other remuneration for services which demonstrates exceptional ability;
5. Evidence of membership in professional associations;
6. Evidence of recognition for achievements and significant contributions to the industry or field by peers, government entities, or professional or business organizations; or
7. Other comparable evidence.[35]

Generally, an alien seeking classification under this category must have a job offer.[36]

2.3 Other Workers[37]

This category includes professional employees with bachelor's degrees, skilled workers with two years of train-

---

[34] 8 U.S.C. § 1153(b)(2).
[35] 8 C.F.R. § 204.5(k)(3)(ii).
[36] 8 C.F.R. § 204.5(k)(4).
[37] 8 U.S.C. § 1153(b)(3).

ing/experience, and certain unskilled workers. A labor certification is required for this category.[38]

2.3.1 Professional Employees with Bachelor's Degrees[39]

In order to qualify for this classification, an alien must possess a bachelor's degree and such a degree must be the normal requirement for entry into the occupation in which the alien is to be employed in the United States.[40] A job offer is required for this classification.[41]

2.3.2 Skilled Workers[42]

Skilled workers are aliens coming to the United States to fill positions which require a minimum of two years of training or experience. *A job offer is required for this classification.

2.3.3 Unskilled Workers[43]

Unskilled workers are aliens coming to the United States to fill positions which require less than two years of training or experience. Only 10,000 visas per year are available to unskilled workers and thus, the current backlog of persons waiting for such visas is quite large and the wait for such a visa is estimated to be in the five- to ten-year range. A job offer is required for this classification.

2.4 Special Immigrants[44]

This category covers several miscellaneous types of immigrants, including ministers and religious workers.

---

[38] 8 U.S.C. § 1153(b)(3)(C).
[39] 8 C.F.R. § 204.5(l).
[40] 8 C.F.R. § 204.5(l)(3)(ii)(C).
[41] 8 C.F.R. § 204.5(l)(3)(i).
[42] 8 C.F.R. § 204.5(l).
[43] 8 C.F.R. § 204.5(l).
[44] 8 U.S.C. § 1153(b)(4); 8 C.F.R. § 204.5(m).

2.5 Investors[45]

This category permits individuals with at least one million dollars to invest in a new commercial enterprise in the United States to obtain permanent resident status. The enterprise in which the investment is made must employ a minimum of ten United States workers on a full-time basis. To qualify, the new commercial enterprise must be: (1) established by the alien; (2) one in which the alien has invested, or is in the process of investing, at least one million dollars (or at least $500,000 if the business is in a rural or high unemployment area); and (3) one which will benefit the United States economy and create full-time employment for no fewer than ten United States workers (not including the immigrant or his immediate family).

An immigrant investor is initially granted conditional permanent resident status for a period of two years. At the end of the two-year period, the United States government may terminate the investor's permanent resident status if it is found that the investor failed to establish the business, did not make the required investment, failed to employ the requisite number of employees, or failed in any other way to meet the requirements of the law.

3.0 SATISFYING THE LABOR CERTIFICATION REQUIREMENT

The purpose of the labor certification requirement is to balance the need to protect the United States labor market from competition from foreign workers with the legitimate interest of United States employers in hiring foreign workers with skills which are not available in the domestic workforce. Labor certification, also sometimes called alien labor certification, is the process by which the Department of Labor tests the labor market to determine whether U.S. workers are available for a particular job. By issuing a labor certification, the Department

---

[45] 8 U.S.C. § 1153(b)(5); 8 C.F.R. § 204.6.

of Labor certifies that U.S. workers are unavailable for the position and that the employer is paying the prevailing wage.[46]

The process for obtaining a labor certification is quite complex and is subject to a myriad of federal regulations. Consequently, the intricacies of the process are beyond the scope of this chapter. A basic outline of the general labor certification process follows.

In general, the first step in connection with any immigrant visa application which requires a labor certification is for the sponsoring employer to file an application with the Job Service Office in the state in which the alien is to be employed. The Job Service Office, in cooperation with the employer, tests the job market by attempting to recruit U.S. workers for the available position. The Job Service Office prepares a job order which is processed through the state recruiting system. The employer also generally posts a notice about the position and advertises the position in an appropriate publication.

The employer is required to evaluate all applicants for the position and may only reject U.S. workers for lawful job-related reasons. Potentially qualified applicants generally must be interviewed by the employer.

At the end of the recruitment period, the employer must submit a written report of the recruitment efforts, which identifies, among other things, the name and address of each applicant and the lawful job-related reasons for rejecting the applicant, assuming no qualified U.S. worker was found.

The Job Service Office will then transmit all relevant documentation to the regional Department of Labor office having jurisdiction over the place of employment. The Regional Certifying Officer then makes a determination as to whether to grant or deny labor certification, basing his/her decision on whether there is an available and qualified U.S. worker and whether the employment of the alien will have an adverse effect on the wages or working conditions of U.S. workers. The Certifying Officer also reviews the employer's recruitment

---

[46] The basic filing instructions for applications for labor certification may be found at 20 C.F.R. §§ 656.20 and 656.21a.

efforts to determine whether more or different efforts should have been made to recruit U.S. workers.

If the labor certification is granted, the employer can proceed with its planned immigrant visa application. If, however, the labor certification is denied, the employer may appeal this denial; unless the appeal is successful, no immigrant visa petition which requires a labor certification can be filed.

4.0 OBTAINING TEMPORARY VISAS FOR WORK IN THE UNITED STATES

Many United States employers employ foreign workers to work on particular projects or matters on a temporary basis. The ability to bring foreign workers to the United States for training, special projects, exchange of information and technology, and cultural exchange is vitally important to the United States' economic and business development.

A variety of nonimmigrant visas are available to business travelers under current law.[47] The nonimmigrant visas which are most commonly used for business travel and temporary work assignments in the United States are as follows:

4.1 B-1 Business Visitor Visa[48]

B-1 visas are reserved for aliens regularly employed outside the United States who must visit the United States for short periods of time (generally, less than six months) to conduct legitimate business activities. Examples of permissible activities include soliciting sales and negotiating contracts for work to be performed outside the United States, purchasing goods produced in the United States, attending conferences or seminars, participating in litigation, consulting with business associates, or conducting market research. The alien may not engage in any ordinary or hands-on labor while in B-1 status. B-1 visa holders generally cannot be paid from United States sources and must maintain an unabandoned foreign residence. B-1 visa holders

---

[47] 8 U.S.C. § 1101(a)(15); 8 C.F.R. § 214.
[48] 8 U.S.C. § 1101(a)(15)(B); 8 C.F.R. § 214.2(b).

must intend to depart the United States at the end of their authorized stay.

4.2 L-1 Intracompany Transferee Visa[49]

This visa is available to an alien employee who, within the three years preceding his filing of an application to enter the United States, has served full-time for at least one year in a managerial, executive or specialized knowledge capacity with the entity seeking to employ him in the United States or with a subsidiary or affiliate of that entity.

The maximum period of authorized admission on an L-1 visa for managers and executives is seven years. For aliens with "specialized knowledge," the maximum authorized period of admission is five years.

An alien having "specialized knowledge" is an alien who "has a special knowledge of the company product and its application in international markets or has an advanced level of knowledge of processes and procedures of the company." This definition permits the transfer of company employees having special expertise with respect to their employer's activities.

"Managerial" is interpreted to mean above "line" supervision; the manager, in effect, must supervise persons who, in turn, exercise some degree of supervision over others. "Functional managers"—those who manage a function or process rather than a person—are also eligible for L-1 visas. The number of employees supervised is no longer the exclusive criteria for determining managerial or executive capacity.

Dependents of L-1 visa holders are eligible for L-2 visas. Dependents cannot work in the United States in this status.

4.3 E-1 and E-2 Treaty Visas[50]

The E-visa category is particularly useful for business personnel seeking entry into the United States for extended periods of time to fulfill an essential role or provide essential

---

[49] 8 U.S.C. § 1101(a)(15)(L); 8 C.F.R. § 214.2(l).
[50] 8 U.S.C. § 1101(a)(15)(E); 8 C.F.R. § 214.2(e).

skills to an enterprise that engages in substantial trade between the United States and a foreign country or that represents a major foreign investment in the United States. To obtain an E visa, an alien must prove that:

1. A treaty exists between the United States and a particular foreign country;
2. Majority (now interpreted to be 50 percent) ownership of the investing or trading company is held by nationals of that foreign country; and
3. The alien seeking entry into the United States is a national of that foreign country.

If any of these elements is missing, the alien and his employer should consider using an H-1B or L-1 visa instead. The alien must also submit evidence that upon his/her entry into the United States he/she will assume a position in management or one involving essential technical skills.

The E-visa category has two separate classifications: E-1 Treaty Trader visas and E-2 Treaty Investor visas. To obtain an E-1 Treaty Trader visa, an alien must prove that his employer is engaged in trade of goods principally between the United States and the alien's own treaty country. Trade in services or technology also suffices to meet the requirements for an E-1 visa. Once it is established that the company is engaged in trade, it must be shown that the trade is "substantial." No set minimum dollar value is used in determining whether trade is substantial. Rather, trade is measured by volume, the number of transactions and whether it is of a continuing nature. Generally, in situations where the volume of trade is low, the number of transactions is large and the history demonstrates a continued course of trade, the chances of qualifying for treaty trader status are increased.

Similarly, to qualify for treaty investor status, the investment must be active and substantial. Whether the investment is "substantial" is to be determined by the Secretary of State after consultation with other appropriate government agencies. Although investments of as little as $20,000 have been deemed sufficient, as a rule of thumb, U.S. consulates usually require an investment of approximately $100,000 to $300,000 depending on the nature of the enterprise in which the investment is made. In general, the substantiality of an investment depends on the nature of the enterprise. Thus, a larger investment would be required for a manufacturing company than for a sales organization.

E-1 and E-2 visas differ from other categories because applicants are processed directly by the State Department's consular officers, not by the INS. E visas can be valid for up to five years and provide for multiple entries into the United States. Some U.S. consulates issue these visas for shorter periods. At the end of each five-year or other valid period, an alien may apply to renew his visa for an additional five years. This ability to renew an E visa indefinitely is a tremendous advantage over other visa categories.

Dependents of the E-visa holders receive the same visa status as the principal alien, i.e., E-1 Treaty Trader or E-2 Treaty Investor.

4.4 H-1B Temporary Worker Visa for Aliens Employed in Specialty Occupations[51]

H-1B visas are well-suited for alien workers who are recent university graduates or professionals who have not yet worked for an overseas affiliate of the employer. Employers seeking H-1B visas for alien employees must prove that the occupation in which they seek to employ the alien employee requires highly specialized knowledge and attainment of a Bachelor's Degree, or its equivalent, as a minimum for entry into the occupation in the United States. No more than 65,000 H-1B visas may be issued in any year.

The Immigration Act of 1990 requires employers who want to hire H-1B workers to file an application with the Secretary of Labor documenting, among other things, that the employer will pay the alien employee at least the greater of the actual wage level at the place of employment, or the prevailing wage for the occupational classification in which the alien is to be

---

[51] 8 U.S.C. § 1101(a)(15)(H)(i); 8 C.F.R. § 214.2(h).

employed in the area of employment; that it will offer working conditions to the alien employee which will not adversely affect the working conditions of other employees; and that there is no strike or lockout at the place of employment. Employers also are to give notice of the filing of an application to employ a temporary worker to the employees' bargaining representative, or to post a notice at the place of employment if there is no bargaining representative.

The Secretary of Labor is authorized to receive, investigate, and adjudicate complaints brought by any aggrieved person or organization (including bargaining representatives) concerning an employer's alleged misrepresentation in such an application. If such a misrepresentation has occurred, an employer may be subject to substantial penalties, including a civil monetary penalty of $1,000 per violation and the denial, for at least a period of one year, of its petitions to employ temporary workers.

H-1B visas are issued for a maximum period of six years. Both the employer and the alien must affirm that the alien plans to stay in the United States only for the duration of the H-1B visa. The alien is expected to return to his home country after his visa expires. Frequently, however, H-1B visa holders convert to permanent resident status before their visas expire. They may do so either based on a family-sponsored petition (e.g., marriage to a U.S. citizen) or a petition by the employer.

Family members of H-1B visa holders receive H-4 visa status. They are not authorized to work in the United States under this status.

4.5 H-3 Temporary Trainee Visa[52]

A company with an established, well-defined training program may bring alien trainees to the United States under H-3 visas. The training program must provide classroom training or a mixture of classroom and practical training which is not available in the alien's home country. It must also prepare the alien to fill a position outside of the United States. The INS will

---

[52] 8 U.S.C. § 1101(a)(15)(H)(iii); 8 C.F.R. § 214.2(h).

not approve an H-3 visa if it believes that the alien is in fact training to fill a position in the United States or engages in productive employment that displaces an American worker. The INS generally restricts H-3 visas to a maximum period of eighteen months.

Dependents of H-3 visa holders may enter the United States with an H-4 visa (the same category used for dependents of H-1B visa holders). They may not work in this status.

4.6 J-1 Exchange Visitor Visa[53]

Although the majority of J-1 Exchange Visitor visa holders are engaged in academic or cultural exchanges, the J-1 visa category offers some benefits to certain narrow classes of business trainees. An exchange visitor program for industrial or business trainees must offer the alien opportunities for observation and practical experience in American business methods and technology. Only organizations approved by the United States Information Agency ("USIA") may sponsor such exchange programs. If an employer does not want to establish a full-fledged program of its own, it may seek to bring J-1 visa holders to the United States under an "umbrella organization."

J-1 visas are valid for the duration of the program, with industrial and business training programs being limited to 18 months. Before proceeding with a J-1 visa petition, however, the alien and his sponsor must ascertain whether the alien will be subject to a two-year foreign residence requirement after acquiring the J-1 visa. Any J-1 exchange visitor subject to this requirement is prohibited from obtaining an H or L visa or permanent resident status until he spends at least two years in his home country after completion of the J-1 program. Waivers are available in some situations.

Dependents of J-1 visa holders may enter the United States on J-2 visas. They are authorized to work only if the INS approves their request for work authorization on grounds of economic necessity.

---

[53] 8 U.S.C. § 1101(a)(15)(J); 8 C.F.R. § 214.2(j).

4.7 O Visa for Aliens of Extraordinary Ability[54]

The Immigration Act of 1990 created a new visa category for aliens of extraordinary ability in the sciences, arts, education, business, and athletics who can demonstrate sustained national or international acclaim and whose entry will substantially benefit the United States. The O category is important under the statutory scheme set up by the Immigration Act of 1990, particularly in view of the 65,000 cap on H-1B visas. In some circumstances, it may be desirable to attempt to classify individuals as O visa holders rather than H-1B visa holders since O visa holders are not limited by an annual numerical cap.

4.8 Q Visas for Participants in International Cultural Exchange Programs[55]

Under the Immigration Act of 1990, a new Q classification was created for aliens coming to the U.S. temporarily (up to a maximum of 15 months) to participate in an international cultural exchange program. The Q alien must maintain a foreign residence and must be paid comparably to U.S. workers.

5.0 THE IMPACT OF THE IMMIGRATION REFORM AND CONTROL ACT OF 1986 ON EMPLOYERS IN THE UNITED STATES

When Congress enacted the Immigration Reform and Control Act of 1986 (IRCA)[56], it drastically changed the obligations of employers with respect to the hiring of new employees. For the first time, employers were required to verify the identity and eligibility for employment of all new hires. Despite repeated calls for repeal of IRCA, the law remains in force today and continues to confound employers and employees alike.

Since April 1991, when the U.S. Immigration and Naturalization Service (INS) announced its intention to step up

---

[54] 8 U.S.C. § 1101(a)(15)(O); 8 C.F.R. § 214.2(o).
[55] 8 U.S.C. § 1101(a)(15)(Q); 8 C.F.R. § 214.2(q).
[56] 8 U.S.C. §§ 1324a and 1324b.

its enforcement efforts, businesses across the country have been the targets of increasingly aggressive INS enforcement actions. As some violating employers have become painfully aware, IRCA subjects employers to investigations and to civil and criminal prosecution for violations of its hiring and paperwork provisions.

5.1 Verification Requirements[57]

IRCA makes it unlawful for an employer to knowingly hire a person who is not authorized to work in the United States. In order to determine which applicants for employment are authorized to work in the United States, IRCA requires employers to complete an employment authorization verification process and, in connection with this process, to complete a Form I-9 for each new hire.

On November 21, 1991, the INS issued a revised Form I-9. On the same date, a revised version of the *Employer Handbook*—the official government publication that provides instructions to employers on how to complete the I-9 Form—also was issued by the INS.

The revised I-9 Form contains three sections: Section One, to be completed by the employee at the time of his/her hire. Section Two, to be completed by the employer within three business days of the date of hire; and Section Three, to be used when it is necessary to update or reverify the employment eligibility of an employee.

Although Section One must be completed by the employee at the time of hire, the employee has three business days from the date of his/her hire to provide the employer with the documentation of identity and work authorization that the employer needs to complete Section Two of the form. If an employee, within three business days of the date of hire, produces a receipt showing that he/she has applied for a work authorization or identity document, the employee may be given 90 days to produce the required documentation.

---

[57] 8 U.S.C. § 1324a; 8 C.F.R. § 274a.

Unlike the former version of the Form I-9, the revised version contains a space to fill in the employee's date of hire. The inclusion of this information on the Form I-9 is designed to make it much easier for the INS to determine whether the employer completed Section Two within three days of the employee's date of hire and to penalize employers who fail to complete Section Two in a timely fashion.

5.2 Employer Penalties[58]

Employers that violate IRCA face potentially staggering monetary penalties. Penalties for knowingly hiring or continuing to employ an alien who is not authorized to work in the United States range from $250 to $2,000 for each unauthorized alien in a first enforcement proceeding against an employer. If an employer is caught a second time, the penalties range from $2,000 to $5,000 per alien; for three-time violators, the penalties range from $3,000 to $10,000 per alien. Paperwork violations can cost an employer anywhere from $100 to $1,000 for each incomplete or missing I-9 Form.

Recent changes to the immigration laws have added new penalties for those who use, accept, or create fraudulent immigration documents.[59] A single violation can result in fines ranging from $250 to $2,000 for each fraudulent document. Subsequent violations can result in fines of up to $5,000 per document. If an employer is found to have engaged in a pattern or practice of hiring or continuing to employ unauthorized aliens, criminal penalties of up to six months in jail and/or fines up to a maximum of $3,000 per alien can be imposed.

5.3 Discrimination Issues[60]

IRCA also prohibits discrimination on the basis of national origin and citizenship status. Many employers, fearful of the heavy penalties that can result from IRCA violations, have

---

[58] 8 U.S.C. § 1324a(e)(4); 8 C.F.R. § 274a.10.
[59] 8 U.S.C. § 1324c
[60] 8 U.S.C. § 1324b.

unintentionally violated IRCA's anti-discrimination provisions by requiring excessive documentation at the time of hire or by attempting to verify the employment eligibility of employees before hire. Employers also have been found to have violated the anti-discrimination provisions by requiring that only some employees (usually foreign-looking or foreign-sounding employees) complete the Form I-9.

It is imperative that an I-9 Form be completed for every employee in a *timely* fashion. Employers must accept any employment eligibility and identify documents that are sufficient to establish identity or work eligibility under the law and that appear to be genuine and to relate to the employee in question. If the documents presented by an employee appear to be forged or altered or do not appear to belong to the person who is presenting them, the employer is under an affirmative obligation to inquire further of the employee. However, the employer must be careful to balance its verification obligations against its duty to avoid discrimination, and should only require additional documentation where a genuine question about an employee's employment eligibility or identity exists.

Chapter 9
DEALING WITH PROBLEM EMPLOYEES

Michael F. Marino
Reed Smith & McClay

1.0 OVERVIEW

Tremendous time and resources are devoted by supervisors, managers, and human resource professionals to dealing with and responding to "problem employees." This generic classification can be used to describe a broad range of employees, from those who have ability but are unwilling to work, those who have a poor attitude, those who are simply incompetent, to those who have engaged in misconduct on or off the job. All such employees result in a tremendous financial burden on employers. The process of hiring, training, and integrating employees into the workforce is expensive and time consuming, yet obviously critical to successful operations. Therefore, when problems arise, they should be responded to quickly and consistently, with fairness and due process.

There is a tendency, however, for employers to procrastinate in responding to these types of issues, particularly if the employee does not respond well to criticism. It is not easy for most people to face confrontation over personnel related matters. In fact, it is often easier to overlook what appear to be minor problems in the hope they will disappear and not have to be confronted. Unfortunately, while employee-related issues can be neglected in the short term, if they are not addressed and resolved, they can become substantial problems resulting in adversarial proceedings and significant expense. Invariably, enormous amounts of time and energy are diverted from productive matters when lawsuits are filed.

With this background in mind, we will review various guidelines and legal issues that should be addressed when dealing with problem employees. Any employee relations program should focus on minimizing problems by responding to problems quickly.

2.0 SIGNS TO LOOK FOR

Regardless of the nature of the problem, most employees not performing at a level expected of them exhibit one or more of the following warning signs:

1. Poor Communication or Interpersonal Skills
2. Poor Attitude
3. Frequent Lateness or Absenteeism
4. Lack of Effort
5. Incompetency

Any demonstration of these characteristics can result in poor performance. These warning signs must be heeded and responsive action taken. It is also important to determine whether personality, drugs or alcohol, family problems, or simply inability is the origin of the problem.

Prior to confronting employees, it is also necessary to review existing policies and practices at the organization. Are there written policies addressing work-related performance? If so, they must be identified and may affect the method of handling the issues raised. If there are no written policies, what has been the practice for handling similarly situated individuals? An essential ingredient in handling these issues is to ensure consistency and uniformity in how problems are addressed. Failing to do so can lead to charges of disparate treatment and result in even more problems. Therefore, before adverse employment action is taken, it is important to review company policies and procedures on hours, absenteeism, scheduling hours of work, lateness, or work-related problems. If such policies exist, they provide a framework to use in addressing the deficiencies in performance with the employee.[1]

The personnel records of such employees also need to be reviewed carefully. Frequently, so called "problem employees" have employee evaluations that make them look like superstar performers. Whether from "halo grading," where one good attribute results in all performance characteristics being marked well, or simply a reluctance by supervisors to confront the situation, it is important to first review carefully the company's policies and practices and the employee's personnel file to determine whether any previous issues have arisen and how this employee would be perceived to the outside world. Supervisors must also understand that documentation is critical in dealing with problem employees.

3.0 REAFFIRMING YOUR "AT WILL" STATUS

The first line of defense of employers in dealing with problem employees is a legal one—preserving the status of "employment at will." While this doctrine has been eroded by statutory protections and various public policy limitations, in virtually all jurisdictions employees are still employed "at will." Accordingly, they may leave employment at anytime and they may be terminated without cause, assuming no other statutory protections or public policy concerns have been violated.[2]

---

[1] If they do not exist, this is a first step that needs to be taken. In order to deal effectively with employee-related issues, there should be written policies and procedures that describe the company's expectations of employees. The lack of such policies leaves the employer vulnerable to attack because of the lack of understanding of what is expected of employees and inconsistent treatment by supervisors in the application of discipline to employees.

[2] Employees are protected under a host of federal laws including, *inter alia*, Title VII of the Civil Rights Act, which prohibits discrimination on the basis of race, color, religion, sex, and national origin; age discrimination; and retaliation provisions of the Fair Labor Standards Act, Occupational Safety and Health Act and ERISA. Employees also try to circumvent their at will status by alleging "contract" or "tort" violations which vary from

Employers can preserve the at will defense by ensuring that applications, offer letters, and policies and procedures all expressly reserve the right to employment at will. Despite the potential for adverse perceptions when maintaining the at will status, raising concerns about job security and due process, this is a legal weapon that is needed by the employer to combat many of the problem employee areas. While lateness or absenteeism are objective violations that can be documented and dealt with, many of the other problem areas are more subjective, and it is important to be able to terminate without cause "for convenience of the employer." In nearly all jurisdictions, this can only be accomplished if the at will doctrine has been **expressly** reaffirmed by stating that an employee may be terminated at anytime with or without cause.[3] With this legal tool in place, employers can assess the employee relations aspects of the issues involved and deal with them appropriately.

4.0 MINIMIZE PROBLEM EMPLOYEES: CAREFULLY SCREEN CANDIDATES THROUGH APPLICATIONS AND INTERVIEWS

No one wants to hire a problem employee. There are many ways that an employer can minimize or at least reduce the likelihood of problems. It is important, therefore, to screen applicants carefully, during the application and interview process.

---

state to state. Regardless of these limitations, employers can substantially protect their right to employment at will by ensuring the doctrine is expressly reaffirmed in their policies and procedures. Specific issues need to be reviewed with your legal counsel.

[3] It is important that such a statement appear on the application, in offer letters and in employee handbooks or personnel policies or procedures to ensure there is no misunderstanding. Employers should also have tear off receipts for the handbooks where employees acknowledge they have read and understand the policies of the company including their status as at will.

4.1 Arrest and Conviction Inquiries

While there are restrictions on such inquiries, employers should determine any prior convictions of applicants. Generally, an applicant's criminal record can be considered only to the extent that an individual's felony and misdemeanor convictions relate to the applicant's suitability for the specific position in question, such as a security position, child-care position, or educational position. Generally, an applicant cannot be asked about any arrests or criminal charges which did not result in conviction or were expunged.[4]

In addition to specific state statutes which may prohibit the consideration of arrests and other pre-conviction criminal charges, employment application questions regarding applicant arrest records or refusal to hire applicants based on their arrest records will generally be held to violate Title VII of the Civil Rights Act of 1964 in view of such policy's potential adverse racial impact and perceived lack of job relatedness.[5]

The EEOC has consistently taken the position that requesting such information may also discourage minority applicants. Therefore, avoiding any such questions on an application or in an interview is advisable. On the other hand, it is appropriate for an employer who learns of a prior arrest to attempt to determine the background and facts involved and whether there would be an effect on the applicant's ability to perform the functions of the position.

Furthermore, while a blanket prohibition against hiring persons with criminal convictions would also violate Title VII,[6] employers may inquire about convictions and may refuse

---

[4] Several states have specific restrictions on an employer's right to inquire about arrest records (e.g., California, Connecticut, Massachusetts, Michigan, Ohio, Oregon, Rhode Island, Virginia, Maryland).

[5] *E.g., Gregory v. Litton Systems, Inc.*, 316 F.Supp. 401 (C.D. Cal. 1970); *aff'd*, 472 F.2d 631 (9th Cir. 1972); *Reynolds v. Sheet Metal Workers Local 102*, 498 F.Supp. 952, 955 (D.D.C. 1980), *aff'd*, 702 F.2d 221 (D.C. Cir. 1981).

[6] *E.g., Green v. Missouri Pacific Railroad Co.*, 523 F.2d 1290 (8th Cir. 1975).

employment based on an individual's criminal conviction. The nature and gravity of the offense, the length of time since the conviction, and the relationship of the conviction to the job in question are all factors to be reviewed. This is an area of inquiry that is legitimate and important.[7] Where a job involves a demonstrable economic or human risk, an employer may legally refuse employment because of an applicant's conviction for a job-related serious crime.[8]

When information is requested regarding convictions from applicants, the EEOC recommends that the following caveat appear on your application forms:

> **Note:** A conviction does not automatically mean you cannot be employed. Factors such as your age at the time of conviction, how long ago it occurred, what you did and the rehabilitation you received will be considered, and we hope you will provide us with such information.

When conducting a criminal record check, remember these points:

a. Do not rely on a telephone check—get a certified copy of any conviction.
b. Check every jurisdiction where the applicant has resided, worked or attended school.
c. Consider using a professional to search police or court records; a mistake could be costly and wrongly identifying someone as have committed a crime can result in a defamation action.

---

[7] *E.g., Richardson v. Hotel Corporation of America*, 332 F.Supp. 519 (E.D. La. 1971), *aff'd*, 468 F.2d 951 (5th Cir. 1972) (hotel could lawfully refuse to employ a black bellman with previous conviction for theft and receiving stolen goods where bellman routinely had access to guests' luggage and guests' rooms in the course of his duties).

[8] *See EEOC v. Caroline Freight Carriers Corp.*, 723 F.Supp. 734 (S.D. Fla. 1989).

d. If the applicant has a conviction, discuss it with him or her. Perhaps the record has been expunged.
   e. Check state laws—some states prohibit such inquiries.

4.2 Reference Checks

A prior employer's recommendation is still one of the best means of discovering information about an individual's ability to perform, despite the fact many employers are reluctant to provide information, fearing exposure to defamation or invasion of privacy suits.

To eliminate exposure to liability when contacting previous employers, keep two concepts in mind which will generally protect employers in disputes concerning employee privacy. First, **consent**—on your employment application, have the applicant provide written consent to having his current and former employers contacted. Second, follow the **need to know** concept—what do you actually need to know that is job related, and who needs to know it. Confine questions to areas pertaining to the applicant's employment relationships; do not ask questions pertaining to the applicant's private life which could result in the forfeiture of an employer's qualified privilege. Furthermore, document the information requested and obtained from each source. Once a reference is obtained, make it available only to individuals who are participating in the selection process. More widespread distribution of information, which could be defamatory, could constitute a "publication" which also may result in loss of an employer's qualified privilege.

4.3 Credit Checks

Two types of credit reports are covered:

4.3.1 Consumer Reports

Any oral or written communication bearing on an individual's creditworthiness, credit standing, character, general reputation, personal characteristics or mode of living.

4.3.2 Investigative Consumer Reports (ICR)

A subdivision of the consumer report derived from personal interviews with friends, neighbors or associates. The definition is broad enough to encompass a typical employment reference check.

The federal Fair Credit Reporting Act,[9] as well as laws in several states, require that employers using "investigative reports" from "consumer reporting agencies" comply with the following disclosure requirements:

(1) An employer who denies a job to an applicant either **wholly** or **partly** because of information contained in a **consumer report** has to notify the applicant of that fact, as well as the name and address of the reporting agency that supplied the report.

(2) Employers using **ICRs** for any employment purpose (hiring, promotion, etc.) must disclose that:
   (a) such a report may be made within three days from the time the report is requested and that it will include information on character, general reputation, personal characteristics and mode of living; and
   (b) upon written request, additional information concerning the nature and scope of the investigation will be provided; this information must be provided within five

---

[9] 15 U.S.C. § 1681 (1976).

days after receiving the individual's request for such information.

(3) The employer is not required to disclose the contents of the investigative report, but only the fact that one was requested and the type of information sought. In addition, pre-notification is not required for employment purposes for which the individual has not specifically applied.[10]

Many states also impose restrictions on the consumer reporting agency with respect to the collection and dissemination of credit information for employment purposes.[11]

4.4 Polygraph Testing

In 1988, Congress enacted the Employee Polygraph Protection Act.[12] The Polygraph Act prohibits most private employers from requiring, requesting, suggesting or causing any employee or applicant to take or submit to a lie detector test. Certain

---

[10] Employers who fail to comply with the foregoing may be subject to the following penalties:
   a. Willful noncompliance may result in actual damages, punitive damages, costs and attorneys' fees.
   b. Negligent noncompliance may result in actual damages and attorneys' fees.
   c. Criminal penalties, including a fine of up to $5,000, are available for willfully obtaining information under false pretenses.
   d. Recently, the Federal Trade Commission reached agreements with four major corporations, McDonnell-Douglas, Macy's of New York, Keystone Carbon Co., and the Kobacker Co., regarding their failure to notify unsuccessful applicants that credit information was a factor in denial of employment. McDonnell-Douglas claimed unfamiliarity with the FCRA. As part of the settlement, all agreed to write rejected applicants, listing the credit bureaus that supplied reports.

[11] See, e.g, Md. Code, Commercial Law, § 14-1210.

[12] (Polygraph Act), 29 U.S.C. § 2001 to 2009 (1090), became law.

positions involving government employees, national security and defense, FBI contractors, providers of security services and those with access to controlled substances are exempted.[13]

Additionally, limited polygraph examinations, with very specific procedures, are allowed for "ongoing investigations" of employee misconduct with respect to controlled substances or economic loss or injury to an employer's business.[14]

Violations of the federal or state polygraph laws can result in the imposition of civil penalties and in some instances can constitute a criminal act.

4.5 Psychological Tests

Psychological tests used by employers range from aptitude tests involving simulated "work-sample" problems to complex exams designed to determine a job applicant's primary character and personality traits. The most commonly used tests in the employment contact are personality inventories and integrated assessment programs.

The EEOC's Uniform Guidelines on Employee Selection Procedures cover any employment procedure that has a disproportionate impact on minorities or women. If a test is shown to have an adverse impact, the employer must produce "empirical data demonstrating that the selection procedure is predictive of or significantly correlated with important elements of job performance."[15] Under the guidelines, employers may be required to compile complex data showing "content validity," "construct validity," "criterion-related validity," or "job-relatedness" to prove that the test does not disproportionately screen out minorities and women.

Some courts have held that psychological testing is justified where public safety outweighs the individual's right to privacy. Psychological testing used to screen out unstable or disturbed applicants from jobs in which they would pose a significant

---

[13] 29 U.S.C. § 2006.
[14] 29 U.S.C. § 2006(F)(2)(B).
[15] 29 C.F.R. § 1607.5(B).

threat to public safety is reasonable and justifiable, these courts have concluded.

4.6 Honesty Tests

Written honesty tests are psychological tests designed to determine the integrity of people who take them. Most honesty tests are designed to measure attitudes toward theft.

Honesty tests usually comprise true-false, yes-no, or multiple choice questions, and they take about one hour to complete. The tests contain questions designed to measure applicants' willingness to steal and whether they condone or rationalize dishonest behavior. Other questions are designed to determine whether applicants are lying in an attempt to "outsmart" the test. Still others are merely filler questions that are not scored. Only the test manufacturers know which questions are which and how they are weighted. The tests usually are scored by computer, and some companies can score tests before the job applicant leaves. Applicants are categorized as high-risk, medium-risk, or low-risk, depending on their scores.

An argument can be made that each interview-type question on these tests is subject to challenge for its disparate impact on minorities and on the basis that it is not job-related. Individual questions also could be challenged on privacy grounds by job applicants, especially those seeking public-sector jobs.

Thoughtful consideration should be given to any decision involving honesty testing. In food service and retail operations, such tests are particularly popular and may be of some value, considering the enormous losses suffered by business as a result of employee theft. Nevertheless, the validity of such tests should be weighed carefully along with other information regarding an employee's background before a final employment decision is made.

4.7 Prior Military Service

For reasons similar to the discussion regarding arrests, employers should not reject applicants simply because they receive less than honorable discharges.[16] Since merely posing questions regarding discharge may deter minority applicants, the employer is best served to avoid an inquiry on the type of discharge unless "business necessity" requires it. In the event such information is solicited, a qualifying statement similar to that of information regarding convictions should be provided. It is useful, and important, to determine what type of skills and expertise an applicant may have developed through military service, and questions on this type of information are permissible. Military service can be evidence of established job related skills and should not be over looked.

4.8 Driving Records

In specific situations, an employer may be interested in an applicant's driving record. Because of concerns with the Americans With Disabilities Act, the Rehabilitation Act of 1973 and state disability laws, the employer should solicit only such information when driving is an essential function of the job. If it is an essential function of the job, the employer should also ensure that having a certain type of driving record is consistent with business necessity. In order to obtain the applicant's consent to review such information and avoid administrative headaches, the employer should require that driving applicants must provide a copy of their driving record from the DMV if driving is an essential element of the position being filled.

In some states, an individual's driving record may be requested only when his or her job responsibilities will involve the operation of a motor vehicle.[17]

All of these inquiries are important to ensure the competency and background of applicants seeking employment.

---

[16] EEOC Decision No. 74-25 (1973).
[17] *See, e.g.,* Virginia Code § 46.1-31(6).

5.0 TOOLS FOR THE EMPLOYER TO UTILIZE DURING EMPLOYMENT IN DEALING WITH PROBLEM EMPLOYEES

The most important means of dealing with problem employees is through first-line supervision. The individuals who work with the employee every day need to have the responsibility and accountability for ensuring problem employees are dealt with. Accomplishing this requires providing training and education to supervisors, and ensuring that they know who they should seek assistance from in the human resources department.

Critical to this effort is the proper use of disciplinary procedures. All employers should have a basic system that identifies what is expected of employees with respect to performance. Employees need to be put on notice of these expectations. No system is effective, however, unless the supervisors are held accountable for addressing employee problems as they arise. This requires the use of verbal counseling and written warnings at the first sign of problems. Sometimes employees simply need to be verbally reminded as to what the rules are and that they will be expected to be able to act properly and in accordance with expectations.

For problem employees, more effort is needed, and therefore, documentation is important. Counseling sessions, letters of warning, or reprimands all need to be communicated to the employee with copies placed in the personnel file. All too often, supervisors maintain they did raise issues with employees but no record exists to demonstrate that counseling took place, and the issue becomes a credibility contest. There must be the "paper trail" which clearly shows that the employee acknowledged having received warning notices, even if the employee's view of the facts differs. The importance of proper documentation cannot be over emphasized.

Where serious allegations or incidents have arisen (such as allegations of sexual harassment or that drug or alcohol use is involved) a more formal investigation should take place. This requires the involvement of the human resources department or the use of outside professionals. Where allegations of wrongdoing or misconduct are involved, it is necessary to conduct an investigation to demonstrate that the company was responsive and made every effort to correct the situation—to minimize the potential of liability on the part of the company for not taking action in response to the wrongdoing of one of the employees.

6.0 INVESTIGATION OF THE FACTS

Establishment of the facts through proper investigations is the key to dealing with employees who may have engaged in misconduct. Obtaining all the facts, and not acting solely on appearances is crucial. If erratic, uncharacteristic behavior is the problem, a drug test may be in order.[18] With drug- and alcohol-related problems, many employers first refer employees with problems to employee assistance programs if the abuse has not yet resulted in a problem at work (or if the employee was not caught in a drug screen), and if the employee comes forward voluntarily. For employees who can make a contribution, and are willing to undergo rehabilitation, referrals to employee assistance programs and treatment programs can be a cost-effective way of retaining a good employee.[19]

On the other hand, an employee must be made aware that alcohol or drug abuse will not be tolerated and to enter a rehabilitation program requires a definite commitment to avoiding future problems. To ensure this is the case, a "last clear chance" agreement should be executed with the employee. By signing this agreement, the employee indicates a willingness to enter into a rehabilitation program and consents, in advance, to random drug testing and complete disclosure to the employer of the medical progress being made. Such agreements should be handled formally with the employee understanding fully their

---

[18] Drug testing programs need to be carefully considered as to what the employers objectives are. Most employers use applicant screening, "cause" or reasonable basis testing, i.e. if an accident occurs or behavior is unusual.

[19] Employees with drug-related problems also may have protection under the Americans with Disabilities Act, if they are now clean and are enrolled in a drug rehabilitation program.

significance, and that failure to follow the agreement will result in termination.

Regardless of what the nature of the problem, the key to success is immediately taking on the problem and dealing with it. Investigation, counseling, confrontation, documentation, discipline and discharge—these are all steps to be taken in response to any of the warning signs previously discussed.

7.0 SPECIAL TOOLS FOR MONITORING PROBLEM EMPLOYEES

7.1 Surveillance

Workplace surveillance has always been a means of quality control and theft prevention. Today employers monitor employees not only to improve efficiency and to remedy job safety, but to detect possible drug dealing or substance abuse and to protect business secrets.

There are two basic types of surveillance that may affect employees: (i) surveillance at work; and (ii) surveillance at an employee's home or other off-the-job locations.

7.1.1 Surveillance at Work

Surveillance at work occurs, not only as a way of detecting possible employee misconduct, but also as a means of monitoring manufacturing. The employer must ensure all employees are aware and on notice they are subject to being monitored in the manner contemplated. This reduces the "reasonable expectation of privacy," and also the employee's continued employment in view of such warnings constitutes implied consent. If phone calls are monitored, customers should also be put on notice.[20]

---

[20] It is important that every employer know about certain specific statutes that can affect the legality of employee electronic surveillance or phone call monitoring. The Federal Omnibus Crime Control and Safe Streets Act of 1968 makes it a crime to "intentionally intercept . . . any wire, oral or electronic communication." 12 U.S.C. § 2511(1)(a). This federal ban on intercepting "oral" communications is directed at "bugging," while the prohibition on intercepting wire or electronic communications is directed at "wiretapping." The law is intended as a comprehensive ban on wiretapping

It is important to note that the general restrictions of the federal wiretap law—and the exceptions—apply to interception of calls between an employee and a third party. It is not unlawful under federal law for one person to listen to or record telephone conversations of another person if at least one party to the conversation has consented to the interception.[21] Under federal law, an employer can tape-record telephone conversations to which it is a party as part of an investigation into employee misconduct.

State wiretapping statutes often are more restrictive than the Federal Omnibus Crime Control and Safe Streets Act. For example, while the Federal statute permits the tape-recording of telephone conversations so long as one party gives his or her consent,[22] some states prohibit any such tape-recording or require an intermittent "beep" to alert the parties the call is being taped.[23] State statutes must be reviewed carefully before any tape recording program is put into place.

Finally, some states also have laws which specifically limit an employer's right to engage in covert surveillance of employees, whether it involves electronic surveillance, a disguised "spotter" or "shopping investigators."

It is important that certain safeguards be kept in mind before monitoring or recording calls:

a. Inform all employees prior to implementation of the monitors.
b. Outline definitive monitoring procedures and inform the employee recording the activities to terminate interception regardless of the call's

---

and electronic surveillance by people other than law enforcement agents, with certain limited exceptions.

[21] *United States v. Boley*, 730 F.2d 1326 (8th Cir. 1984).

[22] 18 U.S.C. § 2511(2)(c).

[23] Both the federal and various state wiretapping statutes are riddled with complex exceptions and technicalities, so it would be a good idea to seek legal advice prior to embarking on a major program involving electronic monitoring or surveillance. *See, e.g.*, Va. Code §§ 19.2-61 *et seq.* (1990).

contents, within the briefest period of time necessary to identify the call as personal.
c. Specify the purpose for monitoring so as to establish guidelines for employee's unauthorized use of company phones.
d. Of course, the easiest solution would be to provide employees with a phone for personal calls in order to insulate them from monitoring and recording systems. *See* Barnett & Maker, "In the Ordinary Course of Business:" The Legal Limits of Workplace Wiretapping, 758, 759.

Electronic mail has become a popular means of communication for employees in recent years. Some employees assume that messages sent via electronic mail are confidential. In order to avoid problems related to the monitoring of electronic mail messages, employers should enact policies which specify that the communications are to be related solely to work and that employees are subject to monitoring by the employer. By doing so, the employer has placed the employee on notice that there is no expectation of privacy as to electronic mail communications.

As one additional note, surveillance or photographs of employees during the performance of their duties has been held not to be an unreasonable invasion of privacy if the photographs are taken as part of a work efficiency study.[24] However, do not "make an example" of an employee by using their photos. For example, if you want to prevent a proliferation of on-the-job accidents after one employee suffers a serious injury at work, do not set an example by distributing a picture of the injured individual's wound to all of his fellow employees. At least one

---

[24] *See Thomas v. General Electric Co.*, 207 F. Supp. 792, 799 (W.D. Ky. 1962). However, photographing employees as part of an advertising campaign, absent consent, may constitute an unreasonable invasion of privacy. *Caesar v. Chemical Bank*, 460 N.Y.S.2d 235 (1983), *affirmed*, 483 N.Y.S. 2d 16 (1st Dept. 1984), *appeal granted, question certified*, 489 N.Y.S.2d 854 (1st Dept. 1985).

court has held this type of "scare tactic" to constitute an invasion of the injured employee's privacy.[25]

7.1.2 Surveillance at Home

When would you ever want to engage in surveillance of an employee at home, and when would surveillance at home be permissible?

The most frequent context in which individuals are observed in their homes involves claimed disabilities—an employee claims that he is incapacitated by an injury which renders him unable to perform work and files a worker's compensation claim. The company's need for accurate information concerning disability stems either from (a) a desire to confirm that the employee's injury is in fact severe enough to render the employee eligible for workers' compensation, or (b) to establish the extent of the injury with a view towards requiring the employee to report to work.

Under state "trespassing" or "invasion of privacy" laws, the validity of an employer's attempts to engage in surveillance of an individual at home will be evaluated using the same balancing test that has already been mentioned. That is, does the employer's reasonable right to know outweigh the employee's reasonable expectation of privacy at home.

It is important to realize that when you are talking about an employee's "reasonable expectation of privacy at home", you are dealing with an expectation of privacy which is greater than the privacy that an employee is entitled to at work.[26] However, an employee's expectation of privacy even at home is not absolute. Thus, in one case,[27] Oregon's Supreme Court upheld an employer's decision to hire private investigators who took eighteen rolls of movies showing an employee performing

---

[25] *See Lambert v. Dow Chemical Co.*, 215 So.2d 673 (La. App. 1st Cir. 1968).

[26] *See generally Pemberton v. Bethlehem Steel Corp.*, 502 A.2d 1101 (Md.App.), *cert. denied*, 479 U.S. 984 (1986).

[27] *See McLain v. Boise Cascade Corp.*, 271 Or. 549, 533 P.2d 343 (1975).

various tasks at home (such as mowing his lawn and rototilling his garden) when the employee claimed that even the "light duty" assignment given to him by his company aggravated a back injury.

At trial, the employee was awarded $250 in nominal damages for the investigator's trespass on his land, but the employee was denied relief for invasion of privacy. The Oregon Supreme Court emphasized that the employer had a legitimate interest in the employee's medical condition, and the court stated that the surveillance was conducted in a reasonable manner. In the Court's words:

> "[T]he investigators did not question any of [the employee's] neighbors or friends and limited their activities to taking pictures while [the employee] was engaged in various activities outside his home. [The employee] testified that these activities could have been viewed either by neighbors or passersby on the highway. [The employee] further testified that he was not embarrassed or upset by anything that appeared in the films."

Can an employer go too far in engaging in surveillance at an employee's home? What if an employee is absent from work for one week without notice and without calling in? In this situation, even if you fear for the employee's health, can you break into the employee's mobile home and, if he is discovered drunk, discharge him?

In Louisiana, the answer is no. A Louisiana court concluded that the employee in question (who was discovered drunk in his mobile home) stated a cause of action against his employer for invasion of privacy.[28]

In all of these cases the two "magic words" are reasonableness and consent. If an employer's "invasion" of privacy is reasonable, or if the employee does not have a "reasonable" expectation of privacy, there should not be problems with the

---

[28] *See Love v. Southern Bell Telephone Co.*, 263 So.2d 460 (La. App.), *cert. denied*, 266 So.2d 429 (1972).

employer's conduct. When first employed, it is best to have the employee sign consent to employer's right to verify his ability to perform work, whether at work or home. If the employee gives his consent—even by implication (for example, an employee may consent to inquiries as to his medical condition by requesting a disability pension),[29] the consent may be an absolute defense to an employer's invasion of the employee's privacy.

Remember, surveillance or investigation by the employer outside the workplace, whether conducted in the public or private sector, may withstand legal challenge **if it is initiated for business-related purposes and conducted in a reasonable and unobtrusive manner.** Privacy challenges almost always succeed when employers engage in covert investigations in an obviously intrusive manner for reasons unrelated to the job.

7.2 Drug Screens

Beginning in the late 1980's, drug screens and tests became widespread. Many legal challenges involving privacy rights and search and seizure issues arose. Most of the law in this area is now relatively settled for private sector employees. The least controversial use of drug testing is with preemployment applicants. While professional assistance should be obtained in setting up the program, and ensuring proper safeguards are established for protecting the process, applicants may be tested if they receive a "conditional offer" of employment. The employment offer is, therefore, conditioned upon the applicant's negative drug test. If preemployment testing is to be used, notice should be provided and an acknowledgment and consent form signed by the applicant.

If drug tests are to be used during the employment process, the issue can become somewhat more sensitive from an employee relations and legal standpoint. Once again, notice and consent at the outset of employment are the best methods of

---

[29] *See Jeffers v. City of Seattle*, 597 P.2d 899 (Wash. 1979).

minimizing problems and being able to use drug testing to deal with problem employees.[30]

7.3 Searches

With regard to employee searches and in-plant searches of lunch boxes, lockers or automobiles, the company's "reasonable right to know" must be balanced against the employee's "reasonable expectation of privacy."

The Fourth Amendment's prohibition of unreasonable searches and seizures applies only to actions taken by government agencies or officials.[31] Thus, the legality of searches of employer-provided lockers, desks, or offices, or personal items employees bring to the workplace depends largely on whether the employer is public or private and, among private employers, whether they act alone or with the help of the police or other government agencies.

Private-sector employers usually have the right to search property they provide to employees for daily use, such as desks and lockers. In addition, private employers may require employees to submit to searches of packages they bring into or take out of the workplace. The U.S. Constitution does not protect employees from searches by non-governmental employers.

Nevertheless, an increasing number of courts are sustaining claims in the private sector under the tort of intrusion. In a private-sector case where a jury awarded $100,000 in exemplary damages for a search of an employee's purse in a company locker without the worker's consent, the Texas Court of Appeals

---

[30] Some employers, including government contractors and those with DOD contracts and DOT contracts are required to certify that they provide a drug-free workplace. Under the Drug-Free Workplace Act of 1988 all federal contractors whose contracts exceed $25,000, must develop and publish a written drug abuse policy. Under the DOT regulations, an employer is required to test applicants and current employees in "safety-sensitive" positions.

[31] See Burdeau v. McDowell, 256 U.S. 465, 475 (1921).

found that the employer had created a "legitimate expectation of privacy" in the locker assigned to the employee.[32]

Employers can take the following steps to retain the authority to conduct random searches and searches connected to investigations while avoiding giving employees any legally binding expectation of privacy:

- When lockers, desks, or offices are assigned, make it clear to their users that the facility or equipment being assigned may be searched.
- Where offices or lockers have locks, keep duplicate keys to them. If employees are allowed to provide their own locks, require them to provide the employer with duplicate keys or combinations to the locks.
- Establish written policies outlining the circumstances under which searches will be conducted, and publicize these policies to all employees.
- To preserve the right to search at random, conduct random searches several times a year. A written policy that is never used is subject to challenge.
- Have employees confine their personal papers and files to one part of their offices or desks.
- Prohibit or place limits on the number or type of containers, such as luggage and gym bags, that employees can bring on employer property, or arrange for storage outside the entrance where employees will be checked to see they do not bring in such containers. For example, have employees park their cars in a central lot from which they must walk past the guard who conducts the checks.

---

[32] *See K-Mart Corp. v. Trotti*, 677 S.W.2d 632 (Tex. Ct. App. 1984), *writ refused*, 686 S.W.2d 593 (1985).

Dealing with problem employees requires that consideration be given to acting reasonably under the circumstances. Problem employees place a tremendous financial burden on employers. The courts, and other regulatory agencies, are willing to consider this issue—but only if the proper safeguards have been taken by employers. Therefore, the best defense is the pre-screening process. Employees are a valuable asset. An investment should be made in the pre-screening and selection process. Reviews should be made of experience and background of employees. Former employers must be contacted. After hiring takes place, the employer should follow up on warning signs. Policies and procedures that set up a disciplinary procedure need to be implemented and followed. Employers need to ensure that employment-at-will doctrines have been implemented properly. In special circumstances, special tools such as drug and alcohol testing, searches, and surveillance need to be implemented. Drug testing of applicants, and "cause based" policies are most widely utilized and accepted by employees. Professional assistance should be obtained in establishing and implementing drug testing programs. With proper implementation, such programs can benefit all employees.

There will always be problems in businesses and there will always be "problem employees." The key for employers is to act promptly and responsibly in addressing such issues to minimize problems wherever possible.

Chapter 10

PERSONNEL POLICY MANUAL AND EMPLOYEE HANDBOOKS

Jacqueline D. Stanley
Attorney At Law

1.0 OVERVIEW

A personnel policy manual is a document written for the benefit of those persons within an organization who are responsible for implementing the policies and procedures necessary for the organization to fulfill its function and meet its objectives. It contains the policies or general guidelines that regulate organizational actions.[1] These policies may regulate everything from procuring equipment and supplies to the rules regarding visitors or making personal phone calls. Although organizations are not required to develop a personnel policy manual, it would be impossible for most organizations to maintain the consistent and efficient application of their policies and procedures without one.

2.0 BENEFITS

In addition to increased efficiency and consistency of organizational operations, there are two additional benefits of

---

[1] Robert L. Mathis and John H. Jackson, *Personnel: Contemporary Perspectives and Application* (New York, West Publishing Co. 1976), p. 419.

developing a personnel policy manual. First, a personnel policy manual can protect organizations against lawsuits. Litigation commonly occurs when an employee is discharged or terminates their employment. A personnel policy manual will ensure there will be no confusion as to your organization's policies. Without a personnel policy manual to consult, a judge or jury will have to rely on lawyers and the circumstances to tell them your organization's policy.

Secondly, a personnel policy manual can ensure that discipline and rewards are based on an objective standard. When employees know what to expect and feel they are treated fairly and in accordance with an established policy there is little chance for accusations of favoritism or discrimination. Eliminating these feelings will help establish and maintain a positive and productive work force.

3.0 WHO SHOULD WRITE IT?

There are basically three viable options—a lawyer, an employee, or a professional business writer. The advantage of hiring an attorney is their expertise in employment and labor law. However, since they do not typically write for lay audiences they may have difficulty using language that your staff can understand. Because of their expertise, an attorney will probably be the most expensive option, charging from $75.00 or more per hour.

There are two advantages to assigning an employee within the organization to write the policy manual. First, there is no expense incurred other than their usual salary. Second, they will be familiar with the organization's operations and will know how to obtain the information they need. The person selected must not only possess the necessary writing skills to design a personnel policy manual but should also be familiar with the relevant laws in order to write a personnel policy manual.

Many organizations favor the use of professional business writers. They tend to be experienced in developing personnel policy manuals and, therefore, possess the requisite writing skills and familiarity with applicable laws and regulations.

Moreover, their fees will be substantially less than those charged by attorney's.

4.0 ADOPTING POLICIES

A common mistake organizations make when developing a personnel policy manual is to try to duplicate policies contained in manuals from other companies simply for the sake of developing one quickly. Policies should be adopted or enacted for one reason—to facilitate the efficient and consistent operations of your organization.

Asking these five questions for each policy under consideration will help eradicate this mistake.

4.1 Does the Policy Make Sense?

Each policy contained in your personnel policy manual should have a rational basis for its implementation. For example, a policy which requires all employees within an organization to wear business suits and does not provide an exception for factory workers makes little sense. When a policy appears irrational it will meet with resistance and supervisors will eventually stop enforcing it.

> **Comment:** Regardless of how comprehensive, a personnel policy manual cannot replace sound decisionmaking skills of supervisors and managers. They need to be familiar with the contents of the personnel policy manual and not have to refer to it every time a situation arises that requires them to take action. This would be time-consuming and cause lower level employees to question their authority. The policy manual is a guide to ensure that everyone within an organization is moving in the same direction. Supervisors and managers should know their way and only look to the guide when unexpected detours arise or periodically to ensure they are following the prescribed course. Invariably, there will be occasions when a written policy will conflict with what a supervisor or manager would consider to be reasonable. In these instances the judgement of the

person responsible for implementing the policy should prevail. It is important to maintain personnel who are capable of exercising sound judgment while at the same time working within the parameters of the personnel policy manual.

4.2 Does the Policy Pertain to Organizational Operations?

Whether it is complying with governmental regulations or maintaining employees productivity and morale, each policy contained in a personnel policy manual should be designed to fulfill a specific function or meet an established objective of the organization. Policies which do not pertain to organizational operations should be considered unnecessary and could even have the potential to create problems. For example, an organization that does not own vehicles would not need a policy regulating their use. Keep in mind that a primary reason organizations develop personnel policy manuals is to improve operations.

4.3 Can the Policy be Consistently Applied?

A personnel policy manual must be a reliable guide for management decisionmaking and employee conduct. The manner in which policies are stated in the manual should be the way they are routinely applied throughout an organization. For example, if members of management are allowed to work flexible work schedules the policy statement should not state that all employees are expected to arrive at work at or before 9 am. The established policies should reflect how different segments of an organization operate. Inconsistency in the application of policies decreases the effectiveness of the personnel policy manual.

> **Comment:** Unemployment compensation is one area of the law where the consistent application of policies as they appear in personnel policy manual can play a critical role. If an organization fails to comply with a policy as it appears in their manual then an employee who may not otherwise be eligible for unemployment

compensation may receive benefits. As a general rule, courts consider conduct which violates a policy as it appears in a manual to be "misconduct." Employees guilty of "misconduct" are not entitled to unemployment benefits. For example, if an organization's written policy states that an employee will be terminated, if they are late three times within any 30-day period and an employee violates this policy and is terminated then the employee would not be entitled to benefits. However, if the employer ignores the written policy for several months and then terminates the employee, most courts would be unlikely to categorize the tardiness as "misconduct" because the employer has rescinded their written policy by not acting in accordance with it. The employee in this case would probably be entitled to receive at least partial benefits. The same principle would apply in instances where the manual states that an employee will be terminated if late three times within a 30-day period and the employee is terminated after being late two times. Organizations should caution their managers and supervisors that what may appear to be slight deviations in the application of policies can make a big difference.

4.4 Can the Policy be Easily Enforced by Supervisors or Followed by Employees?

There is no point in adopting a policy which supervisors could not enforce or employees could not follow. If a situation arose where an employee needed to respond to a family emergency, supervisors would have difficulty enforcing a policy which prohibited employees from leaving work prior to the end of the business day. The policy would need to contain an exception for certain emergency circumstances in order to be practical. Organizations should change any policy which cannot be enforced by management or followed by employees.

4.5 Can the Policy Adapt to a Broad Range of Circumstances?

A policy prohibiting all unlawful conduct is more effective than a policy prohibiting stealing. Since it is a broader statement, the prohibition of all illegal conduct will not require a separate policy for each illegal activity, nor will it force management to continually create new policies because the specific criminal conduct of the employee is not covered in the manual. Further, if the policies contained in a personnel policy manual are too narrowly focused, then organizations will have to adopt a new policy for every situation that arises, or might conceivably arise, during their day-to-day operations. The personnel policy manual would be so voluminous that management would likely consider it more of a burden than a benefit.

5.0 POLICY SOURCES

Organizations typically look three places to find the policies to incorporate as part of their personnel policy manuals. First, they adopt federal and state government requirements. It is important to consult an attorney on these matters. The laws vary from state-to-state and depend on the number of employees.

Second, they confer with individuals responsible for the day-to-day operations of the organization and those responsible for charting its future growth. These people will know what type of policies are necessary to accomplish these objectives.

Finally, they consult and ask probing questions "what kind of information do they need to perform their jobs?" or "what policies are necessary to create a productive and satisfying work environment?" The following items are topics which generally appear as standard policy provisions:

*Accidents/Injuries	*Overtime
*Affirmative Action	Parking
*Alcohol	*Pay Advances
*Annual Leave	*Pay Periods
Appearance	*Payroll Deductions
Attendance	*Pension Plan
Bonuses	Personal Phone Calls

*Disability
 —Long Term
 —Short Term
*Discipline
*Discrimination
*Drugs
*Education
Emergencies
Employee Conduct
Employee Selection Process
Employee Status
 —Permanent
 —Temporary
 —Part-time
Gift Matching
*Grievance Procedure
*Fraternization
Fringe Benefits
*Health/Welfare Benefits
 —Dental Plan
 —Group Life Insurance
 —Medical Insurance
Holidays
*Hours of Operation
*Jury Duty
*Layoffs/Recalls
Leave of Absence
*Military Reserve Duty
Moonlighting

*Personnel Records
*Pregnancy
*Probation
*Profit Sharing
Promotions
*Raises
*Recruiting
*References
*Retirement Benefits
*Safety and Health
*Salaries
*Separation
Service Awards
*Severance Pay
*Sexual Harassment
*Sick Leave
 Smoking
*Social Security
*Suspension
Tardiness
*Termination
Time Tracking
*Training
Transfers
Tuition Reimbursement
*Unemployment Compensation
*Unions
*Voting
*Workmen's Compensation

* May involve state and federal regulations.

6.0 DRAFTING CONSIDERATIONS

It is important when writing a personnel policy manual that the language be easily understood by those who will need to be most familiar with its contents. Terms that are ambiguous or easily misinterpreted should be defined. For example, an unexcused absence could be defined as any absence that is not approved in advance by the supervisor or in which the employee fails to notify the supervisor within one hour after the work day begins. Organizations should also specifically list any exceptions that may apply to a particular policy. For example, exceptions to the policy regarding unexcused absences might include the unexpected hospitalization of the employee or death of a member of the employee's immediate family (spouse, children, parents or sibling).

The language used in personnel policy manuals should also be general enough to avoid legal entanglements but precise enough that management will know how to perform and employees will know what to expect. Employees in jurisdictions that recognize the employment-at-will doctrine sometimes try to rely on an organization's personnel manual to create an employment contract. The employment-at-will doctrine acknowledges that a contractual relationship exists between employers and their employees. However, it maintains that the contract can be dissolved by either party. As a general rule, employment contracts require additional consideration and must be for a definite period. Pay particular attention not to use any language which would appear to create a contract or that would suggest that the contents of the manual establish an agreement between the organization and its employees. Statements such as "hard working employees will always have a job with our organization" or "as long as employees comply with the policies contained in this manual, their position will be secure" are two examples of the kind of language to avoid.

The following statements are sample provisions as they might appear in a personnel policy manual:

Raises/Promotions—Each employee will be evaluated for a raise and/or promotion each year on the anniversary date of their employment. With the exception of cost-of-living raises, all other raises and promotions are based strictly on merit. Factors such as attendance, work performance and attitude will be considered.

Equal Opportunity—Discrimination on the basis of age, race, religion, natural origin, physical handicap or any other factor that does not relate to an employee's ability to perform is prohibited.

Sexual Harassment—Any conduct which might reasonably be construed as sexual harassment or capable of creating a hostile environment is strictly prohibited. Examples of such conduct include but are not limited to the following:

1. Lewd remarks or jokes
2. Inappropriate physical contact or touching
3. Displaying obscene material or paraphernalia

Each employee has an affirmative duty to immediately report such conduct to their supervisor or someone in the Human Resources Department.

Smoking—Smoking is not prohibited or restricted to a particular area. In the event a conflict arises between a smoker and a non-smoker, the rights of the non-smoker to enjoy a pollution-free work environment shall prevail.

Personal Appearance—Employees are permitted to dress in a casual yet professional manner. Under no circumstances will jeans, short pants, jogging suits, or tennis shoes be considered acceptable. Employees who report to work in unacceptable attire shall be sent home to change.

Safety—Employees have an affirmative obligation to familiarize themselves with the posted OSHA rules and regulations. Any conduct or activity which is in violation of these rules or regulations or which could endanger the health, safety and welfare of employees is prohibited and can result in termination.

Salaries—An employee's salary level shall be determined at the time of their employment. The following factors shall be considered:

1. Experience
2. Education/Training
3. Prevailing market wage

Drugs/Alcohol—Employees are prohibited from using illicit drugs or alcohol in the work place or working while under the influence of these substances. Employees who violate this policy shall be given one opportunity to seek treatment. Failure to seek or successfully complete treatment will result in immediate termination.

Once the first draft is completed, have an attorney review the contents and then ask members of management if there are any glaring omissions. Also solicit their input on how the manual can be improved.

7.0 OPEN VS. CLOSED POLICY STATEMENTS

The policies contained in most personnel policy manuals can be classified into two categories: open policy statements and closed policy. Here is an example of each with respect to personal calls.

Open: Employees shall limit the number of personal phone calls they make and accept each day.
Closed: Only emergency phone calls will be permitted during working hours. Personal phone calls should be restricted to lunch and break periods.

Open policy statements do not specifically prohibit any behavior and give employees discretion in how to govern their conduct. Closed policy statements, on the other hand, contain specific directives. They state affirmatively what employees can and cannot do.

The difference between the two can sometimes be difficult to distinguish. The form specific policies should take will depend on the policy and the circumstances. Initially, many organizations begin with open policy statements, and, when problems arise or employees appear to abuse a policy, they enact closed policy statements. It is easier to terminate an employee for violating a closed policy because specific infractions are easier to document. As a general rule, the more important a policy is to organizational operations, the more important it is to adopt a closed policy statement.

8.0 FORMS

The personnel policy manual should also contain any forms necessary to implement an organizations policies and procedures. The forms should be standardized and used consistently throughout the organization. They should be inserted next to the particular policy in which they relate and solicit all information needed to implement the policy. Instructions should be included on the reverse side of each form. If at all possible, forms should be self-explanatory and require little time to complete. Each form should indicate what to do with it once it is complete.

To ensure that a form will simplify rather than complicate procedures, it may be helpful to conduct the following self-audit of each form and its correlating policy:

1. Is the policy clear about who is required to use the form?
2. Will the ultimate user of the form understand its purpose?
3. Does the policy state where the forms will be located and where to submit completed forms?
4. Is the policy clear about when the form should be used?
5. Is the policy clear on how to complete the form?

9.0 REVIEW AND REVISION

Many organizations make the mistake of developing their personnel policy manual and then filing it away. An organization's personnel policy manual is just like the organization itself. It is not static or lifeless. A successful personnel policy manual is dynamic and should reflect whatever changes and growth the organization experiences.

It is generally a good idea to appoint a person in the personnel or human resources department to maintain the personnel policy manual and to conduct the reviews at the end of each fiscal year. Selecting a specific date each year will ensure that the updates are done regularly.

During the annual review, organizations can conduct the following self-audit of each policy contained in their policy manual:

1. Are there any recurring misunderstandings amount supervisors and managers?
2. Has the policy been consistently applied?
3. Does the policy advance organizational objectives?
4. Is the policy current?
5. Is the policy cost effective?[2]

Don't wait for the annual review date to make changes. Organizations should update their personnel policy manual whenever they undergo any major change in policy or whenever there is a significant number of small changes. Employees must be aware of any changes in the personnel policy manual. There are several ways to keep employees informed:

1. Post the updates on the employee bulletin board.
2. Send each employee a memo or electronic mail message.
3. Publish the updates in an employee newsletter.
4. Announce the changes at employee staff meetings.

10.0 LOCATION

The personnel policy manual should be located in places that are convenient and accessible to members of management. Each department should have a copy. If your organization has a library, that would be an ideal location for the personnel policy manual. If at all possible, supervisors should not possess

---

[2] Donald Crane, *Personnel: The Management Of Human Resources, 2nd Edition* (California, Wadsworth Publishing Co., 1979), p.52.

the only copies of the manual. Many employees may feel uncomfortable asking them for a copy. All of your employees should be aware of the exact locations of the personnel policy manual.

Make them aware of its location through the same methods used to make them aware of changes and updates in the personnel policy manual.

11.0 EMPLOYEE HANDBOOK

Since the personnel policy manual was designed for supervisors and upper level management, the policies and information contained in a personnel policy manual must be available so that it can be conveyed to lower level employees. The most obvious means of conveying the information in the personnel policy manual to employees is by reading the information to them or letting them read it when they begin employment. However, this process can be time consuming and likely to create confusion. For this reason, most organizations publish an "employee handbook" or "human resource manual." These terms are often used interchangeably because, in most larger organizations, the human resources department is responsible for the development and distribution of employee handbooks.

An employee handbook is not the same as a personnel policy manual although the terms are often mistakenly used interchangeably. The information in the employee handbook summarizes the information in the personnel policy manual.[3] The difference between the two can be easily seen by considering the following example:

Personnel Policy Manual—Moonlighting
  Purpose—To ensure employees are able to maintain reasonable performance standards.
  Definition—Employment in addition to employment with the organization.

---

[3] Susan L. Brock and Sally R. Cabbell, *Writing a Human Resources Manual* (Los Altos, Calif., Crisp Publications, 1989).

General Policy—Employees who intend to moonlight should first obtain permission of their supervisor. Employees shall be granted permission to moonlight as long as the employment does not interfere with their work schedule or work performance.

Employee Handbook—Moonlighting
We understand that employees may periodically need to supplement their incomes. Moonlighting is permitted as long as employees notify their supervisors in advance and it does not interfere with their employment with the company.

The primary purpose of the employee handbook is to answer two basic questions: what can employees expect from the organization, and what does the organization expect from its employees? The information included in employee handbooks is the kind of information that employees (particularly new employees) will need to perform their jobs. Employees can refer to the handbook on their own time without any interruption in their work schedule. In organizations without an employee handbook, supervisors need to take time to educate employees about the organization's policies and procedures.

Employees handbooks can be given to employees during their initial orientation. Or, they can be mailed to an employee's home since this is where it will be most convenient for them to read it. It is also a good idea to put one copy near the employee bulletin board, in the lounge, break area, and cafeteria. Employees should be told where they can find a copy of the employee handbook.

11.1 What Information Should be Included in an Employee Handbook?

Since the information is written for the benefit of employees, begin by asking them what they want to know. Select a random sample of employees and give them each a questionnaire. Ask them the following questions: "What do you want to know about the organization?" and "what are you confused about or don't understand?" Their responses can serve as the basis of handbook. The following is a list of things most employees will want to know:

1. Salary Guidelines
2. Pay Schedules
3. Types of Benefits
4. Raise Criteria and Frequency
5. Promotion Criteria and Frequency
6. Hours of Operation
7. Overtime Requirement and Salary
8. Types and Amount of Leave
9. Grounds for Termination
10. Types of Fringe Benefits

The supervisors should be consulted, since they work the closest with employees. Consult all or a sampling of the first-line supervisors. Ask them to list the questions employees ask most often and list the things they must constantly remind employees about.

The next place to turn is to the personnel policy manual. Review its contents carefully and select the information that most employees want to know and that is necessary for them to perform their day-to-day duties. Do not attempt to summarize all of the policies contained in the manual. Since the documents were designed for different purposes, it makes sense that there will be information contained in one that does not appear in the other. Employee handbooks often contain information not included in the personnel policy manual. For example, the handbook might include a list of company-sponsored social events, although few organizations find it necessary to adopt written policies regarding these events.

Most handbooks contain a statement that the employee handbook is not a contract between the employee and employer. This is important in the event that an employee attempts to use it as the basis of a lawsuit. Generally, at the beginning of the handbook there is a disclaimer similar to the following: the contents of this employee handbook are not intended to be promises but summaries of the organization's current policies and practices. These policies and practices are subject to change without notice or approval. To ensure that employees can not later claim they were unfamiliar with the disclaimer, it may be necessary to have them sign a statement similar to the following: I have read the contents of the employee handbook. It has been explained and I understand that it is not a contract between me and my employer. It is a summary of the organization's practices and procedures. I also understand that it is subject to change without my prior knowledge or approval. A copy of the statement can be included as part of the employees permanent personnel record.

Since the employee handbook is a more personal document than the personnel policy manual, it will usually contain a letter of welcome or encouragement from the president and information regarding the organization's history:

Who were the founders?
When and where it began?
What does the organization do?
What is the organization's business philosophy?
How has the organization changed over the years?

Employee handbooks will generally include explanations of why particular policies were adopted. The explanation should focus on factors which employees will consider beneficial to them. For example, the reason employees are expected to arrive to work on time can be explained as to ensure that each work station is covered and that a burden is not placed on the other employees. It would not be appropriate to state the reason as ensuring that the organization gets its money's worth out of its employees or any other reason that only reflects an organizational interest. Employees are more likely to adhere to policies which they feel were enacted for their benefit and to maintain a positive attitude toward an organization that they feel is looking out for their best interest.

The following statements are sample provisions as they might appear in an employee handbook:

Opening Statement—This handbook was written to answer most questions employees have when beginning employment. If you have any additional questions, ask your supervisor, or you can refer to the personnel policy manual. A copy is located in each department. This handbook is not a contract. It does not include any expressed or implied promises or agreements. The policies and procedures outlined in this manual were intended to summarize our policies and procedures. They are subject to change or modification without your knowledge or approval.

Hours of Operation—We are open Monday through Friday. Our business day begins at 8:00 am and ends at 6:00 pm. You are entitled to a one hour lunch break. Lunch breaks should be taken between the hour of 11:00 am and 2:00 pm. You are also entitled to one 10-minute break each morning and afternoon.

Pay Schedule—Pay checks will be available in the personnel office on the 15th and 30th day of each month. If the pay day falls on a weekend or holiday, your check will be available on the first working day preceding the weekend or holiday. Pay checks will be mailed to employees who are unable to pick up their pay checks by the close of business on pay day. Pay checks will not be released to anyone other than the employee to whom it belongs.

Raises/Promotions—We believe in rewarding hard working employees. Each year, and more often in cases of exceptional performance, employees will be evaluated for a raise and/or promotion.

Grounds for Termination—There is certain conduct which we consider to be so disruptive that we consider it to be grounds for immediate dismissal. This conduct includes but is not limited to the following:

1. Drugs/Alcohol
2. Unexcused absences
3. Excessive tardiness
4. Fighting

5. Unlawful conduct
6. Poor work performance
7. Insubordination
8. Possession of dangerous weapons
9. Reckless conduct

In most instances we will make every effort to warn and counsel employees about conduct or conditions we feel is not consistent with sustaining employment. However, we reserve the right to discharge any employee with or without cause if we feel that it would serve the best interest of the company and its employees.

Benefits—We offer a very comprehensive health, dental, disability and retirement plan to all of our permanent full-time employees. A comprehensive explanation of the benefits is included in a separate booklet given to each employee when they are hired. Additional copies are available in the personnel department. If you have any questions or need claim forms, contact the plan administrator at extension 1122.

Employee Relations—If at any time during your employment you experience difficulty in working with a co-worker, you are encouraged to first approach the person and try to resolve the problem amicably. If you are unsuccessful, inform your supervisor. They will work with both of you in trying to find a resolution that is satisfactory and conducive to maintaining a pleasant and productive work environment.

Equal Opportunity Employer—It is our sincere belief that a diverse group of employees is an asset. It is for this reason that we do not discriminate on the basis of race, religion, color, natural origin or any other factor not relating to an employees ability to perform.

Sexual Harassment—We are committed to maintaining a work environment in which everyone can feel safe and comfortable. It is our policy to terminate the employment of any employee who sexually harasses another employee or does anything to create a hostile environment. Any employee that is aware of such behavior should immediately report this information to a supervisor or department manager.

Suggestions—We are always looking for ways to improve our performance and save money. Submit your ideas or suggestions in writing to your supervisor. If we use your idea, you will receive a $100.00 bonus.

The employee handbook should be interesting and reader-friendly. If possible, include graphs, diagrams, and pictures. Most readers find it easier to comprehend shorter sentences and paragraphs. Although the length of the handbook will vary it should not exceed 50 pages. The ideal length will allow employees to read it in one sitting.

Packaging is an important consideration in the publication of an employee handbook. The appearance of the employee handbook may mean the difference between whether or not employees bother to read it. Remember, the policies organizations adopt are of no value unless their employees are aware of them. Try to make the cover as appealing as possible and seek professional help if necessary.

To review the points covered thus far, personnel policy manuals play a key role in developing and maintaining the efficient implementation of an organization's practices and procedures. Although organizations are not required to develop personnel policy manuals, there are federal and state regulations governing many of the policies included in the typical manual. It is important that organizations which plan to develop personnel policy manuals consult someone who is experienced in labor and employment law matters. They must also carefully consider the policies they intend to include in the manual to ensure they are geared toward resolving problems instead of creating them.

Chapter 11
PERSONNEL AUDITS

Thomas P. Murphy
Reed Smith Shaw & McClay

1.0 THE VALUE OF SELF-AUDITS

You may have a time bomb ticking away in your personnel policies and practices. Poorly drafted policies or the absence of certain policies can be the launching pad for a multi-million dollar damage award in today's litigation-minded workforce. Employers can no longer passively wait for their first wrongful discharge lawsuit then go out and hire the best labor lawyer in town to try to beat the case. Companies need to take affirmative steps to avoid legal risks and adverse workplace relations from the outset.

One of the best ways of assessing an organization's "Achilles' heel" is by a personnel audit. An employment law audit works just like a financial audit. A careful and thorough personnel audit will help your organization:

- Monitor compliance with the many federal, state and local workplace laws and regulations;
- Target and defuse potential labor relations problems before they explode; and
- Ensure that your policies and procedures are current, sound and effective.

2.0 WHO SHOULD DO THEM?

Any employer is vulnerable to a lawsuit by a disgruntled employee. Large employers. Small employers. Nonprofit organizations or for-profit corporations. The only requirement is that the employer have a "deep pocket!"

Small employers are just as susceptible to suit as large multinational corporations. For instance, labor laws such as the Immigration Reform and Control Act of 1986 apply to all employers regardless of size. The provisions of the Civil Rights Act of 1964 can apply to companies with workforces as small as 15 employees. On July 26, 1994, the Americans With Disabilities Act of 1990 will cover employers with workforces having as few as 15 employees (presently the Act applies to companies with 25 or more employees).

Of course large employers are particularly susceptible to suit because they are viewed by plaintiffs' lawyers as "deep pockets" and are generally treated harshly by jurors. Also, the larger the organization the greater the risk of disparate treatment of employees in areas of discipline. The fact is the larger and more diverse your workforce, the greater the need for a more structured approach to human resources management. A large organization needs a well-drafted employment handbook to increase organizational orderliness and improve employee communications. Also, hiring, training and proper managing of employees are all critical elements of the personnel function.

Multi-state employers need to carefully audit their personnel policies because labor law requirements can vary significantly from state to state. While some state laws mirror the prohibitions of Title VII of the Civil Rights Act of 1964 and generally make it illegal to discriminate in employment decisions on the basis of race, color, religion, sex, disability, or national origin, some states have expanded the Act to include an employee's sexual preference, appearance, political orientation, family responsibilities, matriculation, source of income or place of residence and marital status. A multi-state company is not necessarily protected from liability by simply complying with federal law. Some states' labor laws are broader than federal law.

Government contractors have a number of special federal labor laws they need to strictly comply with as a condition of doing business with the government. Noncompliance can result not only in liability but also "debarment" as a government contractor.

Lastly, any employer interested in positive employee relations needs to consider a personnel audit. Studies show that many employers know surprisingly little about the composition, attitudes and perceptions of their employees. Without this knowledge, employers have increased difficulty in formulating and implementing strategies that maximize the value of their human resource asset. As a result, employment policies miss the mark, salary and benefits are often counterproductive, and employers are surprised when one of their current or past employees alleges discrimination or harassment. A personnel audit can be an ongoing system that provides information and feedback about your employees and what they consider important.

In short, all employers should consider the advantages of a personnel audit. While a personnel audit should not be viewed as a panacea for using every deficiency in the human resources area, it will provide a blueprint of your legal posture in the employment law and labor relations field, pinpoint those facets of your employment relationships which detract from your overall employee relations climate, and hopefully come up with methods for creating a positive employee relations atmosphere. Thus, the audit has the dual objectives of achieving full legal compliance with all applicable labor and employment related laws, and introducing progressive employment and personnel policies and methods of their implementation.

3.0 TECHNIQUES TO PINPOINT YOUR COMPANY'S STRENGTH'S AND WEAKNESSES

As seen so often in the financial area, audits are most successful in terms of accuracy, candor and reliability when done by an outside third party. An experienced employment law auditor is someone who can:

- Understand the important workplace and legal issues;
- ask the right questions; and
- identify and prioritize the tasks necessary to achieve legal compliance and a positive employee relations climate.

A successful personnel audit must be conducted in a thorough manner covering the following topics:

A. Review of Employee Handbooks and Personnel Policies
   1) "Union Free" Statements
   2) Disclaimers
   3) No Distribution Rules
   4) No Solicitation Rules
   5) Standard Policy Clauses
   6) Work Rules and Progressive Discipline
   7) Grievance and Complaint Procedures
   8) "Open Door" Policy
   9) "Probationary" Policy
   10) Other Potential Problem Areas
B. Individual Employment Contracts
   1) Duration
   2) Protection of Intellectual Property Rights
   3) Confidential Information
   4) Employee Benefits
   5) Conflict of Interest
   6) Non-Compete Clauses
   7) Standard Protective Language
   8) Golden Handcuff Provisions
C. Review of Recruitment and Hiring Procedures
   1) Limiting Applicant Intake
   2) Application Duration
   3) Examination of Recruitment Sources
   4) Legal Review of Application Forms
   5) Interviewing Techniques and Screening Processes
   6) Tests and Testing Procedures
   7) Applicant Flow Data
   8) Use of Statistics

9) Union Considerations
10) Minority Recruitment
11) Measuring Turnover
12) Physical Examinations
- D. Orientation
    1) Introduction and Training
    2) Apprentice Programs
    3) Plant Tour and Plant History
    4) Films and Video Presentations
- E. Promotions and Transfers
    1) Bid and Posting Procedures
    2) Seniority Considerations
    3) Other Selection Criteria
    4) Favoritism Issues
    5) Affirmative Action Obligations
    6) Requested vs. Forced Transfers
    7) Documentation/Recordkeeping
- F. Compensation Package
    1) Comparability and Competitiveness
    2) Periodic Reviews
    3) Merit Increases
    4) Bonuses and Incentives
    5) Other Compensation
- G. Benefit Packages
    1) Comparability
    2) Employee Awareness
    3) Part-Time Employees
    4) Individual Allowances
    5) Tax Considerations
    6) Publicizing the "Hidden Pay Check"
    7) Health Insurance
    8) Pension and/or Profit Sharing Programs
    9) IRA's 401(k) Plans
- H. Safety and Health
    1) Legal Obligations
    2) Documentation
    3) Safety Committees
- I. Leave Policies
    1) Sick Leave

2) Vacations
3) Leave Without Pay
4) Disability
5) Maternity
6) Military
7) Bereavement
8) Educational
9) Workers' Compensable Injuries

J. Equal Employment Injuries
1) Workplace Statistical Profile
2) Minority Mobility
3) Affirmative Action Plans (AAP's)
4) Equal Pay Act Compliance
5) Comparable Worth Considerations
6) Sex Discrimination and Sexual Harassment
7) Age Discrimination—Compliance with ADEA
8) Veterans
9) Handicap Discrimination
10) State and Local Discrimination Laws

K. Discipline and Discharge
1) Progressive Discipline
2) Summary Discharge
3) Documentation Procedures
4) Rule-Making and Publication
5) Warning Procedures
6) Uniformity and Consistency
7) Investigation Procedures
8) "Voluntary Resignation" Policies
9) Exit Interviews
10) Termination Forms
11) Defamation/Slander Issues
12) Final Filter Protection

L. Layoffs and Recalls
1) Formalized Procedures
2) Notice Requirements
3) Selection Criteria
4) Alternative Plans
5) Legal Considerations

M. Notice Posting Procedures
   1) State and Local Requirements
   2) Federal Requirements
   3) Penalties for Non-Compliance
   4) Obtaining Posters and Notices
N. Seniority Systems
   1) Recognizing Seniority
   2) Probationary Periods
   3) Vacation Eligibility
   4) Effects on Wages
   5) Two-Tier Systems
O. Communications Programs
   1) Employee Handbook
   2) Employee Newsletters/Magazines
   3) Recruitment Materials
   4) Employee Meetings
   5) Supervisor Meetings
   6) Open Door Policies
   7) Suggestion Boxes
   8) Recognition Programs
   9) Quality Circle/Employee Participation Programs
   10) Bulletin Boards
   11) Employee/Joint Committees
   12) Exit Interviews
   13) Coordination of Programs
   14) Communicating New Policies
P. Auxiliary Services
   1) Uniforms
   2) Tools
   3) Cafeterias and Vending Machines
   4) Breakrooms
   5) Restrooms, Lockers and Showers
   6) Janitorial Services
   7) Parking Areas
   8) Guards and Security Services
   9) Team Sports
   10) Other "Perks"
Q. Overall Policies and Procedures
   1) Attendance

2) Overtime
   3) Work Rules
   4) Progressive Discipline
   5) Light Duty
   6) Flex Hours
   7) Anti-Nepotism
   8) Job References
   9) Policy Change Procedures
R. Company Records
   1) Filing Procedure
   2) Record Retention Requirements
   3) EEO Data
   4) AAP Records
   5) Health and Safety Reports
   6) Wage/Hour Data
   7) OSHA Records
   8) Statistical Information
   9) Contracts and Agreements
   10) Discipline Records
   11) Access Policies

4.0 UNION VULNERABILITY ASSESSMENT

In addition to analyzing the legal implications of your employment policies and procedures, a personnel audit should also focus on the people in your organization and their perceptions of their employment relationships. Do your employees really believe that their employer is following "golden rule theory" of management and that, as employees, they are being treated with the dignity and respect they deserve? Through one-on-one interviews with all levels of management, but concentrating on front-line supervisors, the personnel "auditor" should determine the real and sometimes deep-seated beliefs, and even hostilities, that employees often harbor, toward their employer on such basic subjects as fairness, consistency, trustworthiness, fair and competitive wages and benefits, communications, upward job mobility and basic human values.

This aspect of the personnel audit should culminate in a written report evaluating current employment relations programs and identifying areas of union vulnerability, complete with recommended corrective action.

The goal of this aspect of the personnel audit is to avert costly union organizational drives which can result if management neglects people, policies and procedures or if management fails to properly delegate responsibility for ensuring a progressive and positive employment relations posture. While a union vulnerability assessment, in itself, cannot guarantee that a union organizational drive "won't happen here," it can go a long way toward achieving that objective.

5.0 EMPLOYEE ATTITUDE SURVEY

Another valuable tool providing insight into a company's status of employee relations is an Employment Attitude Survey. The key to such a survey's value is confidentiality; as a result an organization may want to use an outsider to conduct it. It is also critical that it be tailored for your company's special needs.

6.0 THE IMPORTANCE OF FOLLOWING UP ON VULNERABILITIES IDENTIFIED BY THE AUDIT

It goes without saying that it is critical to follow through on any areas of vulnerability identified by the audit. Keep in mind that the audit could turn out to be a two-edged sword. In other words, if your audit identifies that one of your policies is not legally sound (or that your organization is missing an essential policy), and the Company fails to remedy that problem, a court might find that that type of information should be allowed to be presented to a jury. Given the increasing risk of punitive damages in employment cases, that is not the type of information you want presented to twelve reasonable men and women. As a result, many companies will utilize an attorney to conduct (or oversee) a personnel audit because in that case all of the information and documents generated would be protected from disclosure under the attorney-client privilege!

Chapter 12

WORKERS' COMPENSATION

Cynthia Marcotte Stamer
Gardere & Wynne

1.0 INTRODUCTION

In the United States, a tapestry of workers' compensation, occupational safety and employers' liability statutes predominantly govern the legal responsibility of an employer to provide protection and compensation to workers for injuries or diseases that result from industrial or occupational accidents. While federal law specifically governs the workers' compensation obligations of employers in a number of discrete employment relationships[1] and obligations of most employers to maintain work place safety,[2] state workers' compensation laws predominately define the legal responsibility of employers to provide compensation for industrial injuries and occupational diseases for its workers and their families.

---

[1] *See, e.g.*, Longshore and Harbor Workers' Compensation Act, Pub. L. No. 91-173, 83 stat. 742 (codified as amended at 30 U.S.C. §801 (1976)) (1993) ("LHWCA"), the Federal Employer's Compensation Act 5 U.S.C. § 8101 (1993) ("FECA"), and the Federal Employer's Liability Act, 45 U.S.C. § 51 (1993) ("FELA"), the Federal Coal Mine Health and Safety Act of 1969, 30 U.S.C. § 801 (1993) ("FCMHA").

[2] The Occupational Health and Safety Act, 29 U.S.C. §5(a) (1993) ("OSHA"), requires an employer to provide a safe and healthy work environment and authorizes the Occupational Health and Safety Administration to enforce substantial civil, and in some cases criminal sanctions, against employers who fail to comply with occupational safety and health standards.

The ability of an employer to effectively manage its workers' compensation liabilities and costs while meeting other important employment and business objectives fundamentally depends upon an understanding of the legal and practical requirements imposed by these laws and their relationship to the other obligations and objectives of the employer. Based on this understanding, an employer may tailor its workers' compensation compliance strategies and can select appropriate tools for controlling its employment, occupational injury and workers' compensation liabilities and costs in light of the legal parameters of the state workers' compensation systems in which the employer operates and that employer's particular legal, political and business situation.

2.0 HISTORICAL EVOLUTION OF WORKERS' COMPENSATION

The legal right of workers' to compensation for injuries that result from work-site accidents through state workers' compensation systems is a relatively new phenomenon created in response to modern industrial development.[3] Legal principles concerning the obligation of an employer to provide a safe and healthy work environment for its workers and to provide compensation for workers' deaths and injuries only became a common phenomenon within the 20th Century. Before the industrial revolution, injured workers and their families generally enjoyed little or no recourse for injuries arising out of accidents that occurred in the course and scope of employment. Feudalistic employers enjoyed virtually absolute immunity from liability for the accidental death, dismemberment, disability or other injury to workers performing services for the employer. Beginning in the late 19th Century, however, the industrial revolution and growing class

---

[3] 82 Am. Jur. 2d, *Workers' Compensation* § 1 (1992). For additional information regarding the historical evolution of workers' compensation, *see* Larson, 1 LARSON'S WORKMEN'S COMPENSATION §§4.10-5.30 (1992); 99 C.J.S., *Workmen's Compensation* §§ 1 *et. seq.* (1978).

consciousness gradually made continuation of these feudalistic principles politically inviable. In response, the law in many states gradually evolved to include new theories of employer liability intended to provide injured workers recourse for industrial accidents caused by their employer. Early in this transition period, the law in most states evolved to include a common law remedy for a worker injured as a result of the negligence or other tortious actions of his employer. Pursuant to these employers' liability principles,[4] state law often permitted a worker to recover damages from his employer for an injuries if the employee could prove that employer was negligent or otherwise at fault in causing the injury. While these common law employers' liability theories technically made relief available for certain injured workers, practical problems effectively rendered the right of recovery illusory for most injured workers and their families. The necessity of establishing the fault of the employer and legal limitations on the availability of the negligence remedy such as fellow servant doctrine, the assumption of risk doctrine, and the doctrine of contributory negligence, made proof of liability difficult. Employees also faced significant practical barriers to their ability to maintain the litigation against their employers. Employees that attempted to exercise their right to sue an employer lacked the financial resources to maintain litigation. Employers frequently used retaliatory methods such as terminations, harassment, or blacklisting to discourage workers from filing suit and to prevent other workers from providing testimony or other assistance to a worker bringing an action against an employer. As a result, injured workers usually lacked the financial and legal resources to maintain the litigation necessary to obtain compensation from their injuries under a negligence action. Therefore, most injuries to workers remained uncompensated despite the technical availability of a right to pursue recovery under theories of employers' liability such as negligence.

---

[4] 82 Am. Jur. 2d, *Workers' Compensation* § 7 (1992).

As the labor movement gained strength during the early part of the 20th Century, however, labor reformers applied significant political and economic pressure for the adoption of legal reforms that would expand the availability of compensation for injured workers and improve workplace safety. The United States Congress eventually responded to these pressures by enacting federal occupational health and safety laws and various federal workers' compensation acts designed to provide compensation for certain industrial injuries or occupational diseases to federal employees and certain other narrowly defined groups of workers. Meanwhile, state legislatures responded by enacting a statutory scheme of workers' compensation that governed the compensation payable for physical injuries sustained by employees in industrial accidents. For the most part, these state workers' compensation acts created a uniquely statutory system of compensation for injuries having no basis other than that provided by the applicable statute. These statutory workers' compensation systems provided for an award of money relief for an injury, disablement, or death of a worker that results from an industrial or occupational accident, casualty, or disease arising out of an employment based on the existence of an employment relationship covered under the applicable workers' compensation statute, rather than the existence of fault, according to a statutory schedule of compensation. Consequently, virtually every state now maintains a statutory system of workers' compensation pursuant to which injuries arising out of employments covered under the applicable workers' compensation act may be remedied based on the existence of an employment relationship, rather than the existence of fault, according to a statutory schedule of compensation.[5] These state workers' compensation laws generally require that employers provide certain scheduled benefits and other rights in the manner specified by the statute whenever an employee is injured or dies as a result of an accident while performing services in an employment covered

---

[5]*See*, 82 Am. Jur. 2d §§ 1-4 (1992).

under the applicable workers compensation act, regardless of the fault or negligence of the worker or employer. These state workers' compensation statutes also usually prohibit retaliation against workers, establish procedures for the administration of claims and the resolution of disputes within the system, and obligate employers to provide financial security for the workers' compensation rights afforded under the workers' compensation act.

In most states, the statutorily scheduled compensation constitutes the exclusive remedy available to an injured worker or his beneficiaries for injuries or diseases arising out of employments covered by the applicable workers' compensation act. Pursuant to the exclusive remedy doctrine, most workers' compensation laws grant employers immunity from negligence and other tort claims brought by workers seeking to recover damages for injuries received while performing services in covered employments. Compensation generally is awarded in accordance with the statutory schedule without regard to the fault, if any of the employer or employee in bringing about the injury subject to compensation. The workers' compensation law generally forecloses an employee or his beneficiary from seeking to recover compensation or damages for injuries arising out of a covered employment from an employer who complies with the act other than pursuant to the statutory schedule of compensation. Some states provide a limited exception to this rule, however, if the injured employee proves that the injury resulted from conduct of the employer that rises to the level of gross negligence or misconduct,[6] involves intentional acts, or in some cases, violates certain specific statutory requirements.[7]

---

[6] *See, e.g., Woodson v. Rowland*, 407 S.E.2d 222 (N.C. 1991) (holding exclusive remedy doctrine not a bar where the acts or omissions of the employer that caused the injury to the worker were so dangerous that the employer knew injury was substantially certain to result).

[7] *See, e.g.*, Texas Workers' Compensation Act, Vernon's Ann. Civ. St. Art. 8308-401(b) (1992) (an employee or, in the case of a death, his beneficiary may recover exemplary damages if an intentional act or omission of the employer or the employer's gross negligence caused the injury.)

Ordinarily, the exclusive remedy doctrine protects both the employer and its employees and agents from suits brought by injured workers.[8] The states vary regarding the extent to which the exclusive remedy doctrine bars an employee from obtaining damages from providers of workers' compensation services or coverages, however.

On the other hand, the behavior of the worker typically only affects his right to recover workers' compensation benefits if his behavior fell so far below expected standards of employee conduct as to remove the injury from traditional concepts of an injury arising out of or in the course of employment.[9]

3.0 FEDERAL WORKERS' COMPENSATION LAWS

While the majority of this article primarily deals with state workers' compensation laws, federal law specifically governs the liability of employers for paying workers' compensation or other damages for injuries sustained in a number of discrete employment relationships.[10] For instance, injuries sustained by federal civil servants are exclusively covered under the United State's Employees' Compensation Act (USECA) and such employees are not entitled to benefits under any state workers' compensation laws.

The Longshore and Harbor Workers' Compensation Act (LHWCA)[11] is a federal workers compensation act that

---

[8]*See, e.g., Bustamante v. Tuliano*, 591 A.2d 694 (N.J. Super 1991) (suit by officer against fellow officer barred).

[9]For example, in Florida a worker's willful refusal to use a safety appliance or observe safety rules reduces the worker's recovery by 25 percent.

[10]For a more detailed summary of federal workers' compensation and employers' liability laws, *see* 32 Am. Jur. 2d, *Federal Employers' Liability and Compensation Acts* §109 (1992); DeCarlo and Minkowitz, WORKERS COMPENSATION INSURANCE AND LAW PRACTICE; THE NEXT GENERATION, pp. 29-58 (1989).

[11]33 U.S.C. § 933 (1993). *See also*, Joseph J. Lowenthal, Jr., "Longshore Harbor Workers' Compensation Act," *in* WORKPLACE REMEDIES III: WORKERS' COMPENSATION PRACTICE/COMPLEX WORKPLACE LITIGATION FOR THE '90S AND BEYOND (ABA 1992).

applies to employees in navigable waters. As amended in 1972, it provides for the payment of compensation to employees for disability or death from injury occurring upon the navigable waters of the United States, including any adjoining pier, wharf, dry dock, terminal, building way, marine railway, or any other adjoining area customarily used by an employer in loading, unloading, repairing, or building a vessel.[12] In contrast to the USECA, which makes injuries to a federal employee remediable under federal statute rather than state workers compensation laws, situations often arise in which an a state's workers' compensation laws, rather than LHWCA, may apply to an employee. Whether an employee is covered by the federal statute or the state statute depends on two tests, the situs test and the status test. Under the situs test, an employee is covered under the LHWCA if the injury occurred on navigable waters. Under the status test, an employee is covered under the LHWCA if the employee is engaged in maritime employment.[13]

The Merchant Marine Act of 1920, popularly known as the Jones Act, gives seamen a cause of action against their employer and modifies certain common law defenses.[14] A seaman is not entitled to the benefits of state workers' compensation law, but must rely on the Jones Act. The applicability of whether a person is covered under the Jones Act or a state workers compensation law turns on the question of whether or not the person is a "seaman." In its recent decision in *West Virginia University Hospital v. Casey*, the United States Supreme Court, construing the term "seaman" for the

---

[12] 32 Am. Jur. 2d, *Federal Employers' Liability and Compensation Acts* §109 (1992).

[13] *See* generally 3 LARSON, LARSON WORKMENS' COMPENSATION, §89.00 *et seq.*

[14] 32 Am. Jur. 2d, *Federal Employers' Liability and Compensation Acts* §41, 42 (1992). Regarding the availability of damages to survivors of a decedent seaman, *see Miles v. Apex Marine Corp.*, 111 S. Ct. 317, 327 (1990)(holding that while the Jones Act creates a general maritime cause of action for the wrongful death of a seaman, the damages do not include the loss of society to survivors of the seaman or a general maritime survival action for recovery of the lost future wages of the decedent.)

first time in years, ruled that an employee need not aid in the navigation of a vessel to qualify as a seaman if the employee had an employment-related connection with the vessel that included the performance of the "ship's work."[15]

The Federal Coal Mine Health and Safety Act of 1969, as amended, adopted a separate federal system for compensating persons disabled by respiratory and pulmonary disorders (these disorders are commonly known as black lung disease) that typify the poor health of long term coal miners. Miners covered under this federal act are not covered under state workers' compensation laws. A novel aspect of this act is that it allows compensation on proof of complicated pneumoconiosis, without proof of total disability. The Supreme Court rejected a challenge to this provision which allows compensation without proof of income earning capacity.[16]

The Federal Employers' Liability Act (FELA), for instance, regulates the liability of railroad companies to their employees for injuries occurring while the employees are engaged in interstate commerce.[17] FELA applies to any railroad employee whose duties further or substantially affect interstate commerce. FELA gives employees of railroad companies an action in negligence against the employer. As such, FELA actually is a federal employers' liability act, rather than a law of workers' compensation. In fact, FELA is not a workers compensation law at all. Under FELA, the employer can not raise the common-law defenses of the fellow-servant or assumption of risk. The applicability of FELA is very narrow. FELA does not regulate interstate carriers other than railroad companies. Interstate airlines and motor companies are not covered by FELA and are subject to state workers' compensation legislation.

---

[15]111 S.Ct. 807, 817 (1991).

[16]*Usery v. Turner Elkhorn Mining Co.*, 96 S.Ct. 2882 (1976) (The court stated that "Destruction of earning capacity is not the sole legitimate basis for compulsory compensation of employees by their employers. . .)

[17]32 Am. Jur. 2d., *Federal Employers' Liability and Compensation Acts* §5 (1992).

4.0 STATE WORKERS' COMPENSATION LAWS

While federal law regulates workers' compensation for injuries sustained in certain discrete areas of employment, state workers' compensation laws predominately govern the compensability of workplace injuries. Every state now maintains in force a workers' compensation law pursuant to which injuries arising out of employments covered under the applicable workers' compensation act may be remedied based on the existence of an employment relationship.[18] While each state workers' compensation statute contains a number of unique terms and requirements, the workers' compensation statutes of most states share common characteristics and features. These state workers' compensation laws generally require that employers provide certain scheduled benefits and other rights in the manner specified by the statute whenever an employee is injured or dies as a result of an accident while performing services in an employment covered under the applicable workers compensation act. Under these state workers' compensation laws, the entitlement of a worker or his beneficiary to workers' compensation for an industrial injury or disease primarily depends upon the existence of an employment relationship between the injured worker and some employing trade or business, which is covered by the applicable workers' compensation act and the existence of a sufficient casual connection between a physical injury and an employment relationship between the injured worker and his employing entity. A basic understanding of some of the more significant provisions of such acts is helpful to understand the manner in which the compensability of most industrial accidents are remedied in the United States.

---

[18]*See*, 82 Am. Jur. 2d §§ 1-4 (1992).

4.1 Covered Employments

The workers' compensation system of any particular state only applies to those employment relationships covered by the applicable workers compensation law with a trade or business covered by the applicable workers' compensation act.[19] While most modern workers' compensation statutes generally cover most employment relationships created or performed within the state, each state has specific statutory, administrative, or judicial rules that operate exclude certain categories of work and employment from workers' compensation coverage.

Most state workers' compensation laws incorporate a presumption that the workers' compensation law applies to every contract of service or employment other than those specifically exempted.[20] The workers' compensation acts of the states vary regarding the particular employments subject to workers' compensation coverage.[21] State workers' compensation laws generally do not apply to employments covered by a federal workers' compensation law. A particular workers' compensation statute frequently also may exclude other categories of employment relationships from workers' compensation coverage based on a number of factors, including the nature of the relationship between the worker and the employing entity, the nature of the business or occupation to which the worker is rendering services, the number of persons employed by the employing organization, the nature and character of the workers' duties, or a combination of one or more of these factors.[22]

Many states restrict the applicability of workers' compensation coverage based on the nature of the workers' relationship to the employing trade or business. In some states, the employer must contemplate that the performance of services by the worker will be compensated. In these

---

[19] 82 Am. Jur. 2d, *Workers' Compensation*, §§116-138.

[20] *See, e.g.*, GA. CODE ANN. § 34-9-7 (1992).

[21] *See*, 99 C.J.S. *Workmen's Compensation* § 27 (1978).

[22] 88 C.J.S., *Workmen's Compensation* §§ 29-37.

jurisdictions, workers' compensation is not available for injuries sustained in gratuitous workers.[23] In many, but not all, states, the workers' compensation act only applies if the worker performs services in the capacity of a common law employee of a trade, business, or occupation. Under such statutes, the workers' compensation law generally applies only to those employments in which the facts and circumstances demonstrate that the hiring entity possessed the right to control and direct the particular work or undertaking as to the manner or means of its accomplishment.[24] A number of workers' compensation acts expressly exclude workers performing services for a trade or business in the capacity of an independent contractor, partner, or sole proprietor from eligibility for workers' compensation coverage. In other states, however, workers' compensation coverage may extend to independent contractors, sole proprietors, or partners under certain circumstances.[25] Because a number of states have developed special rules regarding the coverage and compensability of injuries sustained by independent contractors, sole proprietors, partners, contract laborers, subcontractors or leased employees, however, the term employment may be more broadly defined by statute or judicial opinion in many states. Indeed, some workers' compensation laws apply to all contracts for hire within the state not specifically excluded from coverage, regardless of the nature of the employment relationship.[26]

Often, special problems arise regarding the characterization of hiring arrangements involving independent contractors or subcontractors. As a general rule, most state workers' compensation laws provide that an employer who engages an independent contractor is not liable for the injuries of the independent contractor or his employees. In many of these jurisdictions, however, several courts have created common law exceptions to this rule. Under certain circumstances, employers

---

[23]*See, Harlow v. Agway, Inc.*, 327 A.2d 856 (Me. 1974).

[24]*See, e.g, Tharpe v. G.E. Moore Co., 174* S.E.2d 397 (S.C. 1970).

[25]*See, e.g.*, S.C. CODE ANN. § 42-1-30 (Law Co-op. 1992)

[26]*See, e.g.*, GA. CODE ANN. § 34-9-1 (1992).

may be required to provide workers' compensation for independent contractors (and the independent contractors employees) hired to do a job. For example, an employer is responsible for injuries to a independent contractor or his employees if the employer retains substantial control over the independent contractor's work.[27] Another judicially created exception is the "inherently dangerous" doctrine. Under this doctrine, an employer who engages a contractor to perform inherently dangerous work is responsible for any injuries to the contractor or the contractor's employees. In other instances, specific statutory provisions may obligate an employer to provide coverage with respect to an independent contractor. When an employer mistakenly believes that it is not responsible for the independent contractor or his employees and fails to maintain workers compensation coverage, many state workers' compensation laws provide that the employer may be responsible in tort for the accidents to these persons.

Under certain workers' compensation laws, the employment of a worker to perform service on an intermittent basis or an indefinite period may cause the employment to be exempt from workers' compensation as "casual employment."[28] Where a workers' compensation law contains a casual employment exemption, the applicability of the exemption generally must be decided based on the facts and circumstances of the particular employment in question.

In many states, the size or nature of the business or occupation to which the worker is rendering services may affect the applicability of the workers' compensation law to a particular employment relationship. Many workers' compensation acts include provisions that provide special rules regarding the application of workers' compensation laws for certain categories of employers. A number of workers'

---

[27]*See,e.g., Kelley v. Howard S. Wright Const. Co*, 582 P.2d 500 (1978). (General contractor responsible in tort for OSHA safety violation which resulted in injury to subcontractor's employee. The basis for the court's determination that the general contractor was liable was the fact that the general contractor had general supervisory and coordinating authority over the sub contractor's work).

[28]*See*, 82 Am. Jur. 2d, *Workers' Compensation* §§121-125 (1992).

compensation laws exclude employments with businesses based on the number of workers' that the business employs.[29] Workers' compensation statutes also often specifically exempt certain employments or occupations such as farm labor[30] and domestic service[31] from workers' compensation coverage. The protection afforded under a workers' compensation act frequently only applies to persons injured while performing, or considered to be performing, services for a trade, business or occupation, profession or vocation that the workers' compensation act identifies as an employer covered by workers' compensation. The determination whether the employing entity is engaged in a trade or business under such workers' compensation act depends on the terms of the applicable workers' compensation statute.[32] Thus, the parameters of the employments covered by workers' compensation vary among the states. Nevertheless, in every jurisdiction, certain enterprises are excluded from status as an employer obligated to provide workers' compensation coverage under the terms of the workers' compensation act. For instance, where a workers' compensation act requires employment in a trade, business, or occupation, courts frequently construe the statute as requiring that the principal's decision to retain the services of a worker be motivated by a pecuniary gain or benefit to bring a trade or

---

[29] *See*, 82 Am. Jur. 2d, Workers' Compensation § 120 (1992); Burton & Schmidle, WORKERS' COMPENSATION DESK BOOK, p.III-5 (1992); DeCarlo and Minkowitz, WORKERS COMPENSATION LAW AND PRACTICE: THE NEXT GENERATION, 70 (1989).

[30] *See*, 82 Am. Jur. 2d, *Workers' Compensation* § 128 (1992); Burton and Schmidle, WORKERS' COMPENSATION DESK BOOK, III-7 (1992); DeCarlo and Minkowitz, WORKERS COMPENSATION LAW AND PRACTICE: THE NEXT GENERATION, 71-74 (1989).

[31] *See*, 82 Am. Jur. 2d, *Workers' Compensation* § 127; Burton and Schmidle, WORKERS' COMPENSATION DESK BOOK, III-9 (1992); DeCarlo and Minkowitz, WORKERS COMPENSATION LAW AND PRACTICE: THE NEXT GENERATION, 75-76 (1989).

[32] *See*, e.g., 99 C.J.S. §§ 37-38.

business within workers' compensation coverage.³³ To the extent that an employment is not subject to one of these or some other exclusion under the applicable provisions of the applicable workers' compensation law, however it generally will be covered by the provisions of the workers' compensation act within that state.

4.2 Compensable Injuries

In order to qualify for compensation payments under any state's workers compensation scheme, a worker generally must suffer an injury that qualifies as a compensable injury. The compensability of an injury usually depends on the nature of the injury and its relationship to an injury or disease arising out of a covered employment. Generally, compensable injuries are those physical injuries sustained in an accident that arises out of and in the course and scope of an employment covered by the workers' compensation law, and not otherwise excluded from compensability under the applicable law.³⁴

The elements that an injury must satisfy to qualify as a compensable injury for workers' compensation purposes depends upon the terms of the particular state workers' compensation law. In most states, however, the elements required to establish compensability are similar. Thus, most states require that for a condition to qualify as a compensable injury, it must be (1) an accidental injury or, in some cases, an occupational disease, that (2) arises out and in the course and scope of covered employment under the workers' compensation law.³⁵

1. Injury. To qualify for compensation under workers' compensation, most workers' compensation laws require that a

---

³³*See also,* 82 Am. Jur. 2d, *Workmen's Compensation* §§ 147-153 (1993). *But see, O'Leary v. Brown-Pacific-Maxon, Inc.,* 340 U.S. 504 (1951) (ruling that an employee need not be engaged at the time of the injury in an activity of benefit to his employer).

³⁴*See, e.g, South Carolina Workers' Compensation Act,* 42 S.C. CODE ANN. § 42-1-160 (Law Co-op 1993).

³⁵*See Doe v. South Carolina State Hospital,* 328 S.E.2d 652 (S.C. Ct. App. 1985).

worker must sustain an "injury" within the course and scope of employment. The term "injury" has been variously construed from state to state.[36] In some states, the statutes define the term "injury" as damage, harm or violence to the physical structure of the body and diseases and infections resulting naturally therefrom. Other jurisdictions define injuries covered by the workers' compensation law more broadly so as to generally include work-related harmful changes to the human organism, arising out of the course and scope of employment.

2. Accidental Injury. Most, but not all,[37] state workers' compensation laws traditionally have restricted compensability to injuries to the physical structure of the body of a worker as a result of an accident rather than as a result of a disease.[38] Under these traditional notions of compensability, the accidental physical injury element resulted in a distinction between the treatment of accidental injuries and occupational diseases. Where applicable, the "accidental injury" element usually requires that the injury or physical condition result from a sudden, unexpected or an instantaneous occurrence.[39] Under this traditional construction, conditions attributable to cumulative exposures to work place traumas, occupational diseases, and other conditions that arose or developed slowly over time as a result of repeated exposure to certain risks in the workplace were viewed as occupational diseases and were not compensable.[40] Accordingly, diseases in any form other than those diseases that resulted naturally and unavoidably

---

[36]*See*, "The Definition of Injury Under the Workers' Compensation Act: Revisited and Redefined," 49 Mont. L. Rev. 341 (Summer 1988).

[37]*See, e.g., Village v. General Motors Corp.*, G.M.A.D, 472 N.E.2d 1079 (Ohio 1984); *Westerhold v. Unitog-Holden Mfg. Co.*, 707 S.W.2d 456 (Mo. App. 1906).

[38]See, e.g., Silkwood v. Kerr-McGee Corp., 667 F.2d 908 (10th Cir. 1977)(interpreting Oklahoma Workers' Compensation Act); Reams v. Burlington Industries, 255 S.E.2d 586 (N.C. App. 1979).

[39]*See, e.g., Landford v. Clinton Cotton Mills*, S.E.2d 36 (S.C. 1944); *Pierce v. Phelps Dodge Corp.*, 26 P.2d 1017 (Ariz. 1933); *McCrory Stores v. Pence*, 453 So.2d 159 (Fla. 1984) (the term "accident" for workers compensation is a sudden or instantaneous act or occurrence.").

[40]*See*, 82 Am. Jur. 2d, *Workers' Compensation* § 321 *et. seq.* (1992).

from an accident historically did not qualify as compensable injuries under state workers' compensation laws. Pursuant to this distinction, disorders such as carpel tunnel which are caused by the repeated or long term exposure of a worker to certain workplace hazards historically did not qualify as compensable injuries. Similarly, the courts in most states traditionally have viewed repetitive trauma disorders, cumulative trauma disorders, occupational diseases, and mental and emotional injuries as developing over time, rather than resulting from a sudden, instantaneous occurrence, construction, and therefore, not compensable injuries.

The treatment of diseases related to employment as compensable injuries for workers' compensation is not uniform, however, and continues to evolve in many jurisdictions, however.[41] Originally, the term "injury" or "physical injury" predominantly were construed to exclude occupational diseases and cumulative trauma disorders. Under most modern workers' compensation laws, however, many occupational diseases and cumulative trauma now qualify for compensation, either pursuant to express statutory provisions or based on judicially expansive constructions of the term "injury."[42] A large number of workers' compensation cases involve claims relating to carpel tunnel syndrome.[43] These and other cumulative trauma

---

[41] For additional information regarding the treatment of occupational diseases, *see also*, DeCarlo and Minkowitz, WORKERS COMPENSATION INSURANCE AND LAW PRACTICE: THE NEXT GENERATION 259-269 (1989); 82 Am. Jur. 2d, *Workers' Compensation* § 326 *et. seq.* (1992).

[42] *See, e.g.*, Decarlo and Minkowitz, "Workers' Compensation and Employers' Liability Law: Recent Developments," 26 TORT & INS. LAW J. 444, 447-448 (Winter 1991).

[43] *See*, George E. Scheer, M.D.,"Carpel Tunnel Syndrome," *in* WORKPLACE REMEDIES III; WORKERS' COMPENSATION PRACTICE/COMPLEX WORKPLACE LITIGATION FOR THE '90S AND BEYOND (1992); Richard K. Johnson, "Carpel Tunnel Syndrome: The Petitioner's Perspective," *in* WORKPLACE REMEDIES III; WORKERS' COMPENSATION PRACTICE/COMPLEX WORKPLACE LITIGATION FOR THE '90S AND BEYOND (1992); "Carpel Tunnel Syndrome: The Defense Perspective," *in* WORKPLACE REMEDIES III; WORKERS' COMPENSATION PRACTICE/COMPLEX WORKPLACE LITIGATION FOR THE '90S AND BEYOND (1992).

disorder claims generally qualify as compensable injuries if demonstrated to sufficiently relate to employment.[44]

The jurisdictions differ regarding the compensability of mental and emotional disorders as injuries.[45] The courts in a number of jurisdictions have begun to expand the concept of an "accidental injury" or "compensable injury" to include certain mental or emotional disorders as compensable injuries.[46] While some jurisdictions have required that there be some physical trauma or injury which led to the mental injury[47], other jurisdictions have not required a physically traumatic injury as a prerequisite.[48] Other jurisdictions, however, restrict the conditions under which mental and emotional injuries qualify for compensation. In New York, for example, the right to recover for mental injury is restricted if the injury is solely mental and based upon work-related stress directly resulting from certain employment actions undertaken by the employer in good faith.[49]

---

[44]*See, e.g.*, *McLaughlin v. Self-Insurance Services*, 361 N.W.2d 585 (Neb. 1985).

[45]For additional information regarding the treatment of mental and emotional disorders and stress claims, *see also*, DeCarlo and Minkowitz, WORKERS COMPENSATION INSURANCE AND LAW PRACTICE: THE NEXT GENERATION 259-269 (1989); 82 Am. Jur. 2d, Workers' Compensation § 337 *et. seq.* (1992).

[46]*Averill v. Dreher-Holloway*, 593 A.2d 1149 (N.H. 1991); *Gacioch v. Stroh Brewing Co.*, 466 N.W.2d 302 (Mich. App. 1990); *Wolf v. Sibley, Lindsay & Curr Co.*, (N.Y. 2d 1975), 303 N.E. 2d 603 (1975). *Also generally see*, 82 Am. Jur. 2d, *Workers' Compensation* §322 *et. seq.*; DeCarlo and Minkowitz, "Workers' Compensation and Employers' Liability Law: Recent Developments," 26 TORT & INSURANCE LAW J. 444, 445 (Winter 1991).

[47]*See, e.g. Hemphill Drug Co. v. Mann* 274, So.2d 117 (Miss. 1973) (psychosis manifesting itself in hallucinations, delusions held compensable where there was clear evidence of causal relationship between work-related accident resulting in serious injury).

[48]*See, e.g., Jones v. Hartford Accident & Indemnity Co.*, 811 S.W.2d 516 (Tenn. 1991) (holding an employee may recover for emotional stress that resulted in a purely emotional injury); *Wolfe v. Sibley, Lindsay & Curr Co.*, 330 N.E.2d 603 (1975).

[49]*See*, DeCarlo and Minkowitz, "Workers' Compensation and Employers' Liability Law: Recent Developments," 26 TORT & INSURANCE L. J. 444, 449 (Winter, 1991).

3. Within the Course and Scope of Employment. The compensable injury must result from an accident that occurs "within the course and scope of employment" in order to qualify as compensable injuries under a workers' compensation system. This "course and scope of employment" requirement regulates whether the worker's injury is sufficiently related to his employment to justify compensation. An injury is said to arise in the course of employment when it takes place within the period of the employment, at a place where the employee reasonably may be, and while he is fulfilling his duties or engaged in doing something incidental thereto.[50] Therefore, an accidental injury occurring while an employee is engaging in an activity for the benefit of an employer usually qualifies as compensable. Acts of employees reasonably necessary to maintain the life, comfort or convenience of the employee while carrying out his duties for the employer even though not acts of service are considered "incidental employment risks" included within the course and scope of employment.[51] Sometimes, injuries that occur during social or recreational activities are compensable. These are usually considered within the scope of employment when the employer derives substantial direct benefit from the activity or the employer requires participation or the activities occur on the employer's premises during a lunch or recreational period.[52]

However, there are very distinct limitations which apply to the "course of employment" requirement. For instance, courts will not compensate an employee for an injury that occurs during the normal working hours if it occurs as a result of an employee's "frolic and detour." An employee generally will be considered on a "frolic and detour" if, for example, an employee deviates from his normal business for the employer and engages in a purely personal errand for the worker's own convenience.

---

[50]*See*, Larson, *Larson Workmen's Compensation*, §14.00 (1992).

[51]Where an employee is washing up after work, satisfying his thirst, seeking fresh air, answering telephone calls, eating lunch, or even going to the toilet. Such personal acts have been considered incidental to employment and thus compensable. *Indiana & Michigan Electric Comp. v. Morgan*, 494 N.E.2d 991 (Ind. App. 1986).

[52]*See, e.g.*, Larson, LARSON'S WORKMENS' COMPENSATION §22.00 (1992).

Likewise, under the "going and coming" rule adhered to by most jurisdictions, accidents that occur as the worker is going or coming from his employer's workplace usually are not considered to occur within the course and scope of employment.[53]

4. Injuries Ineligible For Compensation. Most workers' compensation laws expressly exclude certain injuries from eligibility for compensation. The applicable exclusions vary from states to state. All workers' compensation systems, for instance, exclude injuries and illnesses arising out of risks unrelated to employment from eligibility for compensation. State workers' compensation laws frequently also provide that self-inflicted injuries, injuries sustained while the worker as was engaged in horseplay or certain other categories of misconduct are not compensable.

5.0 COMPENSATION AND BENEFITS

Most state workers' compensation laws provide monetary compensation in accordance with a schedule of compensation established under the applicable workers' compensation statute to an injured workers for certain medical expenses, lost earnings, permanent disablements, death, or certain other losses arising out of a compensable injury. The compensation payable to an injured workers, or in the case of a death, his surviving dependents, usually is fixed by the applicable statute and is determined based on a statutory formula or schedule. Usually, the amount of compensation payable is subject to arbitrary minimums and maximum limits set forth in the applicable statute. The recovery of this relatively modest, but assured compensation usually constitutes the exclusive means through which an employee or his dependent may obtain a remedy for his injury. The workers' compensation statute usually bars a

---

[53]*See, e.g. Santa Rosa Junior College v. Workers' Compensation Appeals Board*, 708 P. 2d 673 (Cal. 1985) (A professor who frequently took work home with knowledge and implicit permission of employer was not covered when killed on the way to his office at home). Compare *Wilson v. Workers Comp. App. Board*, 545 P. 2d 225 (Cal. 1976).

worker from suing his employer for damages for any injury sustained in an employment covered by the workers' compensation law. Employees often retain the right to sue third parties whose negligence cause the injury remains, however, subject to an obligation to apply the proceeds recovered from the third party to reimburse the employer for the compensation outlay.

5.1 Medical Expense Compensation

All workers' compensation laws generally pay compensation to an injured worker for costs and expenses that he actually incurs for necessary medical treatment and care of compensable injuries. The medical expense compensation provided to an injured worker usually covers one hundred percent of the actual medical charges and expenses appropriately incurred for medically necessary treatment of physical injuries sustained in a compensable accident for an unlimited time period following the accident. In some cases, the workers' compensation statute may exclude coverage for treatments, charges or expenses that are not medically necessary or appropriate for the treatment of the particular injury sustained by the workers. Certain state workers' compensation laws include medical fee schedules that regulate the amount of compensation that will be paid for the supplies, care or treatment received by an injured worker. In other states, the medical compensation may be limited to some percentage of the usual charge made for the treatment within the area in which the treatment was rendered. Under certain circumstances, certain types of treatment or supplies may be excluded from coverage under the express terms of the applicable workers' compensation law.

Since the 1970s, many jurisdictions have guaranteed to the injured worker the right to select the treating physician. Many employers view the latitude enjoyed by employees to select physicians as a major contributor to systemic fraud, spiraling health care costs, and excessive periods of disability that has made workers' compensation such a significant, or in some cases a prohibitive, operating expense for many employers. In the last several years, however, a growing number of states have amended their rules to provide employers and insurers with greater input in the selection of the treating physician.[54]

5.2 Wage Loss Compensation

All workers' compensation systems also generally compensate an injured worker for a portion of lost earnings, if any, incurred by the worker during periods of disability that result from a compensable injury. If a compensable injury disables the worker's ability to engage in employment for a period that extends beyond the applicable statutory elimination period, the workers' compensation law usually will provide wage replacement compensation for each week that the worker is disabled from employment as a result of a compensable injury, up to the maximum period, if any, specified by the statute.[55] Temporary wage replacement compensation payments received by a worker generally are included in the taxable income of the worker for federal income tax purposes.[56]

Ordinarily, the amount of the wage replacement compensation is a scheduled amount, calculated under a statutory formula based on a percentage of the weekly wage or spendable earnings of the worker at the time of his accident, subject to certain arbitrary minimums and maximums established by the applicable workers' compensation law. In the majority of states, the wage replacement compensation equals 66 2/3 percent of the workers' weekly wage.[57] In the District

---

[54]*See* "Pennsylvania House, Senate Approve Workers' Comp. Bill," NATIONAL UNDERWRITER, June 28, 1993 at 28.

[55]*See*, South Carolina Workers' Compensation Act, S.C. CODE ANN. §42-1-20 (1976).

[56]26 U.S.C. 104 (1993).

[57]In 1992, this percentage generally applied in Alabama, Arizona, Arkansas, California, Colorado, Delaware, Florida, Georgia, Hawaii, Illinois, Kansas, Kentucky, Louisiana, Maine, Maryland, Minnesota, Mississippi, Missouri, Montana, Nevada, New Hampshire, New Mexico, New York, North Carolina, North Dakota, Ohio (after the initial 12 weeks of disability), Oklahoma, Pennsylvania, Puerto Rico, Rhode Island, South Carolina, South Dakota, Tennessee, Utah, Vermont, Virgin Islands, Virginia, Wisconsin, and Wyoming.

of Colombia, for example, the wage replacement compensation generally equals the lesser of 66 2/3 percent of the injured employee's wage or 80 percent of his spendable earnings. However, the percentage of wages payable as wage replacement compensation under the workers' compensation statute varies widely from state to state.[58]

Most workers' compensation laws set arbitrary limits on the amount of the temporary wage replacement compensation. All jurisdictions limit the maximum amount of the weekly wage replacement compensation payable under the statute. Some states also guarantee that the amount of the temporary wage replacement compensation will equal some minimum amount set forth in the statutes. The applicable minimums and maximums vary among the jurisdictions. In most jurisdictions, the maximum temporary wage replacement compensation is stated as a limitation on the weekly payment amount. A few jurisdictions impose aggregate limitations on the wage replacement compensation payable with respect to a particular compensable injury. Many workers' compensation statutes reduce the amount of the wage replacement compensation by the amount of certain other types of wage replacement payments to which the injured worker may be entitled during a period of disability. Depending on the jurisdiction, these offsetting benefits may include social security benefits, unemployment insurance benefits, and benefits received under an employer-sponsored pension or disability plan[59]. Under certain circumstances, some workers' compensation acts also provide for increases in the basic weekly wage replacement benefit payment based on the number of dependent children,

---

[58]In 1992, for example, Alaska, Connecticut, Iowa and Michigan, generally calculated the basic weekly wage replacement benefit payable during periods of disability at 80 percent of the employee's spendable earnings. In contrast, the applicable percentage was 60-75 percent in Washington, 67 percent in Idaho; 60 percent in Massachusetts; and between 70 and 75 percent in New Jersey, West Virginia, Ohio, and Texas.

[59]Provisions requiring the offset of workers' compensation benefits by benefits payable under an employer-sponsored benefit plan may be unenforceable under certain circumstances. *See Shaw v. Delta Airlines*, 103 S. Ct. 2890 (1983).

if any, supported by the injured employee or other extenuating circumstances.

The duration of temporary wage replacement payments varies among the states. Payments of wage replacement compensation usually begins after the covered worker satisfies the elimination period applicable under the workers' compensation statute. To satisfy the elimination period, the compensable injury usually must precipitate the worker from earning his pre-injury wage for the number of days specified in the workers' compensation law. If a worker satisfies the applicable elimination period, he usually will qualify for wage replacement compensation retroactively to the beginning of his period of incapacity. In most jurisdictions an injured worker generally remains entitled to receive wage replacement compensation throughout the period that he remains disabled.[60] In all jurisdictions, eligibility for wage replacement compensation terminates when the worker has recovered from his injury under the terms of the applicable workers' compensation statute. In most jurisdiction, entitlement to temporary wage replacement compensation continues as long as the injury prevents the employee from obtaining and retaining employment at wages equivalent to his pre-injury wage because of a compensable injury.[61] In a number of jurisdictions, however, the statute limits the time period for which wage replacement compensation is payable. A minority of the states limit the period of eligibility of an injured worker for wage replacement compensation to the shorter of the period of disability or the date that the medical condition of the injured worker reaches some statutorily established level of

---

[60]In 1992, these jurisdictions generally included Alabama, Arizona, California, Colorado, Connecticut, Delaware, Georgia, Hawaii, Illinois, Iowa, Kansas, Kentucky, Louisiana, Maine, Maryland, Michigan, Montana, Nebraska, Nevada, New Hampshire, New York, North Carolina, North Dakota, Ohio, Oregon, Pennsylvania, Rhode Island, South Dakota, Tennessee, Vermont, Virginia Islands, Washington, Wisconsin, and Wyoming.

[61]*See, e.g.*, Texas Workers' Compensation Act, Vernon's Ann.Civ.St. art. 8308-1.03 (1993).

"medical improvement or stability."[62] Certain jurisdictions limit the duration of wage replacement compensation to a specified number of weeks.[63]

5.3 Permanent Disablement Compensation

Most state workers' compensation laws also pay scheduled amounts of compensation to a worker for the severance or permanent disablement of all or a portion of his body as a result of a compensable injury. Compensation for permanent injury or disablement based on the statutory schedule tends to yield a more favorable result to an employer than would apply if the employer were required to pay in a possible tort recovery for an employee's injury. Normally, a worker who succeeds in a obtaining a tort remedy for an injury caused by the negligence of an employer would be entitled to recover in full for past and future wage loss plus damages for pain and suffering. On the other hand, under a workers' compensation statute, a worker is generally not compensated for pain and suffering. Rather, the permanent disablement benefit payable under workers' compensation is usually a scheduled periodic payment based on a specified percentage of the wages of the employee at the time of his injury, calculated in accordance with the statutory schedule.

State workers' compensation statutes differ in the basis upon which they provide permanent disablement compensation and the method of calculation used to determine the amount of compensation payable to a worker as a result of a permanent disablement. Some workers compensation statutes use a "physical impairment" approach. These statutes typically utilize a fixed schedule for a particular disablement or impairment. The loss of an index finger entitles a worker to a certain

---

[62]Alaska, Minnesota, and Texas.

[63]New Mexico (700 weeks [generally; 100 weeks for primary and secondary mental impairment]; Oklahoma (300 weeks); Puerto Rico (312 weeks); South Carolina (500 weeks). Arkansas and Mississippi (450 weeks), Florida (260 weeks), Indiana (500 weeks), Massachusetts (156 weeks), Missouri and New Jersey (400 weeks).

amount of money whereas the loss of a leg would entitle a worker to another sum. Under this type of system, "the loss of a left index finger will result in the same measure of benefit whether the injured worker is a professional violinist or a receptionist."[64]

Other state workers' compensation statutes adhere to a "loss of wage earning" theory in calculating benefits. These statutes ordinarily determined the amount of recovery a worker receives based on whether the worker has lost any capacity to earn income in the worker's field. Often, these statutes distinguish between a functional impairment of the body and an occupational impairment. Thus, a right-handed teacher who loses her left index finger is entitled to nothing under this type of system if there is no loss of ability to teach, whereas a concert pianist is entitled to benefits under the workers' compensation statute since wages are definitely diminished, if not destroyed. While this approach may seem harsh, the logic behind this theory is that a workers' compensation statute is not a health insurance statute, but rather a wage loss statute. However, some states do temper the harshness of a pure "loss of earning" statute with a supplement in order to reflect the loss of bodily integrity.

Traditionally, many workers' compensation statutes have paid, or permitted payment of, the disablement compensation in the form of a lump sum payment. Other workers' compensation statutes require that disablement compensation be paid in a periodic form. Lump sum payments have been criticized a number of grounds. For instance, certain policy makers have argued that lump sum payments frequently are squandered by their recipients for purposes unrelated to rehabilitation or provision of security for lost future earning capacity. Others have argued that such payments encourage fraud by providing incentives to exaggerate the magnitude and permanence of a disablement. In response to these criticisms,

---

[64]Matthew W. Finkin et al., LEGAL PROTECTION FOR THE INDIVIDUAL EMPLOYEE, 625 (1989).

many states have amended their workers' compensation statutes to prohibit lump sum payment of disablement benefits.

5.4 Death Compensation For Survivors

All workers' compensation systems provide protection for the surviving spouse and dependent children, if any, of a worker in the event that the worker dies from compensable injuries sustained within the course and scope of an employment covered by the applicable workers' compensation statute. Nearly all jurisdictions pay the death benefit under a workers' compensation statute as a weekly or monthly annuity benefit for a fixed period set forth in the applicable statute. The amount of the weekly or monthly benefit payable as a result of the death of a covered worker usually equals a statutorily prescribed percentage of the wages of the covered worker at the time of his death (the "basic death benefit"), adjusted in accordance with any other applicable provision of the workers' compensation statute. The amount of the death benefit typically is subject to certain minimum and maximums established under workers' compensation statutes or other adjustments percentage.

The percentage of the covered workers' wage applied to calculate the death benefit varies among the jurisdictions. In a majority of jurisdictions, the basic death benefit payable where a covered employee is survived by a spouse and children is 66 2/3 of the weekly wage of the deceased employee at the time of his death.[65] Significant variation exists among the percentages applied in the remaining jurisdictions to determine the basic death benefit payable under such circumstances. Many states increase the percentage of the workers' weekly wage used to calculate the death benefit if the deceased worker leaves behind dependent children as well as a spouse. For instance, in

---

[65]*In* 1992, these jurisdictions included Alabama, Arizona, Arkansas, California, Colorado, District of Colombia, Florida, Georgia, Hawaii, Illinois, Indiana, Kansas, Maine, Maryland, Massachusetts, Minnesota, Mississippi, Missouri, Montana, Nevada, New Mexico, New York, North Carolina, North Dakota, Ohio, Pennsylvania, Tennessee, Utah, and Virginia.

Alabama, the District of Colombia, Florida, Hawaii, Kentucky, Minnesota, Nebraska, New Jersey, Oklahoma, Puerto Rico, Rhode Island, Tennessee, Vermont, the applicable percentage used to determine the basic death benefit amount generally is 50 percent. In contrast, if the covered employee is survived both by a spouse and dependent children, the applicable percentage increases to at least 66 2/3 percent. In contrast, however, the applicable percentage used to calculate the basic death benefit does not fluctuate in response to whether the covered worker is survived by dependent children, rather than a spouse only.[66]

State workers' compensation laws also differ regarding the duration of time that death compensation payments are made to surviving dependents. The majority of jurisdictions cease benefit payments with respect to a child when the child attains a maximum age specified in the applicable statute. Most jurisdictions also provide for the termination of death benefit payments with respect to a surviving spouse on or shortly after the remarriage of the spouse. A minority of jurisdictions limit the duration of death compensation payments to a fixed period of weeks specified in the statute.

5.5 Miscellaneous Benefits

Some jurisdictions liberally construe the term "treatment" required to relieve and to cure a worker of the effects of his compensable injury. As a result, employers in some states are required to pay for a variety of things including expenses incurred for child care[67], transportation costs incurred as a

---

[66]In 1992, these jurisdictions generally included Alaska, California, Colorado, Connecticut, Georgia, Illinois, Indiana, Iowa, Kansas, Maine, Maryland, Massachusetts, Michigan, Missouri, Nevada, New Mexico, New York, North Carolina, North Dakota, Ohio, South Carolina, Texas, Utah, Virginia and West Virginia.

[67]*See, e.g., Doctors Hosp. of Lake Worth v. Robinson*, 411 So.2d 958 (Fla. App. 1982) (Since injured worker could not care for her child due to work related injury, worker suffered from depression. The court determined that it was necessary that worker's daughter be placed in a nursery school at the employer's expense in order to facilitate the worker's recovery).

result of medical treatment for the injury,[68] nursing services in the home, and the building of an addition to a house.[69]

5.6 Prohibitions Against Discrimination Against Employees Claiming Workers' Compensation Benefits

To prevent employers from using intimidation tactics to deter employees from claiming their rightful compensation, many state workers' compensation statutes include provisions expressly prohibiting employers from discharging or otherwise discriminating against employees for claiming workers' compensation benefits or rights.[70] In a number of other states, courts recognize a common law cause of action based on public policy grounds, pursuant to which employees may recover against an employer for discrimination or retaliation against the worker for exercising his workers' compensation rights.[71] The sanction for violations of these prohibitions vary among the states. In some states, for instance, willful discrimination or attempts to obstruct or impede the filing of claims for workers' compensation constitutes a misdemeanor punishable by fines, imprisonment, or both.[72] In some states, retaliation exposes

---

[68]*See, e.g. Smith v. Chase Bank Co.*, 634 P.2d 809 (Ok. App. 1981) (Court held that employer had to pay transportation expenses for a 240 mile round trip to injured worker's physician since worker had the right to chose her own physician).

[69]*See, e.g., Squeo v. Comfort Control Corp.*, 494 A.2d 313 (N.J. Super 1985) (Worker was quadriplegic as a result of work-related injury. Worker was institutionalized and severely depressed as a result of the institutionalization. Court held that the employer was required to pay for the cost of building an addition to the worker's parent's house so that the worker could live in the addition. This was considered necessary treatment to relieve the worker of depression).

[70]As of 1991, these states include Alabama, Arkansas, California, Connecticut, Hawaii, Illinois, Indiana, Kansas, Kentucky, Louisiana, Maine, Maryland, Michigan, Missouri, Montana, New Jersey, New York, Ohio, Oklahoma, Oregon, South Carolina, Texas, Vermont, Virginia, and Wisconsin.

[71]*See, Framption v. Central Indiana Gas*, 299 N.W.2d 425 (Ind. 1973); *Kelsey v. Motorola*, 384 N.E.2d 353 (Ill. 1978); *Murphy v. City of Topeka-Shawnee County Department of Labor Services*, 630 P.2d 186 (Kan. App. 1981).

[72]*See* Arkansas Workers Compensation Act, ARK. CODE ANN. § (1992) 81-1335; California Workers' Compensation Act, CAL; WORKERS COMP. CODE § 132a (1992).

the employer to liability to the employee for actual damages as well as significant punitive damage awards.

5.7 Administration and Dispute Resolution

Most workers' compensation statutes require that claims and appeals within the workers' compensation system be administered under detailed administrative rules and procedures and allows such claims to resort to the judicial system only in rare cases. These administration procedures generally were designed to provide an alternative mechanism designed to facilitate the compensation objectives of the statute and to minimize litigation. Therefore, these rules and procedures traditionally tend to incorporate presumptions and procedures that favor the rights of workers over those of the employers. Employers typically are prohibited from retaliation against employees for exercise of their workers' compensation rights and remedies under the applicable workers' compensation statute. Employers may be required to comply with other statutory requirements regarding accident and injury reporting, employee notice and posting requirements, and other administrative and safety guidelines and rules.

5.8 Financial Security Requirements

Most state workers compensation statutes require an employer to secure in advance its ability to fulfill its financial and administrative responsibilities under the applicable workers' compensation statute. To meet this responsibility, workers' compensation laws generally require that an employer purchase workers' compensation insurance from a private insurer, contribute to a state workers' compensation fund or establish certain self-insurance arrangements. The states often differ regarding the means through which employers may meet the financial responsibility requirements of the laws. In the states where workers' compensation is required, an employer may either be required to subscribe to the state-mandated program, or may be required to purchase insurance coverage according to state-mandated coverage requirements from a private insurer. Other jurisdictions permit certain qualifying employers to self-insure some or all of their workers' compensation obligation.

Where an employer chooses or is required to purchase private insurance, state law generally dictates that the policy must meet certain coverage requirements. However, a number of states allow some employers to use policies containing nontraditional coverage or premium terms to meet these requirements. High deductible and retrospectively rated workers' compensation insurance policies, for example, are a permissible means through which employers in many states can reduce their obligation to prefund workers' compensation costs. An employer that meets the underwriting and other requirements for use of these policies may find that these types of arrangements, coupled with other safety and cost-containment programs, are effective means for controlling workers' compensation costs. Under a high deductible policy, employers often may obtain a significant reduction in the amount of the premium charged for their workers' compensation policy if the workers' compensation insurance policy requires the employer to pay a significant deductible for each covered injury. Under a retrospectively-rated policy, an employer negotiates with an insurance carrier for payment of a small amount of pre-paid premium, a periodic payment schedule designed to mirror the periodic amount of projected claims incurred in a given time period up to a certain limit, and retroactive payments after certain amounts of times have elapsed which would be based on actual claims experience over that duration of time. Where the applicable law permits self-insurance, an employer choosing to self-insure usually must obtain approval to self-insure, based on an application that demonstrates that the employer meets the requirements in that state to operate as a self-insurer. To be eligible to self insure, the employer generally must meet certain statutory and regulatory requirements, provide evidence of sufficient financial strength and liquidity to assure that the employer will meet its workers' compensation obligations, a plan for claims administration and a specified amount of security to insure safety guidelines and rules. Under certain circumstances, an employer may be able to further enhance the cost containment potential of a high deductible or retrospective policy arrangement by using it in conjunction with an appropriately designed and administered risk management plan that incorporates features such as rigorous safety and accident prevention programs, fraud prevent procedures, light duty return to work programs, and, in some cases, a carefully designed occupational injury benefit plan that qualifies as an employee welfare benefit plan covered by the Employee Retirement Income Security Act of 1974, as amended ("ERISA"). An employer may find it advantageous to structure a program which uses all these principles in order to stabilize the premium payments to make the employer less vulnerable to claim fluctuations which may be unpredictable in their timing.

5.9 Compulsory Nature of Workers' Compensation

In the majority of states, workers' compensation constitutes the exclusive remedy for industrial injuries and deaths arising out of employments covered under the applicable workers' compensation act. Workers' compensation acts typically preclude or substantially restrict the circumstances under which workers' engaged in employments covered by the workers' compensation act may pursue compensation for industrial injuries based on employers' liability principles rather than under the workers' compensation system. A number of states permit employers to make an advance written election to retain their common law right to pursue damages based on fault in lieu of having any injuries arising out of that employment qualify for workers' compensation.[73]

The majority of workers' compensation acts also generally make workers' compensation coverage compulsory for most employers. Most state workers' compensation acts make

---

[73]*See, e.g.*, Texas Workers' Compensation Act, 23 Vernon's Ann.Civ.Stat. art. 8308-3.08 (1992). *Also see*, 82 Am. Jur. 2d, *Workers' Compensation* §§ 64, 108-115 (1992).

participation in the statutory workers' compensation system compulsory for most employers. While most workers' compensation statutes contain a number of exclusions that operate to exempt certain employers and classes of employments from coverage under its statutory workers' compensation system, only three states[74] presently operate an elective workers' compensation system, under which the majority of employers enjoy the legal right to choose to have their obligation to provide compensation as a result of industrial injuries or deaths determined based on the fault-based employers' liability principles, rather than to participate in that state's no-fault workers' compensation system. In Texas, New Jersey, and South Carolina, employers that elect to participate in the state's workers' compensation system operate in a no-fault workers' compensation system substantially similar to those in effect in mandatory states. While Texas, New Jersey, and South Carolina permit an employer to elect not to subscribe to the workers' compensation systems, each of these jurisdictions places special requirements on employers who elect not to subscribe and the statutory schemes provide significant disincentives to an election by an employer to forego coverage under workers' compensation.[75] Consequently, even

---

[74]The workers' compensation statutes of Texas, New Jersey, and South Carolina technically permit most employers to elect either to have the compensability of industrial injuries determined either based on employment under the workers' compensation act or under principles or employers' liability.

[75]First, uninsured employers face unlimited liability to employees injured by their employer's negligence in the course and scope of their employment for actual, emotional distress, pain and suffering, and punitive damages. Second, the state law usually also limits the ability of uninsured employers to defined themselves against employee negligence suits by barring the availability of common law defenses, including contributory negligence, assumption of the risk, etc. to uninsured employers. Because of the loss of defenses, an employee's negligence case against an uninsured employer is generally easier to establish than a typical negligence case. Third, uninsured employers are also responsible for all legal fees incurred in defending a negligence action by an employee. Furthermore, nonsubscribing employers in these states generally also must arrange to comply with certain accident and injury reporting, employee notice and posting requirements, and other administrative and safety guidelines and rules under state workers' compensation and occupational safety laws. Violation of certain of these requirements by a

(continued...)

where state law permits employers to elect not to obtain workers' compensation coverage, the majority of employers traditionally have elected, or have been presumed to have elected to obtain workers' compensation coverage, rather than to have employers' liability and damage principles used to decide the compensability of injuries to workers based on the fault of the employer.

In response to soaring workers' compensation premiums over the past several years, however, an increasing number of employers across the nation have expressed interest in terminating their participation in state workers' compensation systems. While this interest in "opting out" of state workers' compensation coverage primarily arose from the need or desire of the employer to avoid paying burdensome workers' compensation premiums, employer perceptions that it was more capable than the workers' compensation system of delivering care and managing occupational injury liabilities also fueled this interest. Since the option to terminate participation is not widely available, however, few employers outside the elective workers' compensation jurisdictions have intentionally attempted terminate their participation in the workers' compensation systems of most states.

In Texas and the other elective workers' compensation jurisdictions, however, an increasing number of employers decided during the past decade that they could justify exposing themselves to the risks of nonsubscription given the high cost of workers' compensation coverage.[76] After extraordinary

---

[75](...continued)
nonsubscribing employer can expose it to significant liability. Therefore, an employer should not terminate its participation in the workers' compensation system of any state without obtaining competent legal advice and significant planning and preparation.

[76] As part of their risk management strategy, nonsubscribing employers commonly implement complex risk management strategies and policies that include alternative benefit programs, drug and alcohol policies, hiring and employment practices, safety policies and specialized insurance products. Nonsubscribing employers usually often provide a package of benefits for their employees under an employee benefit plan maintained by the employer, purchase excess general indemnity insurance to cover
(continued...)

increases in premium cost and risk pool assessments during the past decade in Texas, for instance, many Texas employers reevaluated the risks of nonsubscription to workers' compensation coverage in light of the financial and material burdens imposed under workers' compensation. In evaluating these liabilities, numerous Texas employers concluded that they could reduce the frequency and magnitude of the risks associated with nonsubscription to workers' compensation by implementing carefully designed and administered safety, risk management, and insurance arrangements. Given the availability of these risk management tools, many of these Texas employers decided that termination of participation in the Texas workers' compensation system would allow them to realize several practical and procedural advantages in dealing with legal claims.[77] While to date, many of these nonsubscribing employers report that these programs have yielded the nonsubscriber status for many, if not most employers, significantly lower costs on employee injury claims, the experience of most main stream employers as nonsubscribers is rather short. Furthermore, the judgments entered against a number of employers who elected to become nonsubscribers and subsequently were adjudged guilty of negligently causing injury to one of their employees illustrates the risk of unsuccessful efforts to manage these liabilities. Accordingly, the risks of nonsubscription clearly are not justified for certain employers.

---

[76](...continued) extraordinary claims and, in some cases, establish a reserve fund to protect the business.

[77]For instance, since an employee who claims he is injured on the job has the burden in court to not only prove the injury was on the job, but also to show that the injury was caused by employer negligence. By implementing appropriate safety and accident investigation procedures, many Texas employers determined that the employer's exposure to negligence liability would be minimal. In addition, since the employer would have direct control over the handling of the litigation, the so-called nuisance value insurance settlements and enable the employer to vigorously defend against fraudulent claims.

6.0 COORDINATION OF STATEWORKERS' COMPENSATION LAWS

The multistate nature of modern employment creates a number of particular workers compensation issues and concerns relative to the interaction between the workers' compensation systems of various states. Contracts of employment often call for an employee residing in one state to perform services within that state for a employer that operates in another state or for an employee to travel outside the state in which he resides or is hired to perform services for his employer. These arrangements frequently create questions regarding the extent to which a state workers' compensation act may require an employer to maintain workers' compensation system for an employee while the employee is performing services for the employer in another state and the extent to which injuries sustained by such employees are compensable under the workers' compensation acts of the respective states.

6.1 Duty to Maintain Workers' Compensation Coverage in a Foreign State

Employers who employ employees in more than one state or whose employees travel among two or more states on the business of the employer need to carefully evaluate their responsibilities to maintain coverage under the applicable workers' compensation acts in each of these states. State workers compensation acts frequently seek to require an employer to arrange for workers' compensation coverage for an employee performing services on a permanent or temporary basis within the state, regardless of whether the employer maintains offices within the state, the employer hires the employee within the state, or the employee's principally resides or performs services within the state. Since a state workers' compensation act is applicable only to those employment relations within the state's legislative jurisdiction, the ability of an a state to require a nonresident employer to provide workers' compensation coverage for an employee generally depends upon whether the employer has "sufficient contacts" with the state to meet the constitutional prerequisites of jurisdiction.[78] To the extent that an employer has sufficient contacts with a state, however, the state may enforce the requirements of that state's workers' compensation act against the employer regardless of whether the employer or the employee resides within the state. While most workers' compensation acts expressly exempt employees covered by a method of workers' compensation established under federal law from coverage, state workers' compensation acts usually do not provide a similar exemption for employees performing services within the state who are covered by a method of workers' compensation established under the laws of another state, for employees hired outside the state to perform services within the state, or for employees hired within the state while performing services outside the state.

6.2 Coordination of Workers' Compensation Coverage in Multiple States

When an employee who is hired or resides in one state sustains an injury in another state while on the business of his employer, questions frequently arise regarding his entitlement to workers' compensation under the respective states. The compensability of an injury under the laws of a particular state under such circumstances often varies from state to state based on a variety of factors. Depending on the terms of the particular state law, a an injury to an employee might qualify as compensable solely because the employee sustained the injury within the state;[79] the employee was hired or recruited within the state;[80] the employee's principal place of employment is

---

[78]See, 82 Am. Jur. 2d §33-36 (1992).

[79]See, e.g., Baker v. Industrial Com. of Arizona, 375 P.2d 556 (Ariz. 1981); Cook v. Minneapolis Bridge Const. Co., N.W.2d. 792 (Minn. 1950); Smith v. Van Noy Interstate Co., 150 Tenn 25, 262 S.W. 1048 (Tenn. 1924). See also, 82 Am. Jur. 2d §37 (1992).

[80]See, e.g., Alaska Packers Assoc. v. Industrial Accident Com., 294 U.S. 532 (1935); American States Ins. Co. v. Garza, 657 S.W.2d 522 (Tex. App. 1983).

within the state,[81] or the employer does business within the state.[82] In other jurisdictions, a combination of one or more of these factors must be present with respect to the state in order for compensability to attach under its workers' compensation system.[83] Since most workers' compensation statutes are extraterritorial in effect,[84] many workers' compensation statutes provide compensation for an injury sustained outside of the state as long as the employee was engaged in work for an employer engaged in business within the state.[85] As a result, a single injury may qualify for workers' compensation in more than one state workers' compensation systems. In accordance with the recommendation of the National Commission on State Workmen's Compensation Laws,[86] many states require the injured employee to elect compensation in either the state of injury, the state of the principal location of his employment, or in the state of hire. Other state workers' compensation acts allow the employee to simultaneously pursue compensation in the state while pursuing compensation under another state's workers' compensation system, but provide special rules for coordinating the workers' compensation payable under the home state with the workers' compensation, if any, payable under the other state. In some jurisdictions, the workers' compensation act specifies that the its workers' compensation coverage will apply unless the injured employee elects to seek workers' compensation for the injury under the workers' compensation system of another state. In other

---

[81]*U.S. Casualty Co. v. Standard Acc. Ins. Co.*, 136 S.W.2d 504 (Tenn. 1940).

[82]*See, e.g.*, *State ex. rel. Morgan v. Industrial Accident Board*, 300 P.2d 954 (Mont. 1956). *See also*, 82 Am. Jur. 2d §37 (1992).

[83]*See, e.g.*, *Wolf v. Ethyl Corp.*, 335 N.W.2d 42 (Mich. App. 1983) (residence of employee and completion of contract for hire within the state required); *L&A Constr. Co. v. McCharen*, 198 So. 2d 240 (Miss. 1967), *cert. den'd.* 389 U.S. 945 (1967) (domicile of employer and residence of employee within state insufficient where neither injury or hiring occurred within the state).

[84]82 Am. Jur. 2d, *Workers' Compensation* §37 (1992).

[85]*See e.g.*, *Pickett v. Tryon Trucking Co.*, 518 A.2d 500 (N.J. Super 1986).

[86]Report of the National Commission on State Workmen's Compensation Laws, Recommendation No. 2.11. (1972).

jurisdictions, the workers' compensation statute provides that the amount of workers' compensation payable by the home state will be reduced by the amount of any workers' compensation received or payable under another state's workers' compensation system. Frequently, inter-jurisdictional agreements among the states may establish the applicable procedures for determining the compensability of the injury among the various state workers' compensation systems.

7.0 RELATED FEDERAL LAWS

The interplay between state workers' compensation and employer liability laws and federal employment laws such as the Americans With Disabilities Act of 1990, the Employee Retirement Income Security Act of 1974, the Family and Medical Leave Act of 1992, and the Occupational Health and Safety Act creates a number of special issues and concerns. Reaching an appropriate balance between these various regulatory concerns often presents significant challenges.

7.1 The Americans With Disabilities Act and Other Disability Discrimination Laws

The Americans With Disabilities Act of 1990 (ADA),[87] and certain other federal laws[88] prohibit discrimination in employment against persons with disabilities under certain circumstances. While not all occupational injuries or illnesses qualify for protection under these disability discrimination laws,[89] the rights and protection granted to certain employees

---

[87] 42 U.S.C. §§ 12101 et. seq. (1993).

[88] See e.g, Rehabilitation Act of 1973, as amended, 29 U.S.C. §§ 701 et. seq. (1993).

[89] The ADA, for instance, only protect an injured worker if he meet the ADA's definition of a "qualified individual with a disability." In order for an occupational injury to qualify an employee as disabled under the ADA, the injury must result in a mental or physical impairment that substantially limits one or more major life activities, cause the employee to have a record of such impairment; or result in the employee being viewed as having such an impairment.

affected by industrial accidents and occupational diseases under these discrimination laws may significantly impact the obligations that an employer may owe to an injured worker following his injury and the ability of the employer to design strategies to control his workers' compensation costs.

The disability discrimination prohibitions of the ADA, for instance, generally make the use of procedures that discriminate against qualified persons with disabilities to control workers' compensation costs or liabilities illegal under federal law. The Equal Employment Opportunity Commission views the ADA as generally prohibiting an employer from making certain inquiries into an applicant's workers' compensation history as part of its hiring practices, and basing an employment decision on **speculation** that the applicant may cause increased workers' compensation costs in the future.[90] Moreover, after an employee becomes disabled as a result of an occupational injury, the ADA prohibits an employer from refusing to let the individual return to work because the worker is not fully recovered from the injury unless the worker either cannot perform the essential job functions of the job that he holds or desires with or without accommodation; or would pose a significant risk of substantial harm that could not be reduced to an acceptable level with reasonable accommodation.[91] Moreover, the ADA also may expand the obligations that an employer owes to an injured worker who qualifies for protection under the ADA in several other respects. For instance, the ADA generally imposes an affirmative obligation to reasonably accommodate the disabilities of qualified workers who become disabled. Furthermore, the ADA also may obligate an employer to take certain additional precautions to protect the confidentiality of medical information and records of employees and applicants who qualify as disabled. On the other hand, the ADA does not appear to prohibit an employer from refusing to hire, or discharging, an individual who is not

---

[90]*See*, Americans With Disabilities Act of 1990: *EEOC Assistance Manual* (CCH 1990).

[91]*Id.*

currently able to perform a job without posing a significant risk of substantial harm to the health or safety of the individual or others, if the risk cannot be eliminated or reduced by reasonable accommodation. The existing guidance suggests, however, that the employer should be prepared to document an appropriate basis for this determination. Speculation regarding safety risks clearly will not be sufficient to meet this burden.[92]

7.2 Employee Retirement Income Security Act of 1974

Striking a proper balance between its obligation to provide benefits under programs maintained to comply with state workers' compensation laws and the legal rights and its responsibilities under employee benefit programs maintained by the employer which are subject to regulation under the Employee Retirement Income Security Act of 1974, as amended ("ERISA"),[93] often is of critical concern to employers.[94]

Since ERISA took effect, employers frequently have relied upon ERISA to circumvent mandates under state workers' compensation laws that seek to obligate employers to continue to cover and provide pension, health or other benefits under their ERISA plans to employees entitled to receive workers' compensation benefits pursuant to a state's workers' compensation statute. In *District of Colombia v. Greater Washington Board of Trade*,[95] for instance, the United States Supreme Court ruled that ERISA rendered unenforceable a workers' compensation statute that required all employers that provided health benefits to continue providing those benefits to an employee as long as he remained eligible to receive workers' compensation. In recent years, many employers also explored

---

[92]*Id.*

[93]29 U.S.C. § 1101 *et. seq.* (1992).

[94]For a more detailed discussion of the implications of ERISA on workers' compensation obligations and strategies, *see* Gibson, King and Chadwick, *ERISA Premption's Use To Cut Workers' Compensation Costs*, 5 BENEFITS LAW JOURNAL 187 (1992).

[95]113 S. Ct. 580 (1992).

the feasibility of using section 514(b) of ERISA to circumvent adverse consequences of terminating workers' compensation coverage and as a means for more cost-effectively providing appropriate care and coverage to employees who sustain job-related injuries than provided under a state workers' compensation system. Employers subject to a mandatory workers' compensation law who have dropped their workers' compensation coverage in violation of the applicable requirements of a mandatory state workers' compensation act have argued unsuccessfully that the preemptive provisions of ERISA preclude state works' compensation administrators from imposing sanctions against the employer for its noncompliance.[96] Nonsubscribing employers in certain elective jurisdictions, such as Texas, also have been mostly unsuccessful in their efforts to use of the preemptive provisions of ERISA as a bar to negligence actions brought by an injured employee under state workers' compensation law[97] but have experienced greater success in using ERISA as a bar to attempts to regulate employee benefit programs maintained by the employer that provide benefits in the event of occupational injuries.[98]

Sections 4(b)(3) and 514 of ERISA control the legal relationship between ERISA and state workers' compensation laws primarily. Section 514 of ERISA generally provides that ERISA supersedes all state laws that "relate to" an employee benefit plan subject to ERISA except those specifically preserved under section 514(b). Under section 4(b)(3) of ERISA, plans maintained solely to comply with state workers' compensation laws are excluded from regulation by ERISA. The United States Supreme Court has narrowly construed section 4(b)(3) as limited in its application to only those

---

[96] *See, e.g., Employee Staffing Services, Inc. v. Aubey*, No. C92-4096, 1993 WL No. 83310 (N.D. Cal. Mar. 17, 1993).

[97] *See Gibbs v. Service Lloyds Insurance Company*, 711 F. Supp. 874, 876 (E.D. Tex. 1989), *Nunez v. Wyatt Cafeterias*, 771 F. Supp. 165 (N.D. Tex. 1991); *Benson v. Wyatt Cafeterias*, 804 F. Supp. 876 (N.D. Tex., 1991); *but see Diaz v. Texas Health Enterprises, Inc.*, 822 F. Supp. 1258 (W.D. Tex. 1993).

[98] *See, e.g., Gibbs v. Service Lloyds Ins. Co.*, 711 F. Supp. 874, 876 (E.D.Tex. 1989); *Foust v. City Ins. Co.*, 704 F. Supp. 752 (W.D.Tex. 1989).

separately administered plans that, as an administrative unit, provide only those benefits required by the applicable state law.[99] Moreover, the United States Supreme Court, also has ruled that section 4(b)(3) clearly does not allow a state to enforce its workers' compensation law in a manner that regulates an employee benefit plan covered by ERISA. It merely permits a state to require that an employer maintain a workers' compensation arrangement that complies with state law as a separate administrative unit. Such a plan would be exempt under ERISA Section 4(b)(3).[100] Consequently, the effect of ERISA on the obligations imposed on an employer under a particular workers' compensation law depends largely on the nature of the provision of the state workers' compensation law in question.

8.0 OSHA

The Occupational Safety and Health Act of 1970 ("OSHA") imposes on all employers a general duty to furnish its employees a place of employment free from recognized hazards that are causing or are likely to cause death or serious physical harm.[101] An employer also must comply with specific standards or rules promulgated by the Department of Labor.[102] OSHA imposes criminal penalties on employers who willfully violate a standard that causes the death of am employee[103] or knowingly makes false statements, representations or certifications in documents required to be

---

[99]*District of Colombia v. Greater Washington Board of Trade*, 113 S. Ct 580 (1992); *Shaw v. Delta Airlines*, 463 U.S. 85 (1983).

[100]*Shaw v. Delta Airlines, Inc.*, 463 U.S. 85 (1983).

[101]29 U.S.C. §5(a) (1993). *See also*, Robert A. Minor and Jeffrey N. Lindemann, "An Overview of Criminal Liability for Workplace Injuries and Disabilities," *in* WORKPLACE REMEDIES III: WORKERS' COMPENSATION PRACTICE/COMPLEX WORKPLACE LITIGATION FOR THE '90s AND BEYOND (ABA 1992).

[102]29 U.S.C. §5(b) (1993).

[103]29 U.S.C. § 666(e) (1993).

kept under OSHA.[104] When Congress enacted OSHA, it was cognizant of the compromise in the workers compensation system which granted employers immunity from tort immunity and guaranteed employees a certain level of benefits. Therefore, Congress enacted a semi-anti-preemption provision which states that nothing in OSHA shall be construed to supersede or affect any workman compensation law.[105] The courts, relying on this provision and the exclusivity doctrine of workers compensation, have not allowed an employee to sue an employer in a negligence action for violation of OSHA standards. However, an employer who intentionally violates an OSHA standard may be sued under the "intentional wrong" exception to workers compensation recognized in most jurisdictions.

9.0 THE WORKERS' COMPENSATION CRISIS

In recent years, spiraling medical inflation, administrative and regulatory bottlenecks, rampant fraud, insurance company and state fund insolvencies, and other problems touched off a workers' compensation crisis in most states across the nation. The problems are staggering. Ever soaring workers' compensation costs wreak havoc with the balance sheets of employers.[106] Fraud and systemic misappropriation run rampant throughout many systems. Litigation, archaic practices and inefficient administrative procedures impede the delivery medical care and other compensation to legitimately injured

---

[104] 29 U.S.C. §666(f),(g) (1993). *See also*, Robert A. Minor and Jeffrey N. Lindemann, "An Overview of Criminal Liability for Workplace Injuries and Disabilities, *in* "WORKPLACE REMEDIES III: WORKERS' COMPENSATION PRACTICE/COMPLEX WORKPLACE LITIGATION FOR THE '90S AND BEYOND (ABA 1992).

[105] 29 U.S.C. §4(b)(4) (1993).

[106] In New York, for example, employers reacted explosively to a proposed 18.7 percent workers' compensation rate increase during the prior three year period of 28 percent, 15.3 percent, and 15.6 percent respectively. *See*, "New York Considers Another Workers' Compensation Rate Increase," *National Underwriter*, June 28, 1993 at 4, 29. *Also see* "Pennsylvania House Senate Ok Workers' Compensation Reforms, *National Underwriter*, June 28, 1993 at 4, 28.

workers. Statutory restrictions on compensation recoveries constantly face erosion from judicial challenges to administrative compensation awards, retaliation claims, or other emerging legal theories designed to circumvent scheduled compensation limitations or to recapture common law rights of recovery. Meanwhile, new and ever-expanding employer obligations under occupational health and safety, workers' compensation, and employment discrimination laws increasingly place the burden on employers to guarantee the health and safety of their workers. Consequently, employers increasingly view occupational injury and workers' compensation costs and obligations as among their leading concerns.[107]

As the crisis threatens to consume their workers' compensation systems, state legislatures are scrambling to shore up the cracks in the workers' compensation system and to control soaring litigations rates and compensation costs through the adoption of legislative reforms.[108] In many states, these efforts have resulted in sweeping legislative and regulatory reforms. Other states, however, have foregone radical reform in favor of more narrow modifications.

While the government debates proposed legislative solutions to workers' compensation problems, employer attention increasing focuses on the identification of practical strategies for controlling their individual workers' compensation and occupational injury costs; eliminating fraud, administrative inefficiency and other abuses from their workers' compensation programs; developing more cost-effective and efficient mechanisms for preventing and remedying occupational injuries and diseases; and complying with the constantly expanding mandates imposed by federal and state workers' compensation, discrimination, employee benefit, and occupational safety laws and regulations. Therefore, many employers throughout the

---

[107]On June 28, 1993, *National Underwriter*, at 25 announced that the state of the workers' compensation system tied with President Clinton's health care reform proposal as the most worrisome issues of risk managers. Twenty-seven percent of respondents to the survey identified workers' compensation as their top concern.

[108]*See, e.g. National Underwriter*, "New York Considers Another Workers' Compensation Rate Increase," June 28, 1993 at 4.

country are developing and refining their strategies for managing occupational injury and workers' compensation costs in compliance with a complex range of state and federal laws.

As part of these efforts, employers frequently seek to tailor solutions to their individual workers' compensation crisis by using a wide range of creative strategies for minimizing occupational injuries and their associated costs and liabilities. To reduce the frequency and magnitude of their workers' compensation and occupational injury risks and liabilities, employers increasingly use carefully integrated and documented risk management strategies and systems tailored specifically for their particular employment environments. Under these risk management programs, employers may modify the employment culture of their organizations; establish safety policies, procedures and education programs targeted at injury prevention; purchase specialized insurance products and claims administration systems; implement complex accident investigation and claims review procedures; aggressively challenge questionable claims; use a wide range of fraud prevention[109] and medical cost containment strategies,[110] redesign existing employee benefit plans for use as a tool to reduce workers' compensation costs; restructure job descriptions and functions to create light duty or other employment opportunities for workers after an accident or injury; seek to persuade injured workers to comply with health care cost management and utilization procedures or to accept

---

[109] *See,* Kizorek, "A Guide to Video Surveillance of Workers' Compensation Claimants." *in* WORKPLACE REMEDIES III: WORKERS' COMPENSATION PRACTICE/COMPLEX WORKPLACE LITIGATION FOR THE '90s AND BEYOND (ABA 1992); Robert L. Dietz, "Avoiding the Fraudulent Workers' Compensation Claim," *in* WORKPLACE REMEDIES III: WORKERS' COMPENSATION PRACTICE/COMPLEX WORKPLACE LITIGATION FOR THE '90S AND BEYOND (ABA 1992).

[110] *See,* Robert J. Zilg, "Integrated Managed Care and Workers' Compensation: Problems and Opportunities," 5 BENEFITS L.J. 227 (Summer 1992); Stephen W. Cavanaugh, "Medical Costs Containment, Can Reform Succeed? The Louisiana Approach/Experiment, *in* "WORKPLACE REMEDIES III: WORKERS' COMPENSATION PRACTICE/COMPLEX WORKPLACE LITIGATION FOR THE '90S AND BEYOND (ABA 1992).

compensation under ERISA-covered benefit arrangements in lieu of pursuing their workers' compensation rights; and a host of other fraud prevention and risk management procedures. While the design, implementation and administration of the required risk management program can be expensive and require significant diligence, many employers credit the use of such procedures with enabling them to significantly enhance their ability to plan for and control workers' compensation costs and liabilities.

While the components of an effective risk management strategy varies among employers, any successful program for controlling workers' compensation costs and liabilities must be built around comprehensive safety and accident prevention procedures. Safety and prevention offers several benefits. The frequency and severity of occupational injuries and diseases usually directly impacts an employer's workers' compensation costs; higher or more severe claims translate into higher workers' compensation insurance and compensation costs and liabilities. Furthermore, employers increasingly recognize that appropriate safety and accident prevention programs often reduce their susceptibility to fraudulent claims and reduce the future exposure of the employer to liability under federal and state laws regarding worker health and safety and disabilities discrimination. Consequently, many employers directly may realize a reduction in their workers' compensation and occupational injury costs by strengthening their safety, drug and alcohol screening, and employee relations policies and implementing comprehensive plans for dealing with workplace injuries.

To fully take advantage of the opportunities of enhanced workplace safety, employers use a variety of mechanisms to identify and eliminate safety hazards and workers' compensation liability exposures from their work places. Safety initiatives often begin with a safety audit conducted by a qualified risk manager or industrial engineer, who seeks to identify unsafe working conditions that are likely to cause occupational injuries or diseases and to evaluate the feasibility of making cost-effective modifications to correct these safety risks. To the extent possible, most employers find it desirable to conduct this audit within the scope of attorney-client privilege. Based on the results of this audit, an employer may make physical modifications to its workplace; implement or enhance safety and employment procedures, practices, and manuals; strengthen alcohol and drug use and testing policies; or modify the employment culture of their organization.

Employers also generally adopt a more active role in investigating workplace accidents and challenging fraudulent or otherwise noncompensable claims. Most workers' compensation statutes contain provisions through which employers and insurers can challenge questionable reports of accident or injury and suspicious medical charges or diagnoses. To enhance their ability to effectively exercise these rights, many employers to use claims adjusters, risk managers or other workers' compensation experts or consultants to investigate accidents and monitor the administration of occupational accident and workers' compensation claims to ensure that the employer's rights and interests are protected to the extent permitted under the applicable workers' compensation statute. In conducting these investigations, employers or claims adjusters often will look indicia of a potentially fraudulent claim, which justify further investigation. These may include ambiguous or overly specific claims; inconsistencies between the initial accident description by the claimant and other subsequently obtained information; unwitnessed accidents that occur in an improbable or unlikely manner; patterns of suspicious claims from the claimant or his section of the company; claims occurring in a close proximity to a reduction in force, termination, disciplinary action, or period of vacation or recreational activity, or having other suspicious time elements; inconsistencies between the nature and extent of the injury; outside reasons for the employee wishing to avoid returning to work, such as personal problems; or the employee benefit coverage that enable the employee to simultaneously collect workers' compensation and other pension or disability benefit payments that may eliminate the incentive for the employee to return to work.[111] The existence of such suspicious facts often justifies further investigation, using surveillance[112] or other methods. To the extent provided in the workers' compensation statute, employers frequently will monitor information about a claim; document and report suspected fraud;[113] present evidence at administrative or judicial proceeding to contest certain claims or their compensability; or communicate with the workers' compensation insurance carrier or state mandated fund regarding proposals to settle a claim. Many employers are taking advantage of these and other rights available under the applicable workers' compensation statute to develop strategies for working within the system to defeat and deter meritless claims and control costs.

The significant increase in the cost of conventional workers' compensation coverage also increased the attractiveness to employers of self-insured or other nontraditional methods for meeting the financial responsibility requirements of workers' compensation laws and funding workers' compensation liabilities. These efforts are reflected in the growing popularity of self-insurance as a means for providing workers' compensation benefits and the widespread use of nontraditional workers' compensation insurance arrangements that contain features such as retrospective rating, high deductibles or self-insured retention features. The use of such arrangements can yield certain cash flow advantages for an employer. Unless the

---

[111]*See*, Dietz, "Avoiding the Fraudulent Workers' Compensation Claim, *in* "WORKPLACE REMEDIES III; WORKERS' COMPENSATION PRACTICAL/COMPLEX WORKPLACE LITIGATION FOR THE '90S AND BEYOND (ABA 1990).

[112]*See*, O'Kasey, "Dirty Dancing: The Effective Use of Surveillance in the Defense of Workers' Compensation Cases," *in* WORKERS' COMPENSATION REMEDIES III: WORKERS COMPENSATION PRACTICE/COMPLEX WORKPLACE LITIGATION FOR THE '90S AND BEYOND (ABA 1990).

[113]*See*, Dietz, "Avoiding the Fraudulent Workers' Compensation Claim," *in* WORKPLACE REMEDIES III: WORKERS' COMPENSATION PRACTICAL/COMPLEX WORKPLACE LITIGATION FOR THE '90s AND BEYOND (ABA 1990).

employer effectively reduces the occurrence and severity of compensable injuries, however, these nontraditional products ultimately only enable the employer to delay, but not avoid, the payment of costs attributable to injuries. Accordingly, employers that use such products must couple their use with other strategies for controlling workers' compensation claims and costs.

To augment their safety and insurance strategies, employers are using a wide range of approaches. Some employers find it helpful to improve working relationships and communications among its workers' compensation, risk management and human resource departments; its claims insurer or adjusters; and employees and their health care providers to ensure that questionable claims are fully investigated and prosecuted and that all parties cooperate to ensure that timely arrangements are made to identify and provide treatments that will maximize the expeditious recovery of an injured worker, and to take advantage of appropriate opportunities to return the employee to employment by providing reasonable accommodations or light duty work, rehabilitation or retraining opportunities to the injured worker where appropriate. A growing number of employers also are exploring opportunities to reduce cost, litigation, time and effort through enhanced coordination of workers' compensation with other employment and employee benefit programs, including implementation of 24-hour benefit programs under which claims for occupational and non-occupational injuries and illnesses are administered under a single integrated arrangement.[114]

In a number of states, employers also may explore reducing their workers' compensation costs and liabilities by changing the manner in which they retain workers' to perform services. While the regulators and legislators of many states are engaged in ongoing discussions regarding the need to reform rules regarding the treatment of leased employee, independent

---

[114]*See, e.g.*, "Clinton Plan Worries Risk Managers, NU Poll Finds," *National Underwriter*, June 28, 1993 at 1 and 25 and "ITT Finds Managed DI Plan is Valuable Sales Tool," *National Underwriter*, July 5, 1993 at 16.

contractor, and other contract labor relationships for workers' compensation purposes, certain jurisdictions currently allow employers to avoid workers' compensation liabilities or costs by entering into certain appropriately designed contract labor arrangements for the performance of tasks with independent contractors, subcontractors, employee leasing firms, manpower service firms. For instance, in recent years, employers in certain states have reduced their workers' compensation premiums or occupational injury costs by outsourcing tasks associated with heightened workers' compensation exposures. Employers using such arrangements should carefully analyze the treatment of such arrangements under state workers' compensation laws and regulations, however, to verify the manner in which state law requires the employer to classify such workers for workers' compensation purposes and the obligations that are imposed on the parties to such arrangements under state law. Many state workers compensation statutes or regulations require that certain contract labor arrangements meet certain documentation and other conditions to qualify for the treatment intended by the employer. Where state law permits the use of such strategies, special caution should be taken to ensure that these rules are observed. Failure to comply with the regulatory or judicial law of a state regarding the use of contract labor, the offending party can face significant liability.

10.0 CONCLUSION

The growing complexity and expense of the workers' compensation environment presents numerous financial and practical challenges for employers. To cope with these challenges, employers must clearly understand the nature of their obligations under a wide range of federal and state workers' compensation, occupational disease, occupational health and safety, employment, insurance, and benefits laws and regulations. The respective rights and responsibilities of employers under these laws and the administrative and judicial authority promulgated thereunder constantly are subject to debate and modification. Ultimately, the degree of success that an employer achieves in managing the financial and legal liabilities under workers' compensation laws and the range of strategies available to an employer for dealing with its workers' compensation challenges depends on the ability of the employer to assimilate accurately and respond creatively to these constantly changing responsibilities.[115]

---

[115]*Cautionary Note: This paper is intended only to be a brief discussion of the laws and issues discussed herein. It is not intended to be a comprehensive analysis of each and every aspect of such provisions. Because of the generality of the discussion and because interpretive guidance is still developing regarding the laws discussed in this paper, the information contained herein may not be applicable in all situations and may not, after the date of this publication, even reflect the most current authority. For these reasons, nothing contained in this paper should be relied or acted upon without the benefit of legal advice based upon the particular circumstances presented. For additional information, please contact the author.*

INDEX

Ability
  Americans With Disabilities Act of 1990, 53-54
  testing, vs disability testing, Americans with Disabilities Act of 1990, 59-60
Access, to employment opportunity, disabled individual, Americans With Disabilities Act of 1990, 71-76
Accommodations, duty to make, under Americans with Disabilities Act of 1990, 60-71
  "undue hardship" defense, 68-69
ADA. See Americans With Disabilities Act of 1990
Adoption of child. See Family and Medical Leave Act of 1993
Advanced degree, professionals with, permanent residenceby employment, 191
Affirmative action, 1-20
  communication, documentation, 16-17
  training, 16-17
  current practices, 19-20
  Executive Order 11246, 2-3
  Executive Order 11375, 2-3
  good faith efforts, documentation, 16-17
  historical perspective, 1-4
    Title VII of the Civil Rights Act of 1964, 1-4
  narrative report, 13
  Office of Federal Contract Compliance Programs, 5-6
    audit, 17-19
    Executive Order 11246, 5-6
    Executive Order 11375, 5-6
    jurisdictional requirements, 5-6
    written affirmative action plan, 6
  Rehabilitation Act of 1973, 3-4
  statistical components, of affirmative action plan, 8-12
  Supreme Court, attitude toward, 6
  training, documentation, 16-17
  Vietnam Era Veterans Readjustment Assistance Act of 1974, 4
Affirmative action plan
  applicant flow, statistical component, applicant defined, 11-12
  components of, 6-7
  creating, 7-8
  narrative section of, 13-15
  Office of Federal Contract Compliance Programs, 6
  personnel actions, statistical component
    applicant flow, 11
    demotion, 11

    lay offs, 11
    negative action, 10-11
    positive action, 10
  preparation of, overview, 12
  statistical component, 8-12
    employees included, 8-9
  personnel actions, 10
Alcohol
  abuse, Americans With Disabilities Act of 1990, 51-52
  testing. See Drug testing
Americans With Disabilities Act of 1990, 44-76
  ability testing, vs disability testing, 59-60
  access to employment opportunity, 71-76
    contractual arrangements, 74-75
    health insurance, 72-74
    interference, 76
    leave policy, 74
    non-segregated facility, 72
    retaliation, 76
  accommodations, duty to make, 60-71
    "undue hardship" defense, 68-69
  alcohol, abuse, 51-52
  disability, defined, 45-46
  drug abuse, 51-52
  testing, 161-165
    medical examination, current employee, 162
    pre-employment medical inquiry/examination, 161-162
  essential job function, 49-51
    criteria, 49-50
    evidence, 50
    job description, 51
  hiring/selection requirements, 53-60
    ability, 53-54
    aptitude, 53-54
    disability, nature/severity of, 54-55
    employment standards, 56-58
    medical examination, 55-56
      confidentiality, 56
    mental qualifications, 58
    physical qualifications, 58
    pre-employment inquiry, 53-55
    religious preference, 58
    selection criteria, 57
  mental impairment, 46-47
  past impairments, 48
  physical impairment, 46-47
  qualification for employment, 49
  qualified persons, 45-53
  safety, 58-59
    "direct threat" standard, 58-59
    food-handling, 58-59

substantial limitation, major life activity, 47-48
Anti-Kickback Act of 1986, wage/salary, 92-93
Applicant flow, affirmative action plan, statistical component, 11
applicant defined, 11-12
Approval matrix, Family and Medical Leave Act of 1993, 42
Aptitude, Americans With Disabilities Act of 1990, 53-54
Arrest record, screening problem employees, 210-212
Asylee, U.S., 185
Audit. See also Personnel audit
employee attitude survey, 256
follow-up, 256
Office of Federal Contract Compliance Programs, 17-19
performance, 249-250
requirements, employee benefits, 108
techniques, 250-255
union vulnerability assessment, 255-256
value of, 248

B-1 visa, 196-197
Bachelor's degree, holders of, permanent residence by employment, 193
Balancing test
drug testing, U.S. Constitution, 165-166
U.S. Constitution, drug testing, specific testing program application, 166-173
Benefits, 99-138
audit requirements, 108
compensation limitation, tax issues, 126
cost-of-living chart, adjusted dollar amount, 136
disclosure to participants, 109-111
rules, 105-109
during family leave, 33-35
Form 5500, 105-108
highly compensated employee, tax issues, 123-124
penalty, failure to file, 109
pension, checklist, 138
Pension Benefit Guaranty Corporation premiums, tax issues, 126-127
qualified domestic relations orders, tax issues, 127
qualified retirement plan, 100
reporting rules, 105-109
retirement, 100-104
    defined benefit plan, 100-101
    defined contribution plan, 100-101
    ERISA, 104
    nonqualified retirement program, 102-104
tax qualification requirements. See Tax qualification requirements, benefits
top-heavy plan, tax issues, 124-126
welfare, 104-105
    checklist, 138

Birth of child. See Family and Medical Leave Act of 1993
Blood-borne disease, General Industry Safety and Health Standards, Occupational Safety and Health Act, 147-148
Break time
Fair Labor Standards Act, 85
hours worked, compensation, 85

Certification requirements, Family and Medical Leave Act of 1993, 30-33
Child
adoption of. See Family and Medical Leave Act of 1993
birth of. See Family and Medical Leave Act of 1993
labor, Fair Labor Standards Act, 89-91
Citizenship, and immigration, 183-184
COBRA. See Consolidated Omnibus Reconciliation Act of 1985
Common law employee, Family and Medical Leave Act of 1993, 23-24
Communication, affirmative action, documentation, 16-17
training, 16-17
Comp time, Fair Labor Standards Act, 87
Company policy regarding drugs, drafting of, 174
Compensation
hours worked. See Hours worked, compensation
limitation, tax issues, 126
Confidentiality, medical examination, Americans With Disabilities Act of 1990, 56
Consolidated Omnibus Reconciliation Act of 1985, 127-137
coverage, 130-131, 137
period, 131-132
definitions, 129-130
effective date, 128
election, 131
employers subject to, 128
notification requirements, 132-133
premium, 133
purpose, 128
sanctions, 134-135
termination, 132
Constitution. See U.S. Constitution
Consumer report, screening problem employees, 213
Cost-of-living chart, adjusted dollar amount, 136
Credit check, screening problem employees, 212
Current practices, affirmative action, 19-20

Davis Bacon Act, wage/salary, 92-93
Defined contribution retirement benefit plan, 101-102
Defined retirement benefit plan, 100-101

Index / 311

Demotion, affirmative action plan, personnel actions, statistical component, 11
Denial of family leave, 38-39
"Direct threat" standard, Americans With Disabilities Act of 1990,
 safety of workplace, 58-59
Disability, defined, 45-46
Disclosure, benefits, to participants, 109-111
Documentation, affirmative action
 communication, 16-17
 good faith efforts, 16-17
 training, 16-17
Driving record, screening problem employees, 217
Drug abuse, Americans With Disabilities Act of 1990, 51-52
Drug screening, of problem employees, 225-226
Drug testing, 160-182
 Americans With Disabilities Act of 1990, 161-165
 employer conduct allowed, 162-165
 medical examination, current employee, 162
 pre-employment medical inquiry/medical examination, 161-162
 company policy regarding drugs, drafting of, 174
 employer conduct allowed, 162-165
 minimizing liability risk, 173-182
 union involvement, 182
 U.S. Constitution, 165-173
 applicant testing, 166-167
 balancing, specific testing program application, 166-173
 balancing test, 165-166
 current employee, 168
 fitness-for-duty testing, 168
 post-accident testing, 170
 random testing, 170-172
 eeasonable suspicion testing, 168-170

E-1 visa, 197-199
E-2 visa, 197-199
Employee
 attitude survey, 256
 eligible for Family and Medical Leave Act of 1993, 25-26
 handbook
 included, statistical component, affirmative action plan, 8-9
 problem. See Problem employees
 self care health leave. See Family and Medical Leave Act of 1993
Employee Retirement Income Security Act of 1974. See ERISA
Employers subject to Family and Medical Leave Act of 1993, 22-25
Employment law
 affirmative action, 1-20
 Americans with Disabilities Act of 1990, 44-76
 benefits, 99-138
 drug testing, 160-182
 Family and Medical Leave Act, 21-43
 immigration, 183-205
 Occupational Safety and Health Act, 139-159
 personnel audit, 248-256
 personnel policy manual, 229-247
 problem employee, 206-228
 salary, 77-98
 visas, 183-205
 wages, 77-98
Employment status clarification, Family and Medical Leave Act of 1993, 41
Entitlements, Family and Medical Leave Act of 1993, 26-37
Environmental controls, General Industry Safety and Health Standards, Occupational Safety and Health Act, 146
Equal Pay Act of 1963, 91-92
ERISA, retirement benefits, 104
Essential job function, Americans With Disabilities Act of 1990, 49-51
 criteria, 49-50
 evidence, 50
 job description, 51
Exceptional ability, permanent residence by employment, 192
Executive Order 11246
 affirmative action, 2-3
 Office of Federal Contract Compliance Programs, 5-6
Executive Order 11375
 affirmative action, 2-3
 Office of Federal Contract Compliance Programs, 5-6
Extraordinary ability, individuals with, immigration, 188-189

Fair Labor Standards Act, 78-91
 break time, 85
 child labor, 89-91
 comp time, 87
 covered employees/employers, 78-79
 enforcement, 88-89
 exemptions, 79-80
 hours worked, compensation, 81-87
 break time, 85
 meal period, 85
 meeting time, 86
 minimum wage, 81
 "on call" time, 85
 overtime, 81-84
 sleeping time, 85-86
 training time, 86
 travel time, 86
 waiting time, 84
 "on call" time, 85
 penalty, 88
 recordkeeping checklist, 97-98
 recordkeeping requirements, 87-88

312 / Index

travel time, 86-87
Family and Medical Leave Act of 1993, 21-43
 approval matrix, 42
 benefits, during leave, 33-35
 certification requirements, 30-33
 circumstances in which leave taken, 27-29
 common law employee, 23-24
 denial of family leave, 38-39
 effective date of, 42
 eligibility for leave, 25-26
 employers subject to, 22-25
 employment status clarification, 41
 entitlements, 26-37
 fifty-employee threshold, 22-23
 "integrated employer", 24-25
 job security, 36-37
 notice, 30-33
 notice to employee, 40-41, 43
  with paid leave, coordination, 35-36
 penalty for violation, 39-40
 spouse employed by same employer, 41
 state family leave laws, coordination with, 42
 types of leave, 29-30
Family care leave. See Family and Medical Leave Act of 1993
Fatalities, recordkeeping/reporting, Occupational Safety
 and Health Act, 152-153
Female, affirmative action plan, narrative section, 13-15
Fifty-employee threshold, Family and Medical Leave Act of 1993, 22-23
Fire protection, General Industry Safety and Health Standards,
 Occupational Safety and Health Act, 145
Fitness-for-duty drug testing, U.S. Constitution, 168
FLSA. See Fair Labor Standards Act
FMLA. See Family and Medical Leave Act of 1993
Food-handling, safety of workplace, Americans With Disabilities Act of 1990, 58-59
Form 5500, benefits, 105-108
401(k) plan, testing, tax qualification requirements, 117-121

General duty clause, Occupational Safety and Health Act, 148-150
General Industry Safety and Health Standards, Occupational Safety and Health Act, 140-148
 blood-borne disease, 147-148
 environmental controls, 146
 fire protection, 145
 hazard communication standard, 141-143
 hazardous material, 145-147
 machinery, 144

 material safety data sheet, 141-143
 specific health standards, 145-148
 specific safety standards, 143-145
 structural conditions, 143-144
 toxic substance, 146-147
Good faith efforts, affirmative action, documentation, 16-17

H-3 visa, 200-201
H-1B visa, 199-200
Handbook. See Employee handbook
Hazard communication standard, Occupational Safety and Health Act, General Industry Safety and Health Standards, 141-143
Hazardous material, General Industry Safety and Health Standards, Occupational Safety and Health Act, 145-147
Health insurance, Americans with Disabilities Act of 1990, 72-74
Health leave. See Family and Medical Leave Act of 1993
Highly compensated employee, tax issues, 123-124
Hiring/selection requirements, Americans With Disabilities Act of 1990, 53-60
 ability, 53-54
 aptitude, 53-54
 disability, nature/severity of, 54-55
 employment standards, 56-58
 medical examination, 55-56
  confidentiality, 56
 mental qualifications, 58
 pre-employment inquiry, 53-55
 religious preference, 58
 selection criteria, 57
Honesty test, screening problem employees, 216
Hospitalization, multiple, recordkeeping/reporting, Occupational Safety and Health Act, 152-153
Hours worked compensation
 under Fair Labor Standards Act, 81-87
 waiting time, 84
Fair Labor Standards Act, compensation
 break time, 85
 meal time, 85
 meeting time, 86
 minimum wage, 81
 "on call" time, 85
 overtime, 81-84
 sleeping time, 85-86
 training time, 86
 travel time, 86
 waiting time, 84

Illegal alien, 186
Illness, recordkeeping/reporting, Occupational Safety and Health Act, 153-154

Immigration, 183-205
  asylee, 185
  citizenship, 183-184
  entitlement to lawful status, determination of, 186-187
  illegal alien, 186
  Immigration Reform and Control Act of 1986, 202-205
  labor certification requirement, 194-196
  permanent residence by employment, 187-194
    advanced degree, professionals with, 191
    bachelor's degree, holders of, 193
    exceptional ability, 192
    extraordinary ability, 188-189
    individuals with, 188-189
    investors, 194
    multinational executive, 190-191
    priority workers, 188-191
    professors, outstanding, 189-190
    researchers, outstanding, 189-190
    skilled worker, 193
    unskilled worker, 193
  permanent resident, 184-185
  status, 183-186
  temporary protected status, 185-186
  temporary resident, 185
  temporary visa, 196-202. See Temporary visa
  Immigration Reform and Control Act of 1986, 202-205
Injury, recordkeeping/reporting, Occupational Safety and Health Act, 153-154
"Integrated employer", Family and Medical Leave Act of 1993, 24-25
Investors, permanent residence by employment, 194

J-1 visa, 201
Job applicant. See Applicant
Job description, Americans With Disabilities Act of 1990, essential job function, 51
Job function, Americans With Disabilities Act of 1990. See Essential job function
Job security, family leave, 36-37
Jurisdictional requirements, Office of Federal Contract Compliance Programs, 5-6

L-1 visa, 197
Labor certification, immigration, 194-196
Lay offs, affirmative action plan, personnel actions, statistical component, 11
Leave policy, Americans With Disabilities Act of 1990, 74
Limitation, on major life activity, Americans with Disabilities Act of 1990, 47-48

Machinery, General Industry Safety and Health Standards, Occupational Safety and Health Act, 144
Manual. See Personnel policy manual
Material safety data sheet, Occupational Safety and Health Act, General Industry Safety and Health Standards, 141-143
Meal period, hours worked, compensation, 85
Medical examination, Americans with Disabilities Act of 1990, 55-56
Meeting time, hours worked, compensation, 86
Mental impairment, Americans With Disabilities Act of 1990, 46-47
Mental qualifications, Americans With Disabilities Act of 1990, 58
Military service check, screening problem employees, 216-217
Minority, affirmative action plan, narrative section, 13-15
Monitoring, of problem employees, 220-228
  Drug screening, 225-226
  Search, 226-228
  Surveillance, 220-225
Multinational executive, permanent residence by employment, 190-191

Narrative report, affirmative action, 13
Narrative section, affirmative action plan, 13-15
  female, 13-15
  minority, 13-15
Nonqualified retirement program, 102-104
Notice, Family and Medical Leave Act of 1993, 30-33, 40-41, 43

O visa, 202
Occupational Safety and Health Act, 139-159
  defense, 156-159
    greater hazard, 158
    infeasability of compliance, 157
    isolated incident, 157-158
    multi-employer work site, 158-159
  discrimination, employee seeking rights under, 155-156
  fatalities, 152-153
  general duty clause, 148-150
  General Industry Safety and Health Standards, 140-148
    blood-borne disease, 147-148
    environmental controls, 146
    fire protection, 145
    hazardous material, 145-147
    machinery, 144
    material safety data sheet, 141-143
    specific health standards, 145-148
    structural conditions, 143-144
    toxic substance, 146-147
    universal application, 140-143
  illness, recordkeeping/reporting, 153-154
  injury, recordkeeping/reporting, 153-154

314 / Index

multiple hospitalization, 152-153
recordkeeping, 150-155
reporting, 150-155
variances, 156
OFCCP. See Office of Federal Contract Compliance Programs
Office of Federal Contract Compliance Programs
affirmative action, 5-6
audit, 17-19
Executive Order 11246, 5-6
Executive Order 11375, 5-6
jurisdictional requirements, 5-6
affirmative action, written affirmative action plan, 6
"On call" time
Fair Labor Standards Act, 85
hours worked, compensation, 85
OSHA. See Occupational Safety and Health Act
Outstanding professor/researcher, permanent residence by employment, 189-190
Overtime
calculation chart, 97
hours worked, 81-84
compensation, 81-84

Paid leave, family leave, coordination with, 35-36
Past impairments, Americans with Disabilities Act of 1990, 48
Pension, benefits, checklist, 138
Pension Benefit Guaranty Corporation premiums, tax issues, 126-127
Permanent residence, obtaining by employment. See Immigration, permanent residence by employment
Personnel actions, affirmative action plan, statistical component, 10
applicant flow, 11
demotion, 11
lay offs, 11
negative action, 10-11
positive action, 10
Personnel audit, 248-256
Personnel policy manual, 229-241
benefits, 229-230
drafting, 235-238
forms, 239
location, 240-241
open vs. closed statements, 238-239
policy adoption criteria, 231-234
policy sources, 234-235
review/revision, 239-240
Physical impairment, Americans With Disabilities Act of 1990, 46-47
Physical qualifications, Americans With Disabilities Act of 1990, 58
Policy adoption criteria, personnel policy manual, 231-234
Policy sources, personnel policy manual, 234-235

Polygraph test, screening problem employees, 214-215
Post-accident drug testing, U.S. Constitution, 170
Pre-employment inquiry, Americans With Disabilities Act of 1990, 53-55
Preparation of, affirmative action plan, overview, 12
Priority workers, immigration, 188-191
Problem employees
employer tools, 218-219
investigation, 219-220
monitoring of. See Monitoring
screening, 209-217
signs of, 207-209
Psychological test, screening problem employees, 215-216

Q visa, 202
Qualification for employment, Americans with Disabilities Act of 1990, 49
Qualified domestic relations orders, tax issues, 127
Qualified persons, Americans With Disabilities Act of 1990, 45-53
Qualified retirement plan, 100

Random drug testing, U.S. Constitution, 170-172
Reasonable suspicion drug testing, U.S. Constitution, 168-170
Recordkeeping checklist, Fair Labor Standards Act, 97-98
Recordkeeping requirements, Fair Labor Standards Act, 87-88
Reference check, screening problem employees, 212
Rehabilitation Act of 1973, affirmative action, 3-4
Religious preference, Americans with Disabilities Act of 1990, 58
Retirement benefits, 100-104
defined benefit plan, 100-101
defined contribution plan, 101-102
nonqualified retirement program, 102-104
qualified plan, 100

Safety of workplace, Americans With Disabilities Act of 1990, 58-59
"direct threat" standard, 58-59
food-handling, 58-59
Salary. See Wage/salary
Screening, problem employees, 209-217. See Screening
arrest record, 210-212
consumer report, 213
credit check, 212
driving record, 217
honesty test, 216
military service check, 216-217
polygraph test, 214-215
psychological test, 215-216

reference check, 212
Search
  drugs, minimizing liability for, 173-182
  of problem employees, 226-228
Selection criteria, Americans With Disabilities Act of 1990, 57
Self care health leave. See Family and Medical Leave Act of 1993
  Employee. See Family and Medical Leave Act of 1993
Separate line of business rule, benefits, tax qualification requirements, 121-123
Skilled worker, permanent residence by employment, 193
Sleeping time, hours worked, compensation, 85-86
Spouse, employed by same employer, Family and Medical Leave Act of 1993, 41
State family leave laws, Family and Medical Leave Act of 1993,
  coordination with, 42
State legislation, wage/salary, 93-94
Statistical component, affirmative action plan, 8-12
  employees included, 8-9
  personnel actions, 10
Structural conditions, General Industry Safety and Health Standards, Occupational Safety and Health Act, 143-144
Supreme Court, affirmative action, attitude toward, 6
Surveillance, of problem employees, 220-225
Suspected impairments, Americans With Disabilities Act of 1990, 48

Tax issues
  compensation limitation, 126
  highly compensated employee, 123-124
  Pension Benefit Guaranty Corporation premiums, 126-127
  qualified domestic relations orders, 127
  top-heavy plan, 124-126
Tax qualification requirements, benefits, 111-123
  eligibility, 111
  401(k) plan, testing, 117-121
  minimum coverage rules, 112-114
  minimum participation requirements, 115
  nondiscrimination rules, 114-115
  separate line of business rule, 121-123
  vesting, 115-117
Temporary protected status, immigration, 185-186
Temporary resident, immigration, 185
Temporary visa, 196-202
  B-1 visa, 196-197
  E-1 visa, 197-199
  E-2 visa, 197-199
  H-3 visa, 200-201
  H-1B visa, 199-200

J-1 visa, 201
L-1 visa, 197
O visa, 202
Q visa, 202
Title VII of the Civil Rights Act of 1964, 1-4
Top-heavy benefit plan, tax issues, 124-126
Toxic substance, General Industry Safety and Health Standards, Occupational Safety and Health Act, 146-147
Training, affirmative action, documentation, 16-17
Training time, hours worked, compensation, 86
Travel time
  Fair Labor Standards Act, 86-87
  hours worked, compensation, 86-87

"Undue hardship" defense, Americans With Disabilities Act of 1990,
  accommodations, duty to make, 68-69
Union
  drug testing, involvement in policy, 182
  vulnerability assessment, audit, 255-256
Unskilled worker, permanent residence by employment, 193
U.S. Constitution, drug testing
  applicant testing, 166-167
  balancing, specific testing program application, 166-173
  balancing test, 165-166
  current employee, 168
  fitness-for-duty testing, 168
  post-accident testing, 170
  random testing, 170-172
  reasonable suspicion testing, 168-170

Vesting, benefits, tax qualification requirements, 115-117
Vietnam Era Veterans Readjustment Assistance Act of 1974,
  affirmative action, 4
Visa, temporary. See Temporary visa

Wage/salary, 77-98
  Anti-Kickback Act of 1986, 92-93
  comp time, Fair Labor Standards Act, 87
  Davis Bacon Act, 92-93
  Equal Pay Act of 1963, 91-92
  Fair Labor Standards Act, 77-98
    break time, 85
    child labor, 89-91
    covered employees/employers, 78-79
    enforcement, 88-89
    exemptions, 79-80
    hours worked, compensation, 81-87
    "on call" time, 85
    penalty, 88
    recordkeeping requirements, 87-88
    travel time, 86-87
  overtime, calculation chart, 97
  state legislation, 93-94

Walsh-Healey Government Contracts Act, 92-93
white collar exemption checklist, 94-96
Waiting time, hours worked, compensation, 84
Walsh-Healey Government Contracts Act, wage/salary, 92-93
Welfare, benefits, checklist, 138
Welfare benefits, 104-105
White collar exemption checklist, salary, 94-96
Workers' compensation, 257
   administration and dispute resolution, 285
   Americans With Disabilities and other disability discrimination laws, 294
   compensation and benefits, 275
   compensible injuries, 270
   compulsory nature of workers' compensation, 287
   coordination of state workers' compensation laws, 291
   coordination of workers' compensation coverage
   in multiple states, 293
   covered employments, 266
   death compensation for survivors, 282
   duty to maintain workers' compensation coverage in a forest state, 291
   Employee Retirement Income Security Act of 1974, 296
   federal workers' compensation laws, 262
   financial security requirements, 285
   historical evolution of workers' compensation, 258
   medical expense compensation, 276
   miscellaneous benefits, 283
   OSHA, 298
   permanent disablement compensation, 280
   prohibitions against discrimination against employees claiming workers' compensation benefits, 284
   related federal laws, 294
   state workers' compensation laws, 265
   wage loss compensation, 277
   workers' compensation crisis, 299

About Government Institutes

Government Institutes, Inc. was founded in 1973 to provide continuing education and practical information for your professional development. Specializing in environmental, health and safety concerns, we recognize that you face unique challenges presented by the ever-increasing number of new laws and regulations and the rapid evolution of new technologies, methods and markets.

Our information and continuing education efforts include a Videotape Distribution Service, over 140 courses held nation-wide throughout the year, and over 150 publications, making us the world's largest publisher in these areas.

Government Institutes, Inc.
4 Research Place, Suite 200
Rockville, MD 20850
(301) 921-2300

Other related books published by Government Institutes:

Complying With The Family and Medical Leave Act: A Detailed Guide - This guide provides concise and accurate guidance on the implementation and administration of family leave policies. Consisting of a manual and a disk, this package includes: an indepth analysis of the Act and its regulations; a Model Leave Policy and all the forms needed to simplify the administration of family leave benefits (also included in disk form): important source documents including the Act, its legislative history, and regulations; a quick reference Q&A section, compliance checklists, timelines, selected information on state family leave laws, and helpful charts to assist employers with understanding and ensuring compliance with the Act. Three-ring binder with IBM-Compatible disk/200 pages/Oct '93/$179 ISBN: 0-86587-354-2

Affirmative Action Handbook - This handbook will prove to be extremely useful in helping you to understand affirmative action and to generate your own working program. Covers: Affirmative Action and Supreme Court; Reverse Discrimination as an Issue; Executive Order 11246 (Minorities/Females) Narrative Affirmative Plan Components; Non-construction; Affirmative Action Plans for Individuals with Handicaps and Veterans; Non-construction Contractors; and the Affirmative Action Audit. Also includes helpful forms and worksheets to use in your affirmative action program. Softcover/160 pages/June '92/$65 ISBN: 0-86587-274-0

Affirmative Action Federal Contract Compliance Manual: Desk Audit, Onsite & Corporate Management Review - This practical manual will help contractors to comply more easily with federal affirmative action regulations. Includes: Procedures for conducting the desk audit portion of the compliance review; A guide for Equal Opportunity Specialists in how to conduct onsite compliance investigations and prepare an investigative report and summary; Background information and guidance on evaluating whether a contractor has refrained from unlawful discrimination; and numerous charts and forms for compliance! Softcover/320 pages/Nov '92/$59 ISBN: 0-86587-323-2

Call the above number for our current book/video catalog and course schedule.

Publications (cont'd)

OSHA Compliance Handbook - This practical non-legalese guide, written by W. Scott Railton, will help you meet your OSHA requirements. Covers: OSHA Standards; General Duty Clause; Recordkeeping; Hazard Communication; Inspections; Civil Penalties and Violations; and much more. Softcover/400 pages/May '92/$79 ISBN: 0-86587-290-2

Health and Safety Audits - Written by John W. Spencer, Vice-President of the National Medical Advisory Service, this practical manual will show you how to conduct audits that will lead to the development and management of successful health and safety programs. Softcover/336 pages/May '92/$65 ISBN: 0-86587-297-X

Environmental Law Handbook, 12th Edition - The recognized authority in the field, this invaluable text, written by nationally-recognized legal experts, provides practical and current information on all major environmental areas. Hardcover/670 pages/Apr '93/$68 ISBN: 0-86587-350-X

Environmental Statutes, 1993 Edition - All the major environmental laws incorporated into one convenient source.
Hardcover/1,170 pages/Mar '93/$59 ISBN: 0-86587-352-6
Softcover/1,170 pages/Mar '93/$49 ISBN: 0-86587-351-8

Directory of Environmental Information Sources, 4th Edition - Details hard-to-find Federal Government Resources; State Government Resources; Professional, Scientific, and Trade Organizations; Newsletters, Magazines, and Periodicals; and Databases. Softcover/350 pages/Nov '92/$74 ISBN: 0-86587-326-7

The Greening of American Business: Making Bottom-Line Sense of Environmental Responsibility - Written by leading environmental professionals from industry, law firms, and universities, this book explains how companies are coping with increasing demands that they engage in environmentally-sound business practices. Softcover 350 pages/Oct '92/$24.95 ISBN: 0-86587-295-3

Educational Programs

- Our **COURSES** combine the legal, regulatory, technical, and management aspects of today's key environmental, safety and health issues — such as environmental laws and regulations, environmental management, pollution prevention, OSHA and many other topics. We bring together the leading authorities from industry, business and government to shed light on the problems and challenges you face each day. Please call our Education Department at (301) 921-2345 for more information!

- Our **TRAINING CONSULTING GROUP** can help audit your ES&H training, develop an ES&H training plan, and customize on-site training courses. Our proven and successful ES&H training courses are customized to fit your organizational and industry needs. Your employees learn key environmental concepts and strategies at a convenient location for 30% of the cost to send them to non-customized, off-site courses. Please call our Training Consulting Group at (301) 921-2366 for more information!

Government Institutes, Inc., 4 Research Place, Suite 200, Rockville, MD 20850, (301) 921-2300